best hikes with KIDS
WASHINGTON, DC, THE BELTWAY & BEYOND
S0-ABC-146

Hikers take in the view of the Potomac River's Mather Gorge.

Lotus flowers in bloom at Kenilworth Aquatic Gardens

Previous page: Reflecting ponds along the Little Stoney Mountain Trail at Claude Moore Park

It's fun to rock hop along Donaldson Run at Potomac Overlook Regional Park.

Bouldering kid-style on Northwest Branch

Wineberry picking at Lake Needwood

This specimen sycamore tree at Cabin John Regional Park is 200 years old.

Left: Fossil finding at Calvert Cliffs

You might spot beautiful meadow flowers and butterflies at Banshee Reeks Nature Preserve.

Watch for creatures in the potholes on the Billy Goat trail.

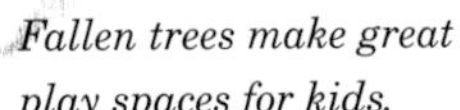

Fallen trees make great play spaces for kids.

Posing where Difficult Run meets the Potomac River

Chillin' after a fun hike

Left: Crossing Scotts Run on cement pillars is a balancing act.

best hikes with

WASHINGTON, DC, THE BELTWAY & BEYOND

Jennifer Chambers

MOUNTAINEERS BOOKS

MOUNTAINEERS
BOOKS

Mountaineers Books is the publishing division of The Mountaineers, an organization founded in 1906 and dedicated to the exploration, preservation, and enjoyment of outdoor and wilderness areas.

1001 SW Klickitat Way, Suite 201, Seattle, WA 98134
800.553.4453, www.mountaineersbooks.org

Printed in the United States of America

First edition, 2014

Copy Editor: Laura Shauger
Layout: Jennifer Shontz, www.redshoedesign.com
Cartographer: Pease Press Cartography

All photographs by the author unless otherwise noted.
Cover photograph: *A family hikes along a mountain trail in Cunningham Falls State Park, Thurmont, Maryland.* Credit: National Geographic Image Collection / Alamy
Frontispiece: *Having fun in the nature exploration area at Wheaton Regional Park*

Library of Congress Cataloging-in-Publication Data
Chambers, Jennifer.
Best hikes with kids : Washington, DC, the beltway & beyond / Jennifer Chambers.
pages cm
Includes index.
ISBN 978-1-59485-782-9 (pbk)—ISBN 978-1-59485-783-6 (ebook)
1. Hiking—Washington Metropolitan Area—Guidebooks. 2. Hiking for children—Washington Metropolitan Area—Guidebooks. 3. Family recreation—Washington Metropolitan Area—Guidebooks. 4. Washington Metropolitan Area—Guidebooks. I. Title.
GV199.42.W17C43 2014
917.53—dc23

2014004786

Printed on recycled paper

ISBN (paperback): 978-1-59485-782-9
ISBN (ebook): 978-1-59485-783-6

CONTENTS

To my husband,
our two children, and
our past and present dogs

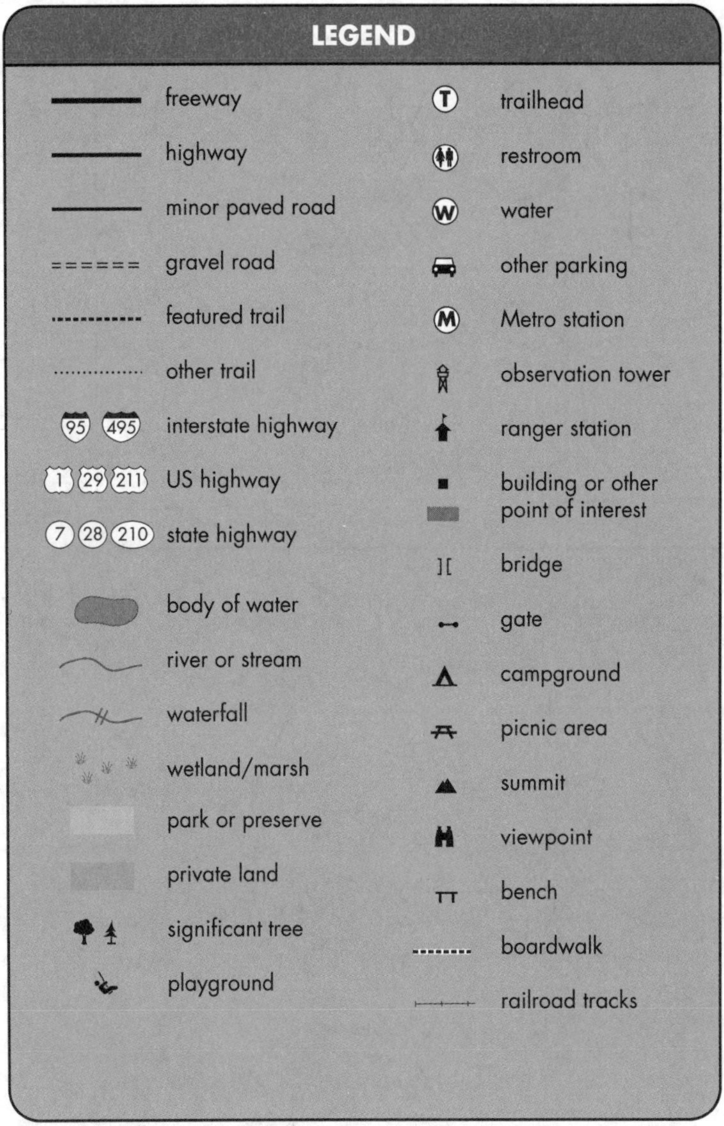

LEGEND

Symbol	Meaning	Symbol	Meaning
	freeway		trailhead
	highway		restroom
	minor paved road		water
	gravel road		other parking
	featured trail		Metro station
	other trail		observation tower
95 495	interstate highway		ranger station
1 29 211	US highway		building or other point of interest
7 28 210	state highway		bridge
	body of water		gate
	river or stream		campground
	waterfall		picnic area
	wetland/marsh		summit
	park or preserve		viewpoint
	private land		bench
	significant tree		boardwalk
	playground		railroad tracks

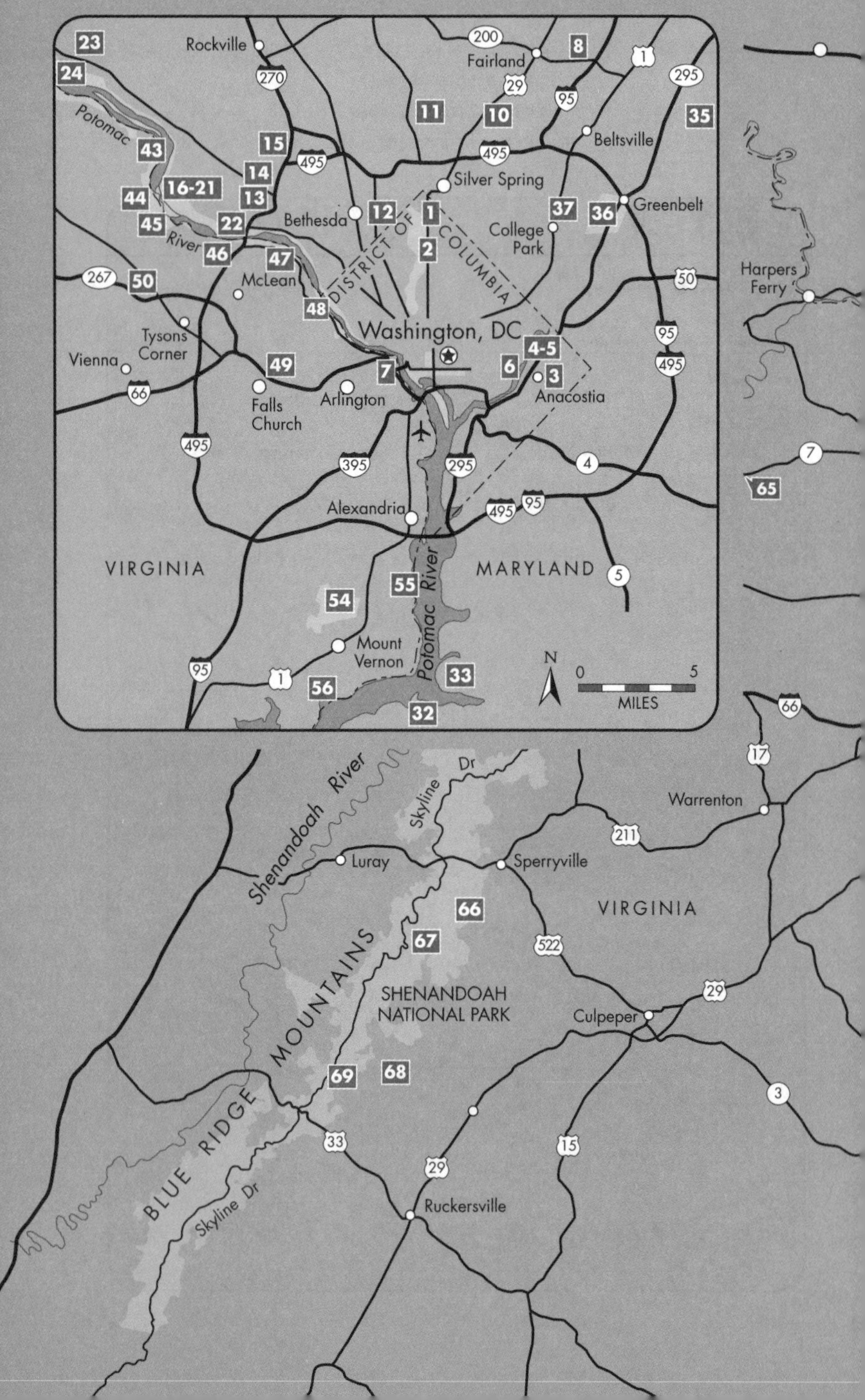

Rockville
Fairland
Potomac
River
Beltsville
Silver Spring
Greenbelt
Bethesda
College Park
DISTRICT OF COLUMBIA
McLean
Harpers Ferry
Tysons Corner
Vienna
Washington, DC
Falls Church
Arlington
Anacostia
Alexandria
VIRGINIA
MARYLAND
Potomac River
Mount Vernon
N
0
5
MILES
Shenandoah River
Skyline Dr
Warrenton
Luray
Sperryville
VIRGINIA
SHENANDOAH NATIONAL PARK
Culpeper
BLUE RIDGE MOUNTAINS
Ruckersville
Skyline Dr

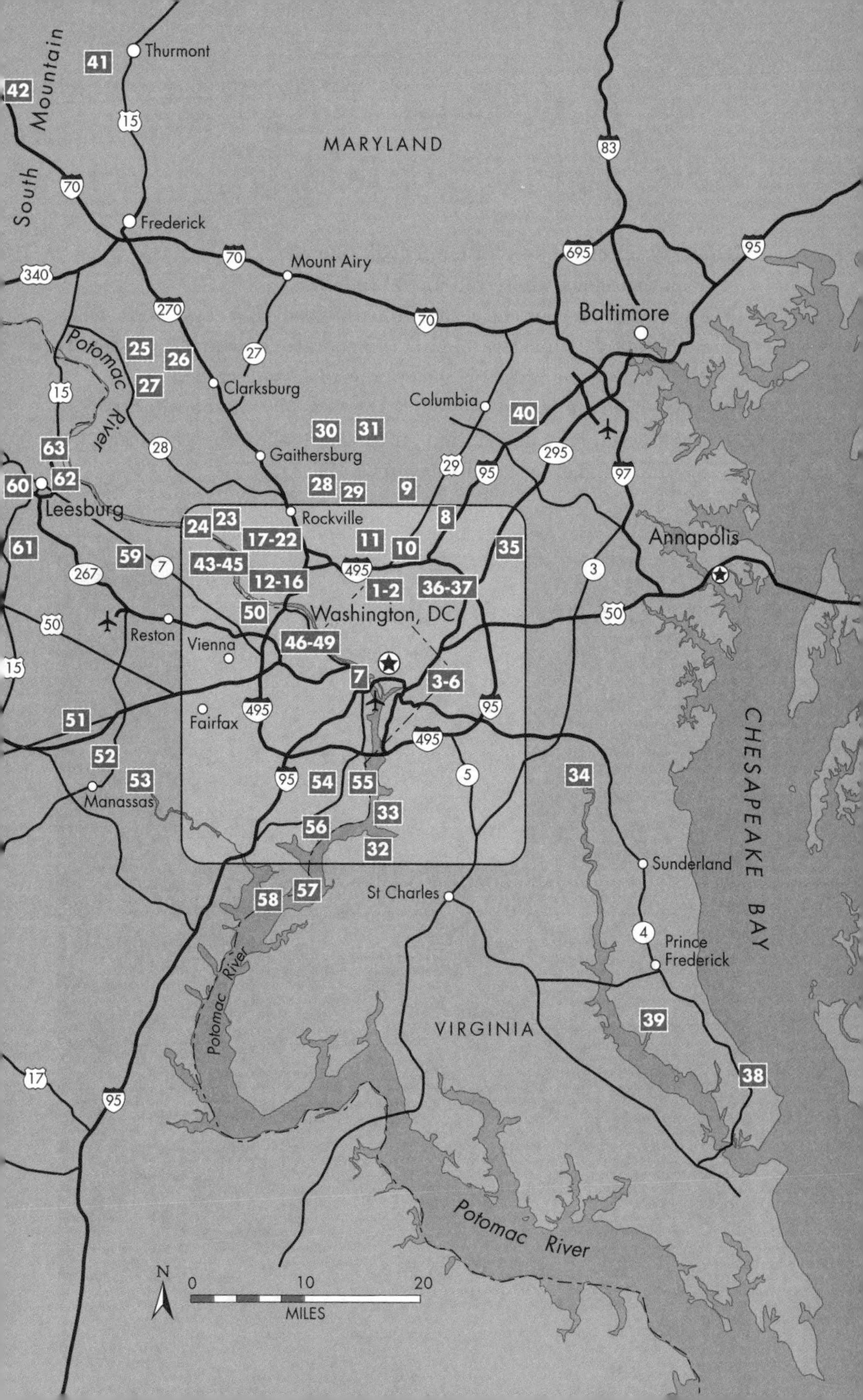

MARYLAND
VIRGINIA
South Mountain
Thurmont
Frederick
Mount Airy
Baltimore
Clarksburg
Columbia
Gaithersburg
Rockville
Leesburg
Annapolis
Washington, DC
Reston
Vienna
Fairfax
Manassas
St Charles
Sunderland
Prince Frederick
Potomac River
CHESAPEAKE BAY
41
42
25
26
27
30
31
28
29
9
8
63
60
62
24
23
17-22
11
10
35
61
59
43-45
12-16
1-2
36-37
50
46-49
7
3-6
51
52
53
54
55
34
33
56
32
58
57
39
38
40
N
0
10
20
MILES

A QUICK GUIDE TO THE HIKES

To quickly select a hike your family will like:

- Pick the region where you intend to hike.
- Narrow down your choices by difficulty level (E = easy; E-M = easy-moderate; M = moderate; M-D = moderate-difficult; D = difficult). Note that some hikes include options of varying difficulty.
- Make sure the trail is accessible the time of year you want to hike.
- See the full hike description for distance, elevation gain, seasonal specifics, and other details. Happy trails!

The split-log bridge over Piney Creek is a fun place to play.

NUMBER AND NAME	DIFFICULTY	SEASON	HIGHLIGHTS
Washington, DC			
1. Rock Creek National Park: Valley to Western Ridge Loop	M–D	Year-round	Hike up and down the valley along Rock Creek.
2. Rock Creek National Park: Rapids Bridge	M	Year-round	Play among boulders along Rock Creek.
3. Fort Dupont National Park: Turkey Trot Trail	E–M	Year-round	Visit a community garden and hike a Kids in Parks TRACK Trail.
4. Kenilworth Aquatic Gardens: River Trail on the Anacostia	E	Year-round	Hike on a peninsula between the marsh and the Anacostia River.
5. Kenilworth Aquatic Gardens: Aquatic Gardens and Boardwalk	E	Year-round	Observe lotus flowers and lilies from May to August.
6. National Arboretum: Asian Garden	E	Year-round	Hike through the Asian Garden and down the bluff to play alongside the Anacostia River.
7. Theodore Roosevelt Island Park: Swamp Trail	E	Year-round	Hike through two different ecosystems—upland forest and marsh—in the middle of the Potomac River.
Maryland: Montgomery County			
8. Holly Trail at Fairland	M	Year-round	Hike up and down rolling hills and over two streams, and have a picnic on the playground at the trailhead in Fairland Recreational Park.
9. Underground Railroad Trail	E–M	Year-round	Experience how slaves escaped to freedom on this interpretive trail.
10. Rachel Carson Greenway Trail	E–M	Year-round	Rock scramble along Northwest Branch as the stream tumbles over boulders.

HIKE NUMBER AND NAME	DIFFICULTY	SEASON	HIGHLIGHTS
11. Wheaton Regional Park	E	Year-round	Visit a nature center, pioneer cabin, and nature exploration area.
12. Woodend Sanctuary	E	Year-round	Hike a nature discovery trail along a stream and pond and through a meadow and forest.
13. Cabin John Trail: MacArthur Boulevard	M	Year-round	Hike up and down the valley to play along Cabin John Stream, and have a picnic on the playground at the trailhead.
14. Cabin John Trail: River Road	E–M	Year-round	Hike through the valley next to Cabin John Stream.
15. Locust Grove Nature Center	E–M	Year-round	Visit an old sycamore tree, nature center, and nature exploration area in Cabin John Regional Park.
16. Ford Mine Trail	M–D	Year-round	Hike up and down rolling hills along the C&O Canal, and tackle six stream crossings.
17. River Trail	E	Year-round	Hike the Potomac River upstream of Great Falls.
18. Gold Mine Trail	M	Year-round	Visit the Great Falls Tavern and the falls on Olmsted Island in the Chesapeake and Ohio Canal National Historical Park.
19. Billy Goat Trail: Section A	D	Year-round	Rock scramble along the Mather Gorge of the Potomac River, climb a cliff, and watch kayakers play in the river rapids.
20. Billy Goat Trail: Section B	M	Year-round	Hike along the Potomac River, climb a rock slab, and observe turtles along the C&O Canal.
21. Berma Road to C&O Canal Towpath	E	Year-round	Hike above and alongside the widest part of the C&O Canal through a unique and rocky ecosystem.
22. Billy Goat Trail: Section C	E–M	Year-round	Watch rock climbers, hike above and along the edge of the Potomac River, and climb rocks along the trail.

23. Muddy Branch Greenway Trail	M	Year-round	Spring is a great time to see amphibians in this trail's vernal pools.
24. Blockhouse Point	M–D	Year-round	Hike under big trees and among lush ferns to two overlooks of the Potomac River.
25. Sugarloaf Mountain Park	D	Year-round	Experience the views from the top of Sugarloaf Mountain.
26. Bucklodge Forest Conservation Park	E–M	Year-round	Discover forest succession on this quiet trail.
27. Turkey Hill Loop	E–M	Year-round	Hike a quiet trail above and next to Little Seneca Lake in Black Hill Regional Park.
28. Lake Needwood	E–M	Year-round	View Lake Needwood from the dam, and explore the lake in a canoe or kayak.
29. Lake Frank	M	Year-round	Play on boulders along Rock Creek North Branch, and visit the lake, a pioneer farmstead, a pond, and the nature center.
30. Blue Mash Trail	E	Year-round	Hike a meadow full of birds, butterflies, and dragonflies.
31. Rachel Carson Conservation Park	M	Year-round	Visit a pond, eat raspberries and blackberries in July, hike along the Hawlings River, and picnic on a car-sized boulder.
Prince Georges County			
32. Marsh Boardwalk at Piscataway	E	Year-round	Visit the National Colonial Farm, and hike along the restored and interpretive shoreline of the Potomac River in Piscataway Park.
33. River Trail: Fort Washington	E–M	Year-round	Explore an 1800s military fort, and hike along the Potomac River and Piscataway Creek.

HIKE NUMBER AND NAME	DIFFICULTY	SEASON	HIGHLIGHTS
34. Jug Bay Natural Area	M	Year-round	Hike through a wetland and to an overlook of Jug Bay, and visit the Rural Life Museums.
35. Patuxent Research Refuge	E	Year-round	Hike an interpretive trail along Cash Lake, and visit the National Wildlife Visitor Center.
36. Greenbelt Park: Azalea Trail	E	Year-round	Challenge yourself and kids at the exercise stations along the trail, and have a picnic at the trailhead playground.
37. Lake Artemesia	E	Year-round	Fish at the pier, and hike the circumference of the lake.
Within Two Hours of DC			
38. Calvert Cliffs State Park: Red Trail	M	Year-round	Hike through an upland forest, along a marsh, and out to the beach on the Chesapeake Bay to swim and hunt for shark's teeth and fossils.
39. Cypress Knee Nature Trail	E	Year-round	Visit the only cypress swamp west of the Chesapeake Bay in Battle Creek Cypress Swamp Sanctuary.
40. Cascade Falls Loop	M–D	Year-round	Splash in two waterfalls, experience the swinging bridge, swim in the river, and visit the ruins of an old mill in Patapsco Valley State Park.
41. Cunningham Falls	M–D	Year-round	Scramble on rocks, and visit the waterfall at Cunningham Falls State Park.
42. Appalachian Trail: Annapolis Rocks	D	Year-round	Have a picnic at a large west-facing rock and enjoy a lot of great rock climbing.

Virginia: Arlington, Fairfax, and Prince William Counties			
43. Riverbend Park	M	Year-round	Visit the nature center, rent boats, and hike to a pond and along the Potomac River.
44. River and Matildaville Loop	M–D	Year-round	Visit Great Falls, rock scramble above the Mather Gorge on the Potomac River to an overlook, and play in an old quarry.
45. Difficult Run and Ridge Trails	M–D	Year-round	Hike along the fast-moving Difficult Run to a waterfall and the run's mouth at the Potomac River in Great Falls Park.
46. Scotts Run Nature Preserve	M	Year-round	Hike in an old-growth forest, along Scotts Run, and to a waterfall on the Potomac River.
47. Turkey Run Loop	M	Year-round	Hike to the Potomac River and along Turkey Run.
48. Potomac Overlook Regional Park	M	Year-round	Visit the nature center and educational gardens, and rock scramble to the Potomac River along Donaldson Run.
49. Upton Hill Regional Park	E	Year-round	This park is full of activities; it offers a playground, miniature golf course, batting cages, and a pool.
50. Wolf Trap Trail	M	Year-round	Hike over ridges along two streams, a pond, and the Theater-in-the-Woods; it's a Kids in Parks TRACK Trail.
51. Stone Bridge Loop	E–M	Year-round	Experience the history of the first and second battles of Manassas during the Civil War on this interpretive trail, and hike a Kids in Parks TRACK Trail.
52. Bluebell Loop	E	Year-round	Enjoy bluebell flowers in April in Bull Run Regional Park.

HIKE NUMBER AND NAME	DIFFICULTY	SEASON	HIGHLIGHTS
53. Bull Run Trail	M	Year-round	Hike along the rocky banks of Bull Run, and visit the ruins of a power plant in Hemlock Overlook Regional Park.
54. Huntley Meadows	E	Year-round	Visit the nature center, and hike on a boardwalk through a huge marsh to view great blue herons, egrets, turtles, and butterflies.
55. Haul Road Trail at Dyke Marsh	E	Year-round	Take in views of the Potomac River from Dyke Marsh Wildlife Preserve.
56. Beaver Pond and Great Blue Heron Trails	E	Year-round	Hike through marshes, along Accotink Creek, and past two vernal pools, and visit a bird blind in Accotink Bay Wildlife Refuge.
57. Woodmarsh Trail	E–M	Year-round	Observe eagles and great blue herons in the Great Marsh in Mason Neck National Wildlife Refuge.
58. Bayview Trail	E	Year-round	Hike along Belmont Bay on the Potomac River, visit two marshes, and play at the trailhead playground in Mason Neck State Park.
Loudoun County			
59. Little Stoney Mountain Trail	E–M	Year-round	Visit the nature center, historical buildings, and the Loudoun Heritage Farm Museum; hike through a forest and around two ponds at Claude Moore Park.
60. Rust Nature Sanctuary	E	Year-round	Visit the natural playground, pollinator's garden, and manor; hike the interpretive trail to a pond.
61. Banshee Reeks Nature Preserve	M	Year-round	Hike through forests and meadows full of flowers and butterflies, to a pond, and along Goose Creek.

62. Red Rock Wilderness Overlook Regional Park	E–M	Year-round	Learn about the antebellum Paxton family farm, and visit an overlook providing beautiful views of the Potomac River.
63. Balls Bluff Battlefield Regional Park	M	Year-round	Hike the interpretive trail to a Civil War battlefield and cemetery.
64. Farmstead Loop	M	Year-round	Play in the creek next to a log-hewn bridge, and hike past a pond and three historical homes at the Blue Ridge Center for Environmental Stewardship.
65. Bears Den Trail Center	M–D	Year-round	Have a picnic, and scramble to a rocky overlook on a ridge facing west.
Shenandoah National Park			
66. Nicholson Hollow Trail	M	Spring to fall	Hike along the Hughes River to a swimming hole.
67. Whiteoak Canyon and Cedar Run Loop	M	Spring to fall	Hike and rock hop along the rapids of Cedar Run and Whiteoak Canyon.
68. Graves Mill Trail	M–D	Spring to fall	Observe beaver habitat, and hike along and cross the fast-moving Rapidan River on boulder stepping-stones
69. Bearfence Trail Loop	D	Spring to fall	Scramble on a narrow ridge at an elevation of 3500 feet.

ACKNOWLEDGMENTS

My father started the spark when I was a kid, but it was ignited when I became a teacher. I witness firsthand the smiles and light in the eyes of my students as they experience the outdoors and its natural beauty when hiking, camping, backpacking, whitewater rafting, rock climbing, and caving. My students fueled a lifelong passion for the outdoors, in particular hiking, and my desire to share it with as many families and children as I can. I created my business, Hiking Along, and many other projects and programs over the last eighteen years—all with one goal: to foster kids' relationships with nature and to instill in them a sense of stewardship.

I introduced my children to hiking when they both were infants. They clung close to my often sweaty body as I joined like-minded parents to hike on the hundreds of miles of trails that the DC area offers. As my children grew, our family adjusted how, when, and where we hiked. Now, I am grateful to be able to share challenging hikes with them in beautiful places like our national parks, the White Mountains, and the Adirondacks. A perfect day for me is discovering the beauty of a new trail with my husband, kids, and our dog. I am indebted to them for the energy they extended to hike many miles with me—even with tired feet—and for their loving and positive support while I wrote this book.

My parents live in Culpeper, Virginia, a beautiful town in the foothills of the Shenandoah Mountains. Whenever we visit, we often spend our afternoons with a picnic lunch on a trail beside a roaring mountain stream. I am thankful for their love of the outdoors and their desire to share their time hiking in Shenandoah National Park, especially for the trips, like Bearfence, that were a great challenge for them. I am so appreciative of their encouragement and loving support of me in all my outdoor adventures.

Hiking with our friends and neighbors made researching and writing this book even more enjoyable. I am grateful for their friendship and companionship on the trail. Thank you very much to these incredible families: Allison, Anderson, Buscaino, Caron, Contreras, Haas, Hunter-Dalby, Kane, Kirchoff-Johnson, Kraus-Jacobsberg, Lang, Levy, Morris, Musheno, Ortman-Fouse, Ratowski-Howe, and Wilson.

Opposite: Playing with the dog in Cabin John Stream

Thank you to these organizations for giving me permission to include their trails in the book, answering my questions, directing me to sources or resources, and providing the maps that the cartographer used to create the maps for this book: Audubon Naturalist Society, Battle Creek Cypress Swamp Sanctuary, Chesapeake and Ohio Canal National Historical Park, Claude Moore Park, Cunningham Falls State Park, George Washington National Parkway, Great Falls Park, Locust Grove Nature Center, Montgomery Parks, National Arboretum, National Capital Parks-East, Patuxent River Park, Potomac Overlook Regional Park, Rock Creek National Park, Shenandoah National Park, and Wolf Trap National Park for the Performing Arts.

Thank you to Kate Rogers and Kirsten Colton at Mountaineers Books and to Craig Romano and Laura Shauger. Craig Romano, author of several Pacific Northwest hiking guidebooks for Mountaineers Books, introduced me to Kate, the publishing house's editor-in-chief, who believed in my abilities to share my knowledge and passion to help engage families in the great outdoors. Laura copyedited the manuscript to make it a more succinct and accessible guidebook for families to use on their hiking adventures. Finally, Kirsten, my project manager, guided me through the labyrinth of publishing this book.

INTRODUCTION

Washington, DC, is known as the political capital of the world, a city inhabited by powerful people. But beyond politics, residents from all walks of life, including the first family, have incredible opportunities to participate in the metropolitan area's rich cultural, historical, artistic, and outdoor adventures. Families can choose from a plethora of outdoor adventures, whether they drive a short distance from their home to an accessible trailhead for a hike or venture farther afield. The DC region offers outdoor enthusiasts many options: backpacking on the Appalachian Trail, whitewater rafting on the Shenandoah River, kayaking and canoeing on the Patuxent River, spelunking in the limestone caves of the Blue Ridge, rock climbing on the metamorphic walls of the Mather Gorge on the Potomac River, fishing in Chesapeake Bay, and hiking on more than a thousand miles of trails. This book is not all-inclusive but describes a potpourri of the best hikes for families in the DC region. Most of them lead to water, rock formations, historical places, nature centers, or parks with activities such as fishing or kayaking.

The Washington region's unique physical features and geologic history provide fantastic places to recreate in nature. A fall line that reaches across the eastern United States has played a predominant role in the geologic history and land formation in the Mid-Atlantic region.

Cash Lake at Patuxent Research Refuge

It marks the difference between the 550-million-year-old metamorphic rock of the Piedmont Plateau west of the fall line and the sand and gravel deposits of the much younger Atlantic Coastal Plain. Evidence of the fall line is present in many of the region's parks from Great Falls Park to Rock Creek National Park to Northwest Branch Park. The fall line's characteristic physical features are steep bluffs, exposed metamorphic cliffs, large boulders, angled rock fractures and formations, and cascading rivers. These physical features offer a wealth of outdoor recreation possibilities from hiking to rock climbing, whitewater rafting, and kayaking.

Areas outside the fall line offer families abundant hiking experiences: the mountains of the Blue Ridge and Appalachian chains, the rolling hills of the Piedmont Plateau, and the wetlands of the Atlantic Coastal Plain. These regions provide incredible opportunities for kids to seek adventures on rocks and in the water, both of which invite a multitude of ways to be creative and engage with nature. Nature's greatest gift to our children is the endless possibilities it offers to discover and question, and trails are the gateway to engaging their curiosity.

Many families have a favorite trail, often close to home; my family's favorite is in Northwest Branch Park. My intention in writing this book was to introduce families to new trails either close to or far away from home so they might add new favorites to their repertoire. Furthermore, I hope families who have never gone hiking might discover a low-cost, minimal-risk activity that enables them to share quality time and make meaningful memories.

ENCOURAGING KIDS TO HIKE

How many times have you suggested a family hike only to be greeted with a crinkled face and a whiney "I don't want to go"? Yet you know that in the end your children always have a great time. How do you turn the initial frown upside-down? These tips will keep your kids coming back for more hiking.

Choose the Right Trail

You know your child the best: his or her interests, energy level, anxieties, and gross motor abilities. A child's age can determine where a family goes hiking; however, some energetic preschoolers with solid motor skills may be able to hike a moderate trail that has some rock scrambling, like Section B of the Billy Goat Trail (see Hike 20). Parents have different philosophies when their child meets challenges outdoors: encouraging them to be independent, enabling them, or somewhere in between. My philosophy is to allow my children and students to meet challenges independently and listen to their intuition, their inner voice. I want them to build self-confidence in their abilities and to know their limits. No matter what, choose a trail that best matches your child's developmental age and ability to help ensure that he or she is smiling at the end of the hike.

Jumping from boulder to boulder on Rock Creek

Offer Choices

Children don't often get to make choices, but when they do, they embrace them. Whenever possible, give your children a choice between a couple of trails. If they don't agree with the options you offer them, model the art of compromise. This approach is particularly beneficial when there is a large age difference among siblings.

Bring a Friend

Sharing a hike with one of your children's friends has many benefits: kids share imaginative play, curiosity, and discovery; distraction from the trail's length and their physical movement on it; challenge and competition; and the potential to introduce a friend to nature.

Hike at Your Child's Pace

Adults have double the leg length and stride of their young children. Embracing children's slower pace can be hard in our fast-paced lives, a pace that often translates into our recreational activities. However, following that old adage "stop and smell the roses" will help you and your children discover the little creatures and variety of plant life that make up a trail's ecosystem. Taking things slowly encourages curiosity and discovery. As they get older, they will match your pace or often surpass it, and you will be the one saying "Wait for me!"

Leave Time for Discovery

It's about the journey, not the destination. What can your children discover about the natural world around them by using their senses: touch, smell, sight, and listening? Encourage your children to ask questions, even if you don't have the answers. Asking questions is the first step in scientific inquiry. To further their curiosity, provide the time and space for them to seek the answer, either through experimenting or reading. Asking questions and seeking answers develops higher order critical thinking and problem solving—essential life skills.

Five-lined skink among the rocks on the Potomac River

Bring Kid Tools

To help encourage children to discover and explore, bring some tools: maybe a camera, hand lenses, binoculars, a bug net, clear plastic or glass containers, a journal, and regular and colored pencils. These tools can help kids engage with nature, hone their observational skills, and ask questions.

Be Flexible

Parents often have an agenda for any activity they engage in with their kids. Hiking offers you the opportunity for your child to set the agenda, even if it is blank and a child just wants to be outside. Highly impulsive and reactive to the stimuli of their environment, children often change their agenda during a hike, so go with the flow. You never know what adventure they will lead you to. Unexpected adventures are sometimes the best and most memorable.

Bring Snacks

I learned this lesson the hard way when one of my children threw a full-blown tantrum on the final stretch of a hike; we were out of snacks, and it was lunchtime. Pack a cooler of drinks and food, and perhaps a special treat, to have when you return to your car after a hike. Children's bodies metabolize food at much higher rates than adults' bodies do. Therefore, they need to graze while hiking to continually refuel. Their need to eat during a hike becomes more prominent when outdoor temperatures are especially cold or hot because it takes more energy to regulate their body temperature in those conditions.

HELPING YOUR KIDS BECOME HIKERS

I began hiking with my daughter when she was an infant. With two months of motherhood under my belt, I was itching to go beyond the streets of my neighborhood and into the woods. I dressed her in a onesie, put her in a snuggie, and sought the shade of mature trees in the deep stream valleys near our home. As she grew, I transitioned her into a hard-framed backpack, which also came in handy during mealtime when camping. Between ages one and two, she rode in the backpack more than she walked, but I gave her every opportunity to hike when she squirmed to get out. Once she was two, I encouraged her to walk more often than she was carried, using the backpack as a respite for when her legs and feet were tired, usually at the end of a hike.

Family portrait atop Annapolis Rocks

A few years later, when my son was a toddler, I switched from the framed kid-carrier to a softer-structured pack because of the ease and convenience of carrying him and packing it. By the time each of my children was four years old, I no longer carried them and instead used the strategies described in the previous section to encourage and motivate them.

Although I never used a jogging stroller, many moms and dads that I have hiked with prefer to use them for either their own physical reasons or the ease of being able to take supplies. The most important thing is being able to get outside on a trail, no matter how. In each hike description, I note whether a hike is passable for jogging strollers.

Parents often wonder—and commonly underestimate—how many miles their child can hike. It depends on your child's activity level, level of perseverance, and how adaptable and flexible they are. For example, a preschooler can hike 2 miles—often longer than parents guess—with minimal elevation change, particularly when hiking with peers, because they help distract each other.

Parents know their children best and what mileage and difficulty level they are able to handle at any given age or time of the day. Some land managers recommend that children be a certain age to hike a particular trail. For example, the C&O Canal National Historical Park recommends that children be eight years old to hike Section A of the Billy Goat Trail (see Hike 19) because the trail has a cliff. This recommendation is based on developmental appropriateness; however, parents make choices based on their familiarity with their child's abilities. Sometimes, though, parents accidentally choose trails that are beyond their child's abilities because they don't know enough about the trail. If you make this mistake, it is important to provide gentle words of encouragement but also to listen and validate their fears.

Overall, there are no hard and fast rules on age appropriateness for mileage and difficulty level. Apply your knowledge of your child to each hiking decision, particularly when deciding whether to challenge them. Choosing the appropriate time to challenge your child on a hike can provide a boost of self-confidence, but if they are not ready, it can have the opposite effect.

HIKING SAFELY

Hiking is one of the safest recreational activities. For most urban trails, putting on a comfortable pair of shoes is the most important step for a successful and enjoyable hike. However, hikers should consider a few hazards that can come into play on any outing: poisonous snakes, poison ivy, ticks, and weather.

Poisonous Snakes

Many species of snakes inhabit the DC region, but only two are poisonous: rattlesnakes and copperhead snakes. Shy and rarely seen, rattlesnakes live in upland forests and rocky outcroppings in northern and western Maryland and west of Fairfax County. They are a threatened species in the Mid-Atlantic due to urbanization and loss of habitat. They rattle their tail to warn people before contact.

Copperhead snakes, on the other hand, are more prevalent. They adapt to a wide range of habitats; they have been found living under trash in the Anacostia neighborhood of DC and sunning themselves at rocky overlooks on the Appalachian Trail. Unlike rattlesnakes, they have no way to warn people who enter their space. Copperheads prefer to conserve their venom, but they will strike if they feel threatened.

Always stay a safe distance away from snakes, and admire their beauty and usefulness in the ecosystem. Don't attempt to handle a snake even if it is nonpoisonous; some snakes will bite to defend themselves. If a rattlesnake or copperhead bites you, seek medical attention immediately.

Poison Ivy

The most common hazard hikers face while on a trail is coming into contact with poison ivy, the feared three-leaf plant. While this plant is not life-threatening, contact with its oil (urushiol) can cause an itchy reaction on human skin. Some people have more severe reactions to poison ivy than others. Oftentimes, we don't know we have come into contact with it until after the rash appears. If you do know that you came into contact with poison ivy, the best remedy is to wash your skin with cold water and soap within a half hour of contact. The oil can also linger on clothing and pet fur; wash any exposed clothes and dogs after hiking. Knowing how to identify the plant, including its vine, will help you avoid it.

Ticks

Insects, including ticks, often get a bad rap because they are perceived as creepy and crawly. However, insects are some of the most beautiful creatures on the planet and are essential in an ecosystem's food web.

Ticks are arachnids, part of the spider family. Many people dislike them because their food source is the blood of mammals, including humans. Ticks are a threat to humans because they carry diseases, such as Lyme disease and Rocky Mountain spotted fever. On their website, the Centers for Disease Control and Prevention offers a complete list and explanation of all the diseases ticks carry.

Ticks don't fly or jump. People come into contact with them when they brush against vegetation. To keep ticks at bay, use an insect repellent with DEET (some people have found lemon eucalyptus oil effective), and wear light-colored long-sleeve shirts and long pants with your pant legs tucked into your socks. Check yourself and your children for ticks after your hike.

Weather

Of the four major hiking hazards, weather can be the most life-threatening. Adverse weather can lead to heatstroke, hypothermia, and lightning strikes. Plan ahead and know the weather forecast so that you and your family are prepared. Bring extra water on hot summer days and raingear and extra clothes on rainy, cold days. Sometimes choosing not to hike is the best decision, particularly when the forecast calls for a storm.

THE TEN ESSENTIALS

When you prepare for a trip, it's critical to think carefully about what to bring. Think of these essentials in terms of either a simple list or a systems approach:

The Ten Essentials

1. Extra clothing
2. Extra food
3. Sunglasses
4. Knife
5. Firestarter
6. First-aid kit
7. Matches in a waterproof container
8. Flashlight
9. Map
10. Compass

The Ten Essentials: A Systems Approach

1. Navigation (map and compass)
2. Sun protection (sunglasses and sunscreen)
3. Insulation (extra clothing)
4. Illumination (headlamp or flashlight)
5. First-aid supplies
6. Fire (firestarter and matches or a lighter)
7. Repair kit and tools (including knife)
8. Nutrition (extra food)
9. Hydration (extra water)
10. Emergency shelter

The American Hiking Society, the national voice for hikers in the United States, promotes its own version of the Ten Essentials for a safe and enjoyable experience on trails.

1. **Appropriate footwear.** Any comfortable shoes that provide foot stability are appropriate for kids. Parents can choose to spend money on hiking boots for kids, but a good pair of sneakers is all that they need to have a safe and fun hike.
2. **Map.** A map provides a sense of place on the trail. Being familiar with your location in relation to your destination will keep you from getting lost, which can happen even on trails in accessible, populated areas.
3. **Extra water.** Water is essential for survival; it helps us maintain proper bodily functions and prevents hypothermia and dehydration. Be sure to bring enough for everyone. If you are hiking with four family members, for instance, pack five water bottles. And on hot days, keep a cooler in the car with some cold water for after your hike.
4. **Extra food.** Children metabolize food much faster than adults do; they often need to graze while hiking to maintain their energy level and prevent crankiness. Don't underestimate your need for food while hiking either. Adults can also become impatient and more easily frustrated when they are hungry.
5. **Raingear and extra clothes.** Checking the day's weather forecast is very important before you head for the trail, but meteorologists are not always right. Pack a raincoat and extra clothes for

those unexpected weather changes. Parents and kids should dress in layers, particularly from fall to spring when temperatures vary throughout the day. Furthermore, you can shed layers during the hike and put them back on when you stop in the shade for a snack or picnic lunch. You might consider purchasing a wicking shirt for your kids; they dry quickly and help regulate body temperatures. Some kids don't like to wear hats, but a hat helps their bodies hold heat on chilly days and keeps the sun off their faces and heads.

6. **Safety items, flashlight, and whistle.** A flashlight or headlamp is important if your family unintentionally ends up hiking after sunset. A whistle is much more effective than your voice when signaling for help.
7. **First-aid kit.** Bring a first-aid kit for those unexpected booboos. Kits are sold at most outdoor retailer stores or can be made at home by putting these items in a zippered pouch: alcohol swabs, antibiotic ointment, various sizes of band-aids and bandages, gauze, first-aid tape, a small pair of scissors, moleskin for hotspots and blisters, a painkiller such as ibuprofen, and an antihistamine such as Benadryl.
8. **Multiuse tool.** These are handy for fixing anything that may break on the trail, removing splinters or embedded ticks, or creating the perfect walking stick.
9. **Sunscreen and hand sanitizer.** Even on a shady forest hike, the sun's rays penetrate through holes in the canopy. You may be exposed to a lot of sun on unexpected play stops along a sunny streambank or on an outcropping of rocks. Apply sunscreen before every hike to prevent the pain and skin damage that results from a sunburn. A small bottle of hand sanitizer stashed in a backpack pocket will help you keep your kid's hands clean—kids use their hands to discover and gain a sense of their world. At the same time, they are always hungry and asking for a snack!

Turkey tail is a beautiful mushroom you might see along the trail.

10. **Backpack.** Where else do you store all these essentials so that you can hike with ease and comfort?

As you gain experience on the trail, you will refine your approach to gear and supplies.

LEAVE NO TRACE

Now that you are totally prepared with the Ten Essentials of hiking, let your thoughts turn to how you could reduce your impact on nature while hiking. Leave No Trace is a set of ethics that helps people limit their footprint on nature when they recreate outdoors. Leave No Trace: The Center for Outdoor Ethics established the seven principles of Leave No Trace in the 1990s when land managers at all levels of government noticed their parks were being heavily impacted by people's outdoor recreation practices. For more than two decades, the organization has molded the initial seven principles to fit the specific practices of different outdoor activities, such as fishing, canoeing, hunting, etc. They also shaped the principles to fit the activities of kids and frontcountry hikers, people who are hiking in accessible, populated areas like the Washington, DC, region.

As parents, we want our kids to explore, discover, and use their imaginations to create adventures. This positive experience keeps them, and you, coming back for more. As they spend more time on a particular trail, your children develop a relationship with that place, which fosters stewardship—a desire to respect and care for the places and experiences that bring positive feelings. It is also our responsibility as parents to model respect and care for nature. Leave No Trace provides the avenue and guidance to be a role model for our children when recreating outdoors. The following questions related to each principle will help guide you and your children to reduce your impact on nature.

1. Plan Ahead and Prepare

Did I remember the Ten Essentials? What is the weather forecast? If I am hiking with a dog, did I remember to bring a leash and poop bags? What do I know about the area my family is hiking in?

2. Stick to the Trails

What color are the blazes? Are there signs that provide direction at each intersection? What happens to plants when I go off-trail? What is the

Tree hollow on the Underground Railroad Trail

best place to sit for a picnic off-trail? Can I find rocks or other durable surfaces? When I need to rest, where is the best place to put my backpack down?

3. Pack Out Your Trash

Did I remember to pack a disposable bag for trash? How can I minimize my trash when preparing for our family hike? Does the area have trash cans, or do I need to bring my trash home? Do I have a method to pick up and carry dog waste? Where are the bathrooms? If there are none, where is the best place to have my child pee or poop? What supplies do I need to pack to dispose of human waste properly? Did my kids help me pick up food bits and garbage after our picnic?

4. Leave What You Find

Do I need to pick that flower for mommy? Can I take a photograph of it? Can I take that turtle shell home? Can I touch it and take a photograph of it?

5. Be Careful with Fire

Can I build a fire in this area? Are there fire rings? Can I bring my own firewood? Or where can I buy some? Is it safer for me to use a stove rather than a fire to cook my meal? Did I put out my fire?

6. Respect Wildlife

Can I pet that rabbit? Can I capture a toad and bring it home? Should I allow my dog to chase a deer? How far away should I stand from a wild animal?

A teachable moment with a toad

7. Be Kind When Sharing the Trail

Will people and children be scared of my unleashed dog? Are my children's screams bothering other hikers who might be watching wildlife? When we meet bikers, hikers, or horseback riders, who yields to whom?

GETTING AROUND THE AREA

Metro reaches every corner of metropolitan Washington from its connected hubs in downtown. From these corners, buses provide point-to-point public transportation. Furthermore, Bike Share provides another green alternative that hikers can use alone or in conjunction with the train and buses. While Bike Share may not be the best option for families with young children, it can add extra adventure to any hiking excursion for families with older children.

Rail

The Washington Metropolitan Area Transit Authority (www.wmata.com), or Metro for short, supplies Washington, DC, and its Maryland and Virginia suburbs with bus and rail transportation.

In Maryland, the Maryland Transit Authority (www.mta.maryland.gov), MARC for short, manages three train lines. The Brunswick line runs from Washington, follows the Potomac River northwest and then crosses it at Harpers Ferry to end in Martinsburg, West Virginia. The Camden and Penn lines run from Washington northeast to Baltimore; the Penn line continues beyond Baltimore.

Both Metro and MARC have trip planners on their websites. Families can type in their current location and a destination and receive an itinerary and departure times for both rail services.

In Virginia, the Virginia Railway Express (www.vre.org), or VRE for short, manages two lines of rail service from Washington, DC, to the Virginia suburbs. The Manassas line runs from Union Station past Manassas to Broad Run. The Fredericksburg line departs Union Station and follows the Potomac River to Fredericksburg.

Bus

The Washington Metropolitan Area Transit Authority (Metro bus) overlaps with county bus systems along major arterial routes from Washington and in some areas within the counties. Each county has its own bus transportation system:

- Arlington County: Arlington Transit (ART), www.arlingtontransit.com
- Fairfax County: Fairfax Connector, www.fairfaxcounty.gov/connector
- Loudoun County: Virginia Regional Transit (VRT), www.vatransit.org
- Montgomery County: Ride On, www.montgomerycountymd.gov/dot-transit
- Prince Georges County: The Bus (operates Monday–Friday, 6:30 AM to 7:00 PM), www.princegeorgescountymd.gov/sites/publicworks/transit/thebus

Bike Share

To shrink your family's carbon footprint and increase your physical activity, bike from the Metro station to the trailhead. Bike Share is available in the District of Columbia; Alexandria and Arlington in Virginia; and Bethesda, Silver Spring, and Rockville in Maryland. To find out more information about how Bike Share works, visit their website (www.capitalbikeshare.com).

HOW TO USE THIS BOOK

This book is packed with information about kid-friendly hikes in the DC region, and this overview will help you understand how details are presented for each hike. The Quick Guide to the Hikes (near the beginning of the book) is a great resource for identifying possible hikes.

Opposite: A hiker perches over Rapidan River rapids.

Playing in a fort on the Gold Mine trail

Before You Go

This section provides information about where to obtain a trail map created by the land manager, the name of the managing agency or park, whether they charge a fee, and the nearest city or town. Note that the maps in this book are intended for planning purposes only; it's always a good idea to pick up a more detailed map for your trip. For details about a park's hours and its contact information, see "Contact Information" in the appendix. If the park's hours are not stated there, then the default is dawn to dusk.

About the Hike

All the hikes in the book are day hikes with a length between 0.25 mile and 5.5 miles.

Difficulty Level

Each hike is rated based on its length, elevation gain, and trail surface, such as rock, boardwalk, dirt, and so on. Each hike is rated as easy, easy/moderate, moderate, moderate/difficult, or difficult.

Seasons

Most of the hikes in this book can be hiked year round. The few exceptions are clearly called out.

Length

Trail length is measured in miles, and the length listed for a particular hike is the entire distance of the described route. This book features three types of hikes: out-and-back, loop (circuit), and a loop combined with a spur. An out-and-back hike means that you return via the same route. One direction is described for each out-and-back hike. A loop hike connects to create a circle. Lastly, a loop-and-spur hike is one that combines both an out-and-back section and a loop.

Hiking Time

Hiking times are calculated at a rate of a half hour for every mile on a flat, dirt trail with time added for elevation gain and more challenging trail surfaces. The time accounts for short stops but not longer ones for picnics or playtime. It's worth noting that kids' hiking speed varies, depending on how they feel.

High Point/Elevation Gain

The high point is the highest elevation that your family reaches on the hike. The elevation gain is the total number of feet the trail climbs.

Access

This category covers the trail surface and jogging-stroller access. Most hikes are on compact soil. However, trail surfaces in the region also include asphalt, boardwalk, grass, rock, and gravel. Rocky trail surfaces require some agility with your feet and possibly your hands, often slowing your child's pace.

Trails are classified into three categories: jogging-stroller friendly, passable for jogging strollers, or not passable for jogging strollers. A hike that is jogging-stroller friendly is on a trail without impediments; you will not need to lift your stroller up a step or over an erosion-control device. A hike that is passable for jogging strollers is on a trail where parents will need to lift a stroller over or traverse rocks, logs, a step or two, or erosion-control devices. A hike that is not passable for jogging strollers is on a trail where a quarter of the trail tread has rocks, logs, stairs, or multiple steps.

Getting There

The driving directions for most hikes begin on Interstate 495 (Capital Beltway), referred to as I-495 throughout. For a few hikes, directions are given both for hikers coming from Maryland and for those coming from Virginia. For hikes that are accessible by public transit, the nearest Metro stop is listed.

On the Trail

Each hike description begins with an overview of the park and then explains why the trail is family-friendly. The description highlights its physical features and activities that are great for kids, and helps parents follow the trail from the trailhead to the end.

COMMON TERMS

The hiking community uses some common terms. Here are the ones I use in this book:

blaze: A mark placed on a tree or rock to indicate to a hiker which trail they are on; often a 2- by 6-inch rectangle in a variety of visible colors.

erosion-control devices: A check dam, water bar, or drainage dip used by trail builders to remove water quickly from the trail tread to prevent sediment runoff.

people's choice trail: An unsanctioned shortcut created by hikers; never blazed or signed; sometimes called a social or use trail.

puncheon: A raised walkway built to traverse through wet areas on a trail; made either of wood or rock and soil.

trail tread: The substance on the surface of a trail.

KEY TO SYMBOLS

The symbols below will help you quickly identify important features, such as restrooms, of the hikes in this book. With the use of the Quick Guide to the Hikes and these symbols, you can choose the best hike for your family on any particular day. Some hikes only fall into one of the categories while others fit multiple. The symbols are located below the "About the Hike" section for each hike.

Accessibility. These trails are easily passable for wheelchairs and strollers, which is different than being passable for jogging strollers. There are no major obstacles that impede passage along the trail; however, inquire about trail conditions before hiking.

Bike paths. The park where the hike is located also has bike paths for families. Some are on paved trails, while in other locations, they are on temporarily closed streets. Therefore, call the park for street closure times.

Campgrounds. At these hike locations, the park offers a campground where families can car-camp or camp at sites along the hike.

Dog-friendly. These hike locations welcome dogs as long as they are on leash. Please remember to pick up after your dog. Some parks are pack-in, pack-out, which includes dog waste.

Drinking water. Water fountains are located at the trailhead or along the hike. However, always bring your own water in case they are turned off for the season or are not functioning.

Fun extras. These hikes are located in parks or public spaces where there are fun activities, such as playgrounds, pools, and nature centers, to experience with kids beyond the hike.

Historical sites. These hikes are in parks or public spaces where families can learn about what historical events, such as Civil War battles, occurred on the land.

Restrooms. Restrooms are located either at the trailhead or along the hike. Some restrooms may be flush toilets and others may be port-a-potties.

Splash zone. On these hikes, families have an opportunity to get their feet wet, wade, or swim in the water.

Wildlife. These hikes are in parks or public spaces where families have an opportunity to observe a variety of wildlife, such as birds and reptiles.

GET OUTSIDE AND HIKE AS A FAMILY

Growing up in the twenty-first century is far different from how most of us grew up in the late twentieth century. If our parents didn't shoo us out the door, then we ran outside on our own, excited to disappear in our neighborhoods, parks, and sometimes the woods in our backyards and did not return until the dinner bell rang. As a kid, I made forts in the woods or in large snowbanks, went sledding, rode my bike, played tag throughout my neighborhood, and played in the creek—all without adult supervision. Much has changed since then. Many kids are overscheduled with homework, sports, and other extracurricular activities; however, this is only one factor contributing to a nature deficit in our children's generation. Other factors include the advent of technology, an increase in stranger danger fed by the media, and decreasing access to green space.

With the decline in the amount of time kids spend outside and in their access to open spaces, environmental educators and advocates have reverted to studies and programming to change the tide of nature

Sharing a moment at Lake Frank

A "we are the champions" moment along the trail

deficit. My parents and grandparents instinctively knew the benefits of outdoor play and exploration in nature: mental and physical well-being and an increase in creativity, imagination, and problem solving. In the twenty-first century, parents, educators, and policy makers need studies to be convinced that children need to put down technological devices, reduce their extracurricular activities, and get outside to play, whether it's in a park, their backyard, or on a trail.

For generations, families have gathered on trails to share quality time together and to explore the extraordinary natural resources that this country has. It is easy to understand why hiking has remained one of the top five outdoor recreational activities for many years: It is inexpensive, does not require much equipment, and is more accessible than other outdoor recreational sports. In light of the decrease in outdoor playtime, hiking provides kids with unstructured opportunities to use their creativity and imagination.

From the mountains in the west, to the Chesapeake Bay in the east, and the multitude of streams and rivers in between, the Washington region provides a wealth of opportunities for families to get outside on a trail to enjoy our rich natural resources. With more than a thousand miles of trails in the wider region, families can choose a trail close to their homes for a short hike or they can travel to a hiking destination to enjoy a full day on the trails. This book serves as a one-stop resource to encourage parents and children to share quality time hiking and experiencing the splendor of nature in the Washington region.

Opposite: Looking for muskrats at Kenilworth Aquatic Gardens

WASHINGTON, DC

ROCK CREEK NATIONAL PARK: VALLEY TO WESTERN RIDGE LOOP

BEFORE YOU GO
Map: Available on park website
Contact: Rock Creek National Park

ABOUT THE HIKE
Moderate/difficult, year-round
Length: 3 miles, loop
Hiking time: 2–2½ hours
High point/elevation gain: 362 feet/232 feet
Access: Compact soil, passable for jogging strollers

GETTING THERE

From I-495 (Capital Beltway), take exit 33 for Connecticut Avenue (MD 185) south toward Chevy Chase, Maryland. Drive 1.4 miles, and turn left onto East-West Highway (MD 410). Drive 1 mile, and turn right onto Beach Drive. Drive 0.8 mile to the parking lot, which is on the left at Boundary Bridge.

ON THE TRAIL

In the Washington, DC, region, there are two parks named Rock Creek. Rock Creek National Park is in the District of Columbia and has been owned and operated by the National Park Service since 1890. Rock Creek Regional Park is in Montgomery County and is owned and operated by Montgomery Parks, also known as the Maryland National Capital Park and Planning Commission. Both parks are buffer zones for Rock Creek and provide ample recreational opportunities for area residents: biking, hiking, fishing, picnicking, kayaking, canoeing, golfing, and horseback riding. Both parks also have nature centers, which provide educational opportunities for families.

The Valley to Western Ridge Loop in the northern section of Rock Creek National Park is a popular destination for trail runners and dog walkers. However, this loop is also a great family hike on the border of Washington, DC, and Montgomery County. The first half is on the Valley Trail, which follows Rock Creek as it meanders to the Potomac River. Saunter through a floodplain and then up the valley walls above the creek for great views. The second half follows a connector trail and the Western Ridge Trail, which allows you to wander through old-growth forest on the western ridge of the park.

Frozen Rock Creek along the Valley Trail

The trailhead is at the end of a small parking lot that holds ten cars. On weekends, Beach Drive is closed to cars from this parking lot to West Beach Drive. Additional sections of Beach Drive in the District of Columbia are closed to vehicles on the weekends.

At the trailhead, turn right on the Valley Trail, and walk over Boundary Bridge. Just after the bridge, a people's choice trail intersects the trail. Continue straight to walk through the floodplain, which can be very wet, particularly in spring. Within a couple tenths of a mile, the Valley Trail curves to the right and intersects the Boundary Trail, which connects to Primrose Road. For the next half mile, the Valley Trail hugs the valley wall to the right just above the floodplain, allowing the trail to stay dry. Young beech trees populate the forest along this section.

BEECH TREES

Beech trees are a shade-tolerant species that prefer older-growth forests. In forests that have been clear-cut for whatever purpose, beech trees have a more difficult time regenerating. In patches of the forest on this hike, young beech trees dominate the understory.

They characteristically grow near mature trees either from their seed (the beechnut) or root suckers. A beech tree produces seeds from the pollination of male and female flowers after it is forty years old. The tree produces seeds every two to eight years and sheds them in the fall after the first hard freeze. Once the seed has germinated, it grows rapidly in a canopy-covered forest but then slows its growth rate after six years. Beech trees don't need to outpace other trees, like the tulip poplar, because they survive well in shade and are not browsed heavily by deer. They are easily recognizable in the forest by their shallow roots that peek aboveground and their silvery, smooth bark that people often unfortunately mar with carvings.

Just before the West Beach Drive Bridge, the trail forks. The left fork connects to West Beach Drive. Take the right fork, and head under the bridge. On the other side, another trail (on your left) from West Beach connects to the Valley Trail. Continue straight and over the pedestrian bridge. The trail follows the creek for a half mile until it climbs 200 feet above the valley wall. Before the trail climbs, a short access trail intersects the Valley Trail on the left, allowing access to Juniper Street. In addition, there is a spot along the trail to access the creek.

The trail curves to the left after climbing about 100 feet and follows the walls of a gulch in and out until it parallels the creek. All the while, the trail continues to ascend. Coming out of the gulch, the trail curves left and, shortly thereafter, intersects the Pine Trail on the left. The Pine Trail connects to 16th Street. Follow the Valley Trail as it curves to the right. Within a few hundred feet, the trail curves again to the left; however, a people's choice trail to the right leads to the end of a peninsula that overlooks Rock Creek, providing great views.

From this peninsula, the Valley Trail descends to an intersection with a connector trail. The Valley Trail continues left and follows Rock Creek south. However, to make the loop with the Western Ridge Trail, continue straight and over the Riley Spring Bridge. Cross Beach Drive

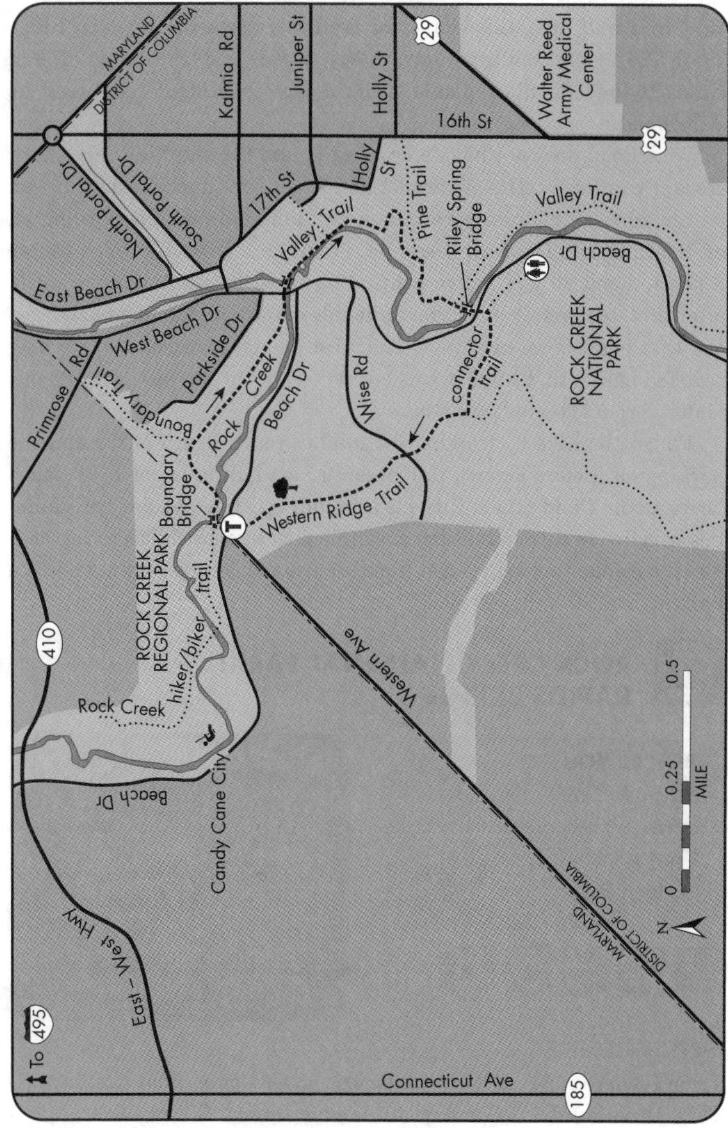

cautiously—there is no crosswalk. Large boulders mark the entrance of the connector trail. Within 100 feet, a trail intersects from the left. Continue straight as the trail ascends the hill with a gulch on the right side. In a half mile, this connector trail intersects the Western Ridge Trail. Turn right and hike toward Wise Road. The trail levels off and curves to the left. Hike 0.3 mile until the Western Ridge Trail intersects Wise Road.

Wise Road does not have a crosswalk, and the sightlines are short; cross it cautiously. The Western Ridge Trail continues straight ahead on the other side. From here, it is a half mile to reach the parking lot on Beach Drive. The trail descends the hill and crosses a gulch to rise a short, steep 20 feet before continuing back downhill again. Shortly after this steep rise, look on the right side of the trail for an amazing red oak that has five fused trunks. The most plausible reason for this five-trunked oak is that after it was cut down within the last century, five viable sprouts created new stems.

Finish the hike by walking 0.1 mile to reach Beach Drive and the parking lot. Before leaving this area, drive a half mile north on Beach Drive to the Candy Cane City playground, which is popular with families who live in this area. It has multiple play sets for children from toddlers to elementary school age. You can also reach it by walking north a half mile on the Valley Trail.

ROCK CREEK NATIONAL PARK: RAPIDS BRIDGE

BEFORE YOU GO
Map: Available at the nature center or on park website
Contact: Rock Creek National Park

ABOUT THE HIKE
Moderate, year-round
Length: 2 miles, loop
Hiking time: 1–1½ hours
High point/elevation gain: 374 feet/230 feet
Access: Compact soil, passable for jogging strollers

GETTING THERE

From I-495 (Capital Beltway), take exit 33 for Connecticut Avenue (MD 185). Drive south on Connecticut Avenue toward Chevy Chase, Maryland, for 3 miles. Enter a traffic circle, and take the fourth exit to stay on Connecticut Avenue. Drive 0.5 mile, and turn left onto Military Road. Drive 1 mile, and turn right onto Glover Road. Drive 0.3 mile, and stay left on Glover Road. Turn left into the driveway for the nature center

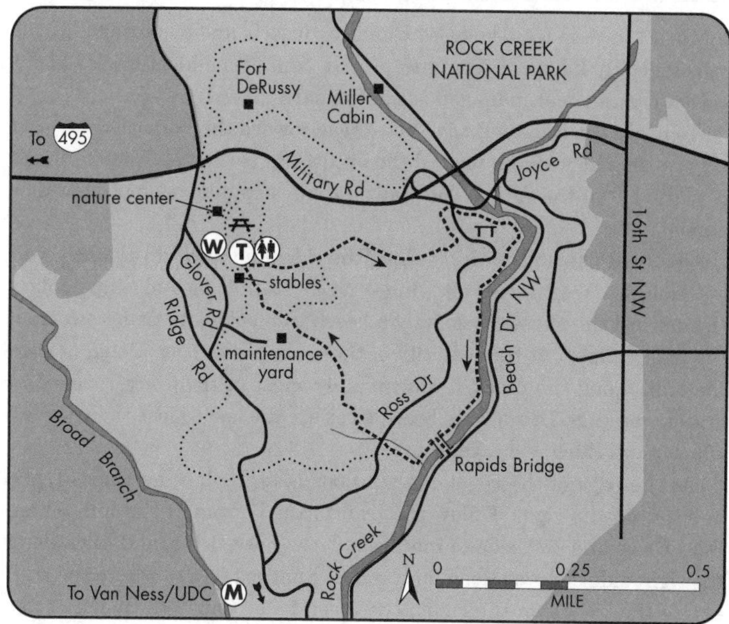

and horse stables. The nature center parking lot is on your left. The closest Metro station is Van Ness/UDC (Red Line).

ON THE TRAIL

Rock Creek National Park was established in 1890 by the federal government. This 1700-acre park extends from the DC–Maryland border south to the Potomac River, creating a buffer zone for the southern half of the 33-mile-long creek. Rock Creek Regional Park was established in the 1930s to provide green space for Montgomery County residents and buffer the northern half of the creek.

The Rock Creek National Park Nature Center is an ideal location to start a family hike. Whether you visit the nature center before or after your hike, you can view their exhibits and live animals, play in their activity room, visit the planetarium (check the website for program times) and small bookstore, and talk to a ranger. Behind the nature center is a half-mile interpretive hike. Grab an interpretive brochure from the nature center or box at the trailhead, and learn about the park's big trees, like the beech tree—nicknamed the graffiti tree. People have left traces of themselves by carving into the beech tree's smooth bark, but this practice damages the tree by inviting insects and bacteria to invade it, potentially killing it. The interpretive trail also educates kids about poison ivy and deer management in the park.

To begin the Rapids Bridge hike, head toward the horse stables, and stay to the left walking toward the outdoor horse corral. The trailhead is to the left of the corral. The trails on this loop hike are not blazed or named.

The trail descends quickly along the ridgeline toward the creek valley. Along the trail, large red, white, and chestnut oaks and tulip poplars rise toward the sky. Occasionally a beech tree pokes its trunk out from the trail's edge, but the majority of them appear farther along, next to the trail along the creek. Unfortunately, most of them are covered in graffiti carvings. In autumn, beech trees are the last to lose their leaves, which gives the forest a yellow glow.

At the edge of the ridge, the trail bends to the left, and Ross Drive appears on the right. Follow the trail to the bottom of the hill, where Ross Drive and Joyce Road intersect. Cross Ross Drive, and hike along the right side of Joyce Road for a couple hundred feet to where the trail enters the woods on the right. The creek is on your left. Shortly after you enter the woods, you will see a bench that overlooks the rapids on Rock Creek. The creek makes a rapid descent here where the Piedmont Plateau meets the Atlantic Coastal Plain.

The trail quickly rises up along the valley wall to then fall back toward the creek where it stays for most of the hike except for one more short rise due to the geologic formation of the valley walls. For a half mile, the trail follows Rock Creek as the water tumbles quickly over large boulders. There are multiple places to play on these boulders and along the creek. The creek constantly changes its path as the water ebbs and flows due to rainfall and stormwater runoff; it carves new streambanks, deposits rocks, and forms sandbars. During a rainstorm, the ferocity of the creek has carried picnic tables, large trees, and often tons of garbage downstream. Look for evidence of how the creek leaves its mark on the land.

Just before turning right to ascend the steep ridge, pass the Rapids Bridge, a pedestrian bridge that crosses Rock Creek to Beach Drive. After turning right, the trail makes a gentle ascent but then quickly turns steep. Ahead is a vehicle bridge on Ross Drive. About three-quarters of the way up the hill, turn right where the trail forks, and head under the vehicle bridge. A feeder creek runs adjacent to the trail

Scrambling on rocks in Rock Creek near Rapids Bridge

on your right in the ravine. After you walk under the bridge, the trail crosses a large culvert over the feeder stream and follows switchbacks up the hill. The trail's curves provide a gentler slope and reduce the erosion of the ridge's sidehill. The curves soon give way to a straighter trail that provides respite for your pounding heart.

Shortly before you reach the horse stables, a trail from the right intersects your path; continue straight toward the stables. Take a break at one of the picnic tables here for a snack or lunch to watch the comings and goings of the horses and their riders. The stables are a busy place, particularly on the weekends.

Pass the picnic tables, and turn right onto the stable's driveway. Just after the building, turn left onto a sidewalk and trail that leads back to the parking lot at the nature center. Picnic tables and benches are scattered around the nature center property in case you brought a picnic lunch.

FORT DUPONT NATIONAL PARK: TURKEY TROT TRAIL

BEFORE YOU GO
Map: Available on Kids in Parks website
Contact: Fort Dupont National Park

ABOUT THE HIKE
Easy/moderate, year-round
Length: 1.25 miles, loop
Hiking time: 1 hour
High point/elevation gain: 236 feet/171 feet
Access: Compact soil and asphalt, passable for jogging strollers

GETTING THERE

From Maryland, take I-495 (Capital Beltway) to exit 19B for US 50. Drive 4.7 miles, and take the exit for I-295. Drive 4.2 miles, and take the exit for Pennsylvania Avenue East. Drive 0.5 mile, and turn left onto Minnesota Avenue. After 0.5 mile, turn right onto Randle Circle. Drive 0.1 mile, and turn right onto Fort Dupont Drive Southeast. Drive 0.25 mile, and turn left into the activity center parking lot.

From Virginia, take I-395 to I-695 (Southeast Freeway). Exit left onto Southwest Freeway. Drive 2 miles. Take the exit for I-295 north and drive 0.8 mile. Take the exit for Pennsylvania Avenue East and drive 0.4 mile. Turn left onto Minnesota Avenue. After 0.5 mile, turn right onto Randle Circle. Drive 0.1 mile, and turn right onto Fort Dupont Drive Southeast. Drive 0.25 mile, and turn left into the activity center parking lot.

The closest Metro stations are Minnesota Avenue (Orange Line) and Benning Road (Blue Line).

ON THE TRAIL

Fort Dupont was one of sixty-eight forts built by the Union Army around Washington, DC, to defend it against the Confederate Army during the Civil War. Today, it is a 376-acre park, one of the largest in DC. The park offers 10 miles of trails, including the 7-mile hiker-biker trail that links many of the Civil War defense structures; ranger-led educational programming at the activity center; an ice skating rink; basketball and tennis courts; athletic fields; picnic areas; and summer concerts.

The Turkey Trot Trail, a 1.25-mile loop, starts at the activity center, passes the summer amphitheater, heads into deciduous forests, along a

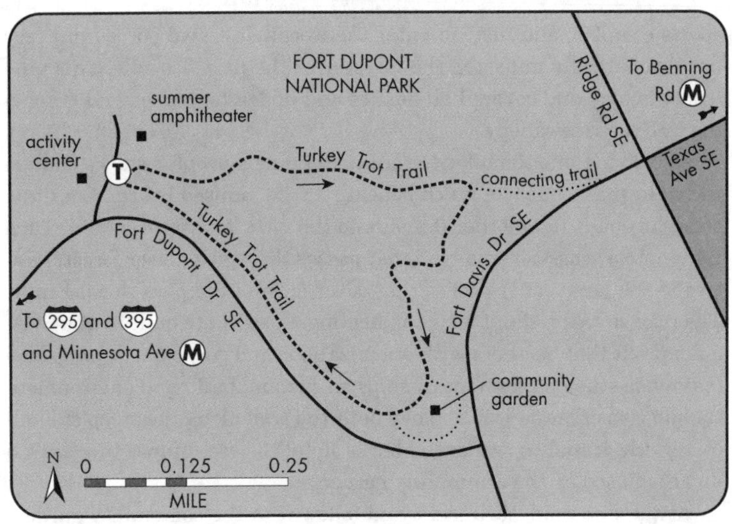

meadow, and by a community garden. Described clockwise, the loop creates a triangle with the first leg a gentle ascent on asphalt and gravel. The second leg follows the sidehill of a gulch to a community garden, and the last leg descends back to the summer amphitheater. The trail is inconsistently signed and blazed; a blue blaze appears occasionally on trees. The intersections are not signed. A new section of the loop built by the Student Conservation Association (SCA) on the second leg is the only part with signs.

Begin the hike at the "Kids in Parks: TRACK Trails" sign at the back right corner of the activity center parking lot. This trail is part of the Kids in Parks TRACK Trails program, which is funded by the Blue Ridge Parkway Foundation. This program's mission is to engage kids with activities and share knowledge about the natural resources found along hikes. The program developed four brochures (available on the Kids in Parks website) for parents and kids for this particular park: Fort Dupont: Animal Athletes, Fort Dupont: Hide and Seek, Fort Dupont: Nature's Relationships, and Fort Dupont: Need for Trees.

After the Kids in Parks sign, follow the trail downhill 100 feet, and turn right on the asphalt trail next to the amphitheater. Follow it through the grassy area of the amphitheater uphill to where the trail tread becomes gravel with a meadow on the left and forest on the right. Pass a trail on the left at the edge of the meadow that leads to the sports complex, and instead enter the woods. Invasive porcelain berry has dramatically impacted the forest over the next 0.1 mile. This vine has entwined and covered all bushes and understory trees and is moving into the tree canopy.

At 0.3 mile into the hike, the trail intersects a people's choice trail on the right that leads to a gulch beneath an old, unused bridge. Continue straight uphill for another 0.1 mile to the next trail intersection. Turn right onto a grass-covered trail that passes through a newer forest, relative to the large canopy trees that cover most of the park, for 0.1 mile. The trail curves right at a sign indicating a new route built by the SCA, a nonprofit that partners with organizations and government programs to provide students with internships on sustainability and environmental and conservation issues. They built the trail along the steep sidehill of a gulch; it makes two switchbacks uphill before intersecting with a dirt road used by the community garden.

At the dirt road, turn right and follow it to the community garden. Each year, DC residents have the opportunity to cultivate a 20-by-25-foot plot of land in Fort Dupont Park after attending a two-hour workshop. Residents may cultivate more than one plot, but they must farm organically, provide an opportunity for interpretation and education, and engage youth in the cultivation process. At the edge of the community garden, turn right and follow the road toward Fort Dupont Drive Southeast with the garden on the left. On the southern edge of the

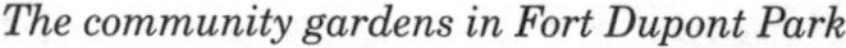

The community gardens in Fort Dupont Park

garden, turn right on a dirt road that becomes a grass-covered trail as it enters the woods. The trail ascends a small hill to then descend all the way back to the amphitheater and activity center.

Fort Dupont participates in the National Park Service Junior Ranger program. Children may obtain a junior ranger booklet during ranger-led programs. Contact the park for a schedule of their programs.

KENILWORTH AQUATIC GARDENS: RIVER TRAIL ON THE ANACOSTIA

BEFORE YOU GO

Map: Available at the visitor center

Contact: Kenilworth Aquatic Gardens

ABOUT THE HIKE

Easy, year-round

Length: 1.4 miles, out and back

Hiking time: 1 hour

High point/elevation gain: 20 feet/no gain

Access: Compact soil, jogging-stroller friendly

GETTING THERE

From I-495 (Capital Beltway), take exit 22B for the Baltimore-Washington Parkway south (MD 295). Drive 6.3 miles, and take the exit for Eastern Avenue, Kenilworth Avenue and the aquatic gardens. Drive 0.3 mile, and turn right onto Quarles Street Northeast. After 0.2 mile, turn left onto Anacostia Avenue Northeast. The gardens are immediately on the right. The closest Metro station is Deanwood (Orange Line).

ON THE TRAIL

Kenilworth Aquatic Gardens is a 12-acre national park that sits on the Anacostia River. The park features forty-five artificial aquatic ponds that showcase lilies and lotus flowers, both native species and species from around the world. In addition, the ponds provide habitat for animals, such as fish, muskrats, turtles, and frogs. Beyond the ponds, walk the River Trail and the boardwalk through the wetlands to observe plant and animal life, such as the great blue heron, which thrives in this wetland. The park has a small visitor center where you can talk with a ranger, read interpretive signs, buy books to expand your child's curiosity, and view paintings of lilies by the former landowner.

The beavers have been busy with this tree!

The River Trail is 1.4 miles out and back on a peninsula between the Anacostia River and its wetlands. The trail is wide and shady with a combination of grass-covered and crushed stone surfaces. From the parking lot, walk 100 yards on a crushed stone path to a four-way intersection where a sign marks the trailhead. Turn right onto the River Trail. Within 100 feet, there is a vernal pool on the right created by flooding of the Anacostia. At this spot and others along the trail, play "I Spy" for evidence of beavers. Kids may notice the telltale pencil point of a small tree trunk or the removal of large sections of bark and cambia on the lower trunks of larger trees.

After the vernal pool, the trail curves right to follow a large marsh on the left. It's straight for 0.1 mile and then makes a sweeping left hook around the large marsh. You can view a variety of plant life, such as cattails, arrow arum, tidal grasses, and trees, and the open water of the wetlands. You can also see turtles, such as eastern painted and snapping turtles, and listen to frogs. If young hikers are really quiet, they may see a frog or beaver, particularly around dawn and dusk. This marsh and those in the park provide a prime example of a freshwater tidal wetland, whose water level rises and falls with the ocean tides.

WETLANDS

Wetland ecosystems have one of the widest arrays of plant and animal life found on earth. Wetlands are giant filters that clean pollutants and thus protect rivers, estuaries, oceans, and groundwater; they also absorb floodwaters and help to prevent land erosion. During dry seasons, they maintain water flow and sustain groundwater aquifers. In terms of their economic value, wetlands are used to grow crops, such as cranberries and rice, and they provide fish and seafood.

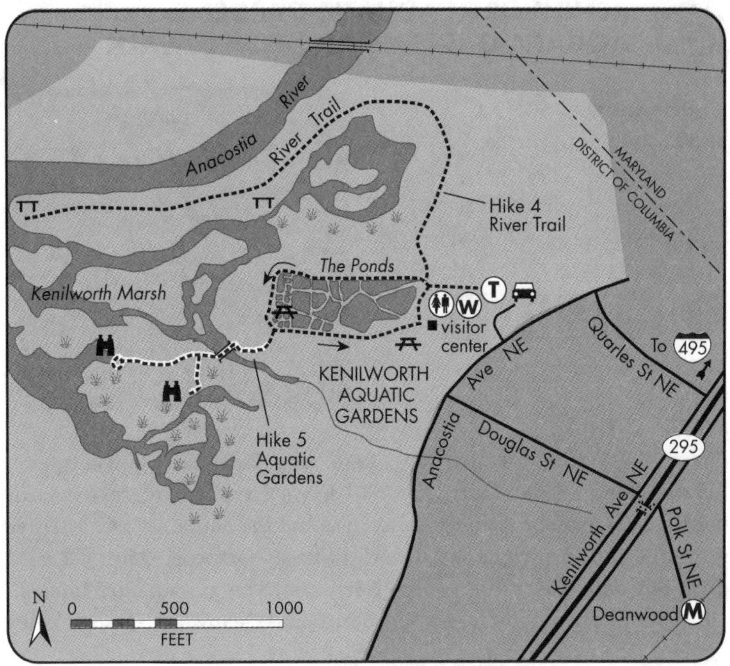

After 0.3 mile on the trail, the vegetation clears on the right to allow you to catch a glimpse of the Anacostia River and watch trains pass over it. From this point, the trail is mostly straight with a few small bends as it traverses the peninsula. The river is on the right and the marsh on the left. After about a half mile, the trail opens to a shady clearing on the marsh side. At the bench here, you can sit and observe wildlife and a great example of where a beaver chewed the bark and cambia off a large tree.

At 0.6 mile, a people's choice trail that accesses the Anacostia River appears on the right. The riverbank has a retaining wall at this spot. Hike a little more than 0.1 mile to the trail's end where the marsh meets the river. Here, there is a bench and a clearing on the river side to access the shoreline. When exploration and playtime are over, turn around and hike back the same way to the trailhead. Before you leave, see the displays at the visitor center and perhaps enjoy a picnic lunch at the tables just beyond it, or hike 1 mile around the ponds and out and back on the boardwalk (see Hike 5).

KENILWORTH AQUATIC GARDENS: AQUATIC GARDENS AND BOARDWALK

BEFORE YOU GO

Map: Available at the visitor center

Contact: Kenilworth Aquatic Gardens

ABOUT THE HIKE

Easy, year-round

Length: 1 mile, loop and spur

Hiking time: 1 hour

High point/elevation gain: 20 feet/no gain

Access: Crushed stone and boardwalk, jogging-stroller friendly

GETTING THERE

From I-495 (Capital Beltway), take exit 22B for the Baltimore-Washington Parkway south (MD 295). Drive 6.3 miles, and take the exit for Eastern Avenue, Kenilworth Avenue and the aquatic gardens. Drive 0.3 mile, and turn right onto Quarles Street Northeast. After 0.2 mile, turn left onto Anacostia Avenue Northeast. The gardens are immediately on the right. The closest Metro station is Deanwood (Orange Line).

Visit the gardens in the summer to see lotus flowers in full bloom.

LILIES AND LOTUS FLOWERS

Many of the ponds hold the lotus flower and different types of lilies. The gardens showcase two major varieties of water lilies: hardy and tropical. The flowers and pads of both types float. Hardy lilies, which bloom in late May, are generally cup-shaped and can be a variety of colors, with white being the most common. Their usually solid green pads are thick and waxy with smooth edges. Tropical lilies in general are more open and star-shaped; their blooms are a variety of colors. Their thin pads have scalloped or toothed edges and often have variegated patterns. Vulnerable to freezing temperatures and ice, tropical lilies bloom from the end of July to early fall.

With its long stem, large leaves, and flower that grows far above the water's surface, the lotus dwarfs the water lilies that inhabit most of the ponds. Each stem boasts one flower with cupped, pink-tipped petals and a yellow stamen and pistil. It blooms from late June to August. The flower opens in the cool morning and closes by nightfall or when temperatures reach 90 degrees Fahrenheit. Upon first blooming, the lotus releases a subtle perfume to attract pollinators, but it doesn't release pollen unless a pollinator becomes trapped inside the closed flower at night. This adaptation increases the flower's genetic diversity by preventing self-pollination. Once the ovules are fertilized and seeds are created, the pistil dries out, and the pod, often characterized as an upside-down showerhead, releases its seeds. Morning is the best time to see the flowers in bloom during summer as they often close in the heat of the afternoon and don't reopen until the next morning.

ON THE TRAIL

Kenilworth Aquatic Gardens is a twelve-acre national park that sits on the Anacostia River. The park features forty-five artificial aquatic ponds that showcase lilies and lotus flowers and both native species and those from around the world. In addition, the ponds provide habitat for animals, such as fish, muskrats, turtles, and frogs. Beyond the ponds, walk the River Trail and the boardwalk through the wetlands to observe plant and animal life, such as the great blue heron, which thrives in this wetland. The park has a small visitor center where you can talk with a ranger, read interpretive signs, buy books to expand your child's curiosity, and view paintings of lilies by the former landowner.

Fifteen years after fighting in the Civil War, Walter Shaw bought thirty acres of land along the Anacostia from his in-laws where he established a business of growing and selling water lilies. His daughter Helen later took over the business and traveled the world to bring more exotic species of lilies to the ponds. By the early 1900s, the Shaw family had become famous for their lily ponds. Thousands of people—including President Calvin Coolidge and his wife, Grace, who visited repeatedly—came to see the ponds. The park was established in 1938 when Congress bought eight acres from the Shaw family to prevent the land from being destroyed; the Army Corps of Engineers wanted to dredge the Anacostia River.

This 1-mile hike winds around the outside of the ponds and out to the end of the boardwalk. The best time to view the flowers is during summer, especially in the morning when they are open. Plus the trail offers little shade. Watch out for abundant poison ivy along this exposed hike.

From the parking lot, follow a crushed stone path for 100 yards to a four-way intersection with the River Trail and the trail around the ponds. To hike the circumference of the ponds counterclockwise, continue straight on the crushed stone path at the trail sign. A majority of the ponds are supported and bordered by grass-covered walking paths to provide visitors with an intimate view of the variety of the lilies and lotus flowers they harbor. You can choose to hike the perimeter of the ponds or divert and walk some of the paths among the ponds.

To reach the boardwalk, hike halfway around the perimeter of the ponds (0.3 mile) and turn right just past a picnic table under a tree. The boardwalk leads above the wetlands, then splits at a Y intersection. Both branches end at two viewpoints with seating and interpretive signs describing the plants that inhabit the marshes and the mechanics of tidal wetlands. The two platforms offer opportunities to watch osprey and great blue herons and maybe catch sight of an eagle. They are also perfect spots to rest and have a snack with your kids.

When you are ready, return the same way on the boardwalk to the trail around the ponds. Take a right and follow it 0.2 mile to a shady area with picnic tables. The trail makes a final curve to the left; the visitor center and restrooms are on the right after the curve. In the greenhouse beside the visitor center, the National Park Service cultivates and grows lilies and lotuses.

The hike ends where it started at the crushed stone path at a four-way trail intersection that leads back to the parking lot. To see more of

Kenilworth Aquatic Gardens, hike 1.4 miles out and back on the River Trail (see Hike 4), which follows a peninsula along the Anacostia River and its wetlands.

NATIONAL ARBORETUM: ASIAN GARDEN

BEFORE YOU GO
Map: Available on the arboretum's website and at the visitor center
Contact: US National Arboretum

ABOUT THE HIKE
Easy, year-round
Length: 1.6 miles, out and back
Hiking time: 1 hour
High point/elevation gain: 148 feet/40 feet
Access: Compact soil and asphalt, jogging-stroller friendly

GETTING THERE

From I-495 (Capital Beltway), take exit 22B for the Baltimore-Washington Parkway south (MD 295). Drive 5.6 miles, and exit for US 50 west. Drive 2.4 miles, and turn left onto Bladensburg Road. Drive 0.4 mile, and turn left onto R Street. At the end, turn right into the National Arboretum. To reach the Asian Garden, drive on Meadow Road to one of three parking areas near the garden. The closest Metro station is Rhode Island Avenue (Red Line).

ON THE TRAIL

The mission of the US National Arboretum, a 446-acre park operated by the US Department of Agriculture, is to research, educate, and create garden displays with a large variety of plant species to enhance the environment. The visitor center has bonsai and aquatic plant life displays that host koi. The arboretum's azaleas, ferns, and Asian plant collections have walking paths to help visitors enjoy the plant life. Most of these paths are compact soil but some are paved.

This hike visits parts of the Dogwood and Asian Gardens, both of which sit on the ridge above the Anacostia River. The Asian Garden displays plant collections from China, Japan, and Korea. In 1996, the arboretum constructed a Chinese-style red pagoda on a ledge among

The red pagoda peeks through the trees in the Asian Garden.

trees, making for excellent photo opportunities.

Start the hike on a paved trail to the left of the dogwood collections sign. After 100 yards, the paved trail ends at a circle with benches. The Dogwood Garden continues down a grassy lane to the left. The best time to see the garden in bloom is the first week of May. Continue straight on the grassy trail almost to the edge of the ridge above the Anacostia River. Turn right onto a trail of compact soil, and follow it above the river. Stay left on this trail along the edge of the ridge above the river, passing intersections with short trails on the right that weave among the gardens.

At 0.2 mile, the trail reaches a point with a bench providing an opportunity to rest, snack, and take in the nice view of the Anacostia River below. Then continue on the trail as it skirts the edge of the ridge and stays along the river. A few more benches sit along the trail overlooking the river.

ANACOSTIA RIVER

The Anacostia River is 9 miles long from its mouth at the Potomac River to its source where the northeast and northwest branches converge to form it. The 176-square-mile Anacostia Watershed covers most of eastern Washington, DC; Montgomery County; and a large portion of Prince Georges County. Thirteen tributaries feed into and create the watershed. The slow-moving, tidal Anacostia has been tagged as "the forgotten river" because of the pollutants, such as trash, that enter it. The river cannot easily rid or flush itself of the pollutants that enter it through storm drains. For several years, the DC government and many organizations have worked hard to clean up and revitalize the river.

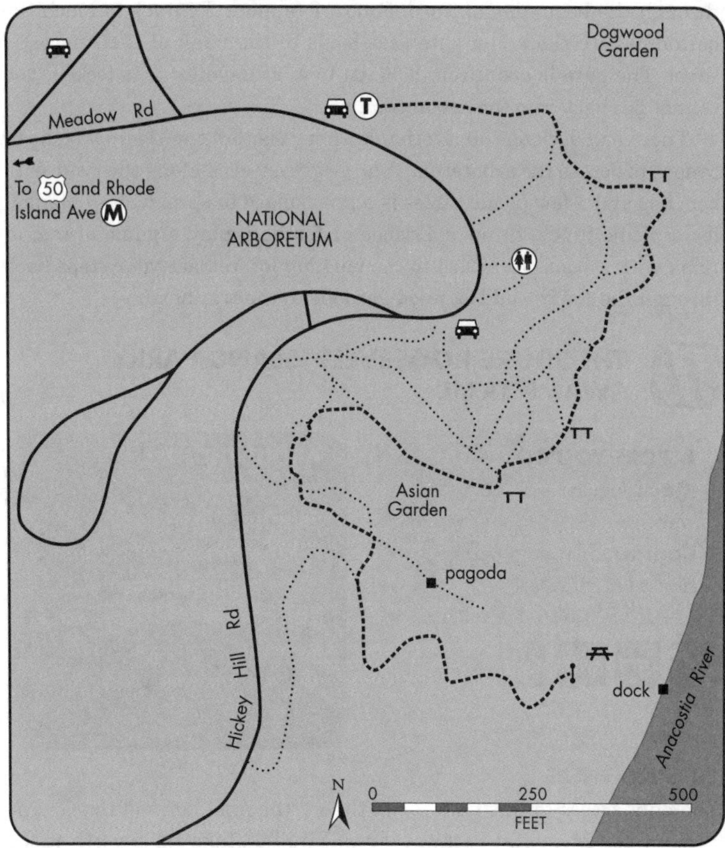

After a third bench, the trail curves right, away from the river. Look to the left, and notice the Chinese pagoda through the trees on the opposite side of the gulch. Walk about 100 yards to another circle; continue around it and out the opposite side. The trail becomes paved again. At the fork, stay left and descend the path, which becomes large crushed stone and descends a few steps before reaching the path that leads to the Chinese pagoda.

Turn right and walk about 100 feet to an intersection with a wide cement path that winds up and down the ridge from Hickey Hill Road to the river. Turn left and follow the S curves downhill, passing magnolia trees. The best time to see them in bloom is from the end of March through the beginning of April. Follow five more S curves to reach the bottom where there is a gate that leads to the bank of the Anacostia River. The gate is open from 8:30 AM to 4:00 PM; once it is locked, you cannot get back into the arboretum.

There is a dock on the riverbank where visitors can tie up kayaks or canoes to access the arboretum. A large grassy area along the river with benches and a few picnic tables is a great place to spread out a blanket for a picnic lunch, throw a Frisbee or football, play a game of tag, or relax with a book. To return to the parking lot, retrace your steps back through the Asian and Dogwood gardens to the trailhead.

THEODORE ROOSEVELT ISLAND PARK: SWAMP TRAIL

BEFORE YOU GO
Map: Available on park website
Contact: Theodore Roosevelt Island Park

ABOUT THE HIKE
Easy, year-round
Length: 2 miles, loop
Hiking time: 1–1½ hours
High point/elevation gain: 93 feet/110 feet
Access: Compact soil and raised boardwalk, passable for jogging strollers

GETTING THERE

The only access to this park is via the northbound lanes of the George Washington Memorial Parkway. From Virginia, take I-395 north to the George Washington Memorial Parkway north. Drive 2.2 miles, and take the exit on the right for Theodore Roosevelt Island. From DC, take Constitution Avenue west over the Roosevelt Bridge. Exit onto the George Washington Memorial Parkway north. Stay in the right lane and take the right exit for Theodore Roosevelt Island. The island is accessible from the Rosslyn Metro station.

ON THE TRAIL

Theodore Roosevelt Island sits in the middle of the Potomac River between Georgetown and Rosslyn, Virginia. The last island in the river as it flows toward the Chesapeake Bay, it straddles the end of the Piedmont Plateau and the beginning of the Atlantic Coastal Plain. An

Rock hopping on Theodore Roosevelt Island

upland forest sits on top of soil-covered metamorphic rock that dominates the northern and western ends of the island. This metamorphic rock is most noticeably exposed in the northeast corner.

A compact soil trail traverses through the upland forest but swampy wetland dominates the landscape of the island's southern and eastern ends, and a raised boardwalk leads through it. A 2-mile loop hike around the circumference of the island takes you on a tour of these two contrasting ecosystems. The hike ends at the monument for Theodore Roosevelt where you and your kids can read famous Roosevelt quotations on four topics—the state, democracy, youth, and nature—on four large stone pillars. The island is a great place for spending a couple hours exploring its rocks, trails, and monument.

To access the Swamp Trail, cross the pedestrian bridge at the end of the parking lot. The trails on Roosevelt Island are restricted to hikers. While crossing the bridge, you and your kids may spy mallard ducks hanging out in this tranquil part of the Potomac. In addition, rowers and kayakers like this quiet, still water between the island and Virginia. At the end of the bridge, turn left to follow the yellow-blazed Swamp Trail clockwise. During periods of heavy rain and flooding, this section can be muddy because it is close to the river.

Along the trail in the northern section of the island, there are many people's choice trails that access the river's edge. The most confusing spot on the trail is in the northwest corner where a people's choice trail goes straight, but the Swamp Trail turns right. At a second intersection

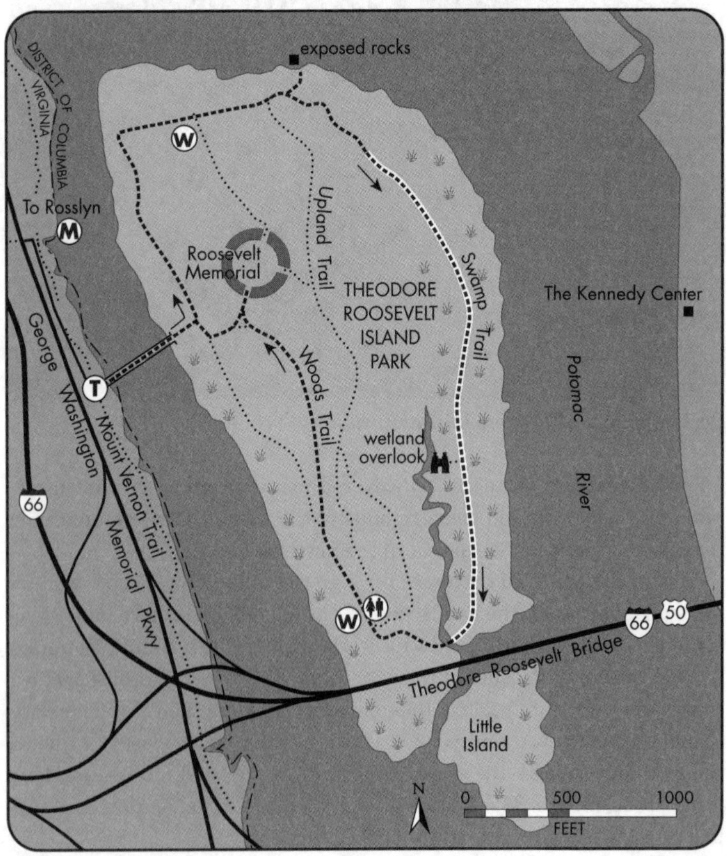

THE ISLAND'S HISTORY

Throughout history, this island has had many names—most notably Mason Island—and owners. The Nacotchtank Indians once inhabited it for fishing. George Mason bought the island in the late 1600s and passed it down through family. The Mason family built a mansion at the high point of the island, but it succumbed to fire in 1869 and again in 1906. Evidence of the mansion doesn't exist anymore because the Civilian Conservation Corps removed the burnt shell in the 1930s. During the Civil War, the Union used the island as a training ground, in particular to train the first black US troops.

In 1932, the Theodore Roosevelt Memorial Association bought the island and gave it to the federal government. Congress appropriated money to create a memorial for Roosevelt in a most apropos setting to honor the conservation and preservation of millions of acres of land in the United States during his presidential terms. The monument was dedicated to the public in 1967.

with a people's choice trail, turn right to follow the yellow blazes of the Swamp Trail. You can go straight on the people's choice trail at this intersection as it links to the Swamp Trail in the northeast corner of the island near exposed metamorphic rock; however, the trail narrows, is not passable for jogging strollers, and is covered with poison ivy. The upland forest here is dense with heavy vine coverage, including natives like poison ivy, the grape vine, and nonnatives like Oriental bittersweet. The Swamp Trail, on the other hand, is a wide path inviting families with young children to cross the northern tip of the island and easily access the raised boardwalk through the wetlands.

Pass two trails that intersect the Swamp Trail from the right: first, the red-blazed Woods Trail and second, the blue-blazed Upland Trail. (The trails on Roosevelt Island are marked with colored blazes instead of their names.) At the intersection with the red-blazed Woods Trail, there is a water fountain. In the northeast corner, there are three trails. The trail to the extreme right is the blue-blazed Upland Trail. Straight ahead is a people's choice trail to an area of large metamorphic rocks at the river's edge—a great spot to let your kids play. Note that these rocks catch a lot of the river debris that flows south; don't be surprised to see a huge pile of tree trunks and limbs and trash in the river below.

The yellow-blazed Swamp Trail continues between the people's choice trail to the rocks and the Upland Trail. In a short distance, the trail changes from compact soil to a raised boardwalk as families leave the upland forest for the swampy wetlands. Like the upland forest, the dense wetlands provide much cover for animals. During spring, you can hear the songs of green and jug o'rum frogs in the wetlands. With pockets of vernal pools scattered everywhere, this area is a ripe breeding ground for amphibians. Along the boardwalk, a few benches and a landing allow you and your kids to observe the wildlife in the inlet.

As you draw closer to the Roosevelt Bridge, the boardwalk curves right and heads over a bridge to the inlet and back onto compact soil. The Swamp Trail curves right again and away from the Roosevelt Bridge. The island's only restroom and second water fountain appear ahead. The Upland Trail intersects from the right here. Continue straight on the Swamp Trail for another 0.2 mile. Where the Swamp Trail forks left and narrows, turn right onto the Woods Trail, and reach the Roosevelt monument in a quarter mile. Before the monument, reach a triangular intersection. To return to the parking lot, turn left. To visit the monument, stay right.

The mostly tree-covered monument makes for a great place to spread out a blanket and share a picnic. Kids find the area a great place to play a game of tag or hide-and-seek due to its many natural hiding places. The large fountains (turned off in winter) provide a peaceful backdrop along with the chirping birds. However, planes flying low to land or take off from Reagan National Airport only a few miles south of Roosevelt Island often break this peace. When you and your kids are ready, return to the trail and walk straight toward the pedestrian bridge.

Opposite: Hiking among the tall trees at Sugarloaf Mountain Park

MARYLAND

MONTGOMERY COUNTY

HOLLY TRAIL AT FAIRLAND

BEFORE YOU GO
Map: Available on the Montgomery Parks website
Contact: Fairland Recreational Park
Nearest city: Burtonsville, MD

ABOUT THE HIKE
Moderate, year-round
Length: 2.5 miles, loop and spur
Hiking time: 1½–2 hours
High point/elevation gain: 456 feet/95 feet
Access: Compact soil, passable for jogging strollers

GETTING THERE

From I-495 eastbound (Capital Beltway), take exit 30A for US 29 (Colesville Road). Drive 7 miles, and turn right on Greencastle Road. Drive 0.5 mile, and turn left into the park. Turn left at the stop sign into the parking lot.

From I-495 westbound, take exit 29 for MD 193 (University Boulevard). Drive 0.5 mile, and turn right onto US 29 (Colesville Road) north. Drive 7 miles, and turn right on Greencastle Road. Drive 0.5 mile, and turn left into the park. Turn left at the stop sign into the parking lot.

ON THE TRAIL

Tucked among neighborhoods in eastern Montgomery County on the border with Prince Georges County, Fairland Recreational Park offers about 5 miles of paved and dirt trails for hikers, mountain bikers, and equestrians, as well as playgrounds, picnic areas, playing fields, basketball courts, an aquatic center, and tennis courts. The Holly Trail in the northernmost section of this 322-acre park is heavily wooded and follows the undulating landscape of ridges and narrow stream valleys around Little Paint Branch. The trail passes close to two neighborhoods and the Gunpowder Golf Course, which allows access to the park via people's choice trails.

The Holly Trail is shared with equestrians and mountain bikers. To sustainably support mountain bikes on it, Montgomery Parks has built drainage dips, banking on downhill turns, natural railings out of tree trunks, and ramps to provide an adventurous ride through the woods.

Hikers carefully cross a stream on the Holly Trail.

As a courtesy, bikers should always yield to hikers and horseback riders, while hikers should always yield to horseback riders.

The hike begins on the paved Little Paint Branch Trail at the end of the parking lot. Follow it between the playground and the bioretention pond for 100 yards until you reach a trail sign and a dirt trail. Make a slight left off the Little Paint Branch Trail to follow the signs for the Holly Trail. Within 100 feet, this connector trail dead-ends into the Crows Foot Trail. Turn left on the Crows Foot Trail, and follow signs for the Holly Trail. At a trail sign 0.2 mile from the start, the Crows Foot Trail turns right; follow the Holly Trail straight. A few people's choice trails from the playground enter the Holly Trail on the left and just beyond is a confusing intersection of trails (all people's choice trails); continue straight on the Holly Trail, following the blue blazes.

The trail follows a sidehill around a gulch that descends toward Little Paint Branch. It curves right around the gulch and then atop a ridge where it turns right again and passes through the cut remnants of a large downed red oak. The trunk provides an excellent natural play space for kids. Along the trail here, there is a lot of mountain laurel. It grows successfully on ridge faces where water can easily drain from the soil. Mountain laurel is often found on eastern-facing sidehills where it receives the weaker morning rays of sunshine.

After the downed red oak, the Holly Trail curves left and descends the sidehill toward a bridge over a small stream that feeds into Little Paint Branch. Cross the bridge a half mile into the hike, and make one switchback to the right up the sidehill on the other side of the stream. On top of the ridge, the trail curves left and two people's choice trails intersect here on the left: one making a shortcut and the other coming from the neighborhood. Furthermore, the trail was relocated to reduce sediment erosion into the Little Paint Branch. Follow the blue blazes straight as the trail descends gradually along the ridge face to the branch instead of taking the trail to the right that descends steeply and has greatly eroded.

In the narrow valley of the branch, the Holly Trail makes a 180-degree turn with banking on the outer edge for mountain bikers. After the turn, cross the branch on rocks. At this crossing, there is a small rockslide with cascading water and some great places to play in the stream on a warm day.

On the other side of the branch, the trail ascends the bank to the right 20 feet and then curves sharply back to the left to stay level for 0.2 mile. With the branch still on the left, pass the foundation of an old building. Just before the intersection with the loop trail, the Holly Trail curves right and ascends the ridge.

Upon reaching the mile-long loop, you can choose to hike the loop clockwise or counterclockwise; both options return to this same spot to backtrack on the Holly Trail to the playground. The blue-blazed loop is marked by a signpost. The loop trail gradually rises on the ridge to follow the natural undulations of the land. On the back side of the loop, the trail comes close to Gunpowder Golf Course and a neighborhood of townhomes. A few people's choice trails provide access to Fairland Recreational Park from the golf course and neighborhood. No matter which direction you hike the loop, the trail follows above the branch for a quarter mile. A mature forest of chestnut and red oaks populates this ridge. While you are hiking, you might hunt for chestnut oak leaves on the ground; look for four-inch oval leaves with large sawtooth lobing.

After hiking 1 mile on the Holly Trail Loop, return to the loop trail sign. Turn off the trail loop and back on the Holly Trail (turn right when

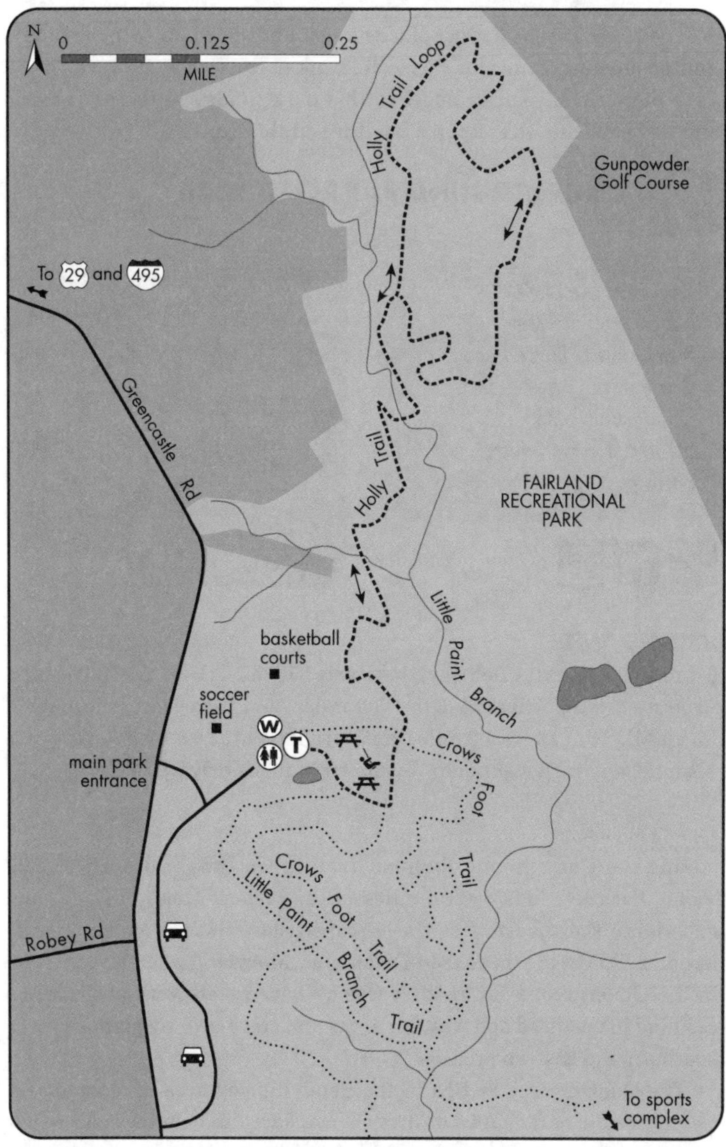

hiking the loop counterclockwise and left when hiking the loop clockwise). Retrace your footsteps for 0.75 mile back across the Little Paint Branch and to the playground.

The Holly Trail is a great place for you and your family if you have a limited amount of time for a peaceful walk in the woods. However, if you have more time, you can linger in this park to play at the playground and have a picnic after a fun adventure on the trail.

UNDERGROUND RAILROAD TRAIL

BEFORE YOU GO
Map: Available on Montgomery Parks website
Contact: Northwest Branch Stream Valley Park
Nearest city: Sandy Spring, MD

ABOUT THE HIKE
Easy/moderate, year-round
Length: 4 miles, out and back
Hiking time: 2–2½ hours
High point/elevation gain: 485 feet/124 feet
Access: Compact soil and a dirt road, passable for jogging strollers

GETTING THERE

From I-495 (Capital Beltway), take exit 31A for MD 97 north (Georgia Avenue) toward Wheaton. Drive 3.5 miles, and turn right onto Layhill Road (MD 182). Drive 4.9 miles, and turn left onto Norwood Road. Drive 0.2 mile, and turn right onto Woodlawn Manor's driveway.

ON THE TRAIL

Hiking the Underground Railroad Trail in Northwest Branch Stream Valley Park lets kids walk 4 miles in the historic shoes of slaves and experience their journey as they escaped slave owners on the path to freedom. Bordering the Mason-Dixon Line, Maryland was a pivotal state in the Underground Railroad. It was a divided state with abolitionists residing in northern and western areas and slave-owning plantations in southern and eastern areas.

The Quakers who settled in the Sandy Spring area of Montgomery County in the early 1700s at first owned slaves to help them farm, but they freed their slaves in the early 1800s. The Quakers and freed slaves worked together as accomplices in the Underground Railroad. Woodlawn Manor and the Sandy Spring Friends Meeting House were used to hide slaves on the run. Woodlawn Manor is the trailhead and first interpretive location for the Underground Railroad Trail. While this trail route doesn't include the Meeting House (built circa 1817), you can extend your hike an additional half mile out and back to visit it.

You can print an interpretive trail guide from the Montgomery Parks website (the park and trail directory section). Along the trail, signs indicate historical features of the Underground Railroad. These small, metal, black-and-white signs, which are also the trail blazes, show a traveling slave. Match these signs with the interpretive guide to learn how runaways traversed the forest from one safe house to another.

Follow the trail as slaves once did on the Underground Railroad.

The trailhead is adjacent to the informational kiosk across from the old stone barn at Woodlawn Manor. Constructed in 1832, this barn was used to stow runaway slaves. After reading the interpretive sign at the trailhead about the Quakers and African Americans in Sandy Spring, walk on the grass with the horse corral fence on the left. Follow the blazes to the left around the horse corral where the trail enters the edge of the woods on the right. Stop to read the interpretive sign about the constellations of the night sky and the nocturnal animals that inhabit the forest. The wood's edge is the second interpretive stop on the trail; as the sign explains, slaves seeking freedom used the cover and density of forests to keep from being spotted by trackers.

Entering the dense woods, ascend slightly to notice raspberry and wineberry scattered as ground cover under the tree canopy. The interpretive guide showcases these brambles as perfect spots for the slaves to escape from the tracker's dogs that were following their scent. Just past the brambles, the trail descends toward a stream. Follow the blaze to the left (not toward Alexander Manor Drive). Make sure to follow the blazes before and after the bridge as a few people's choice trails lead to the Sandy Spring Friends School and their Adventure Park. This area is location four, "Crossing of Paths," on the interpretive guide. Intersecting

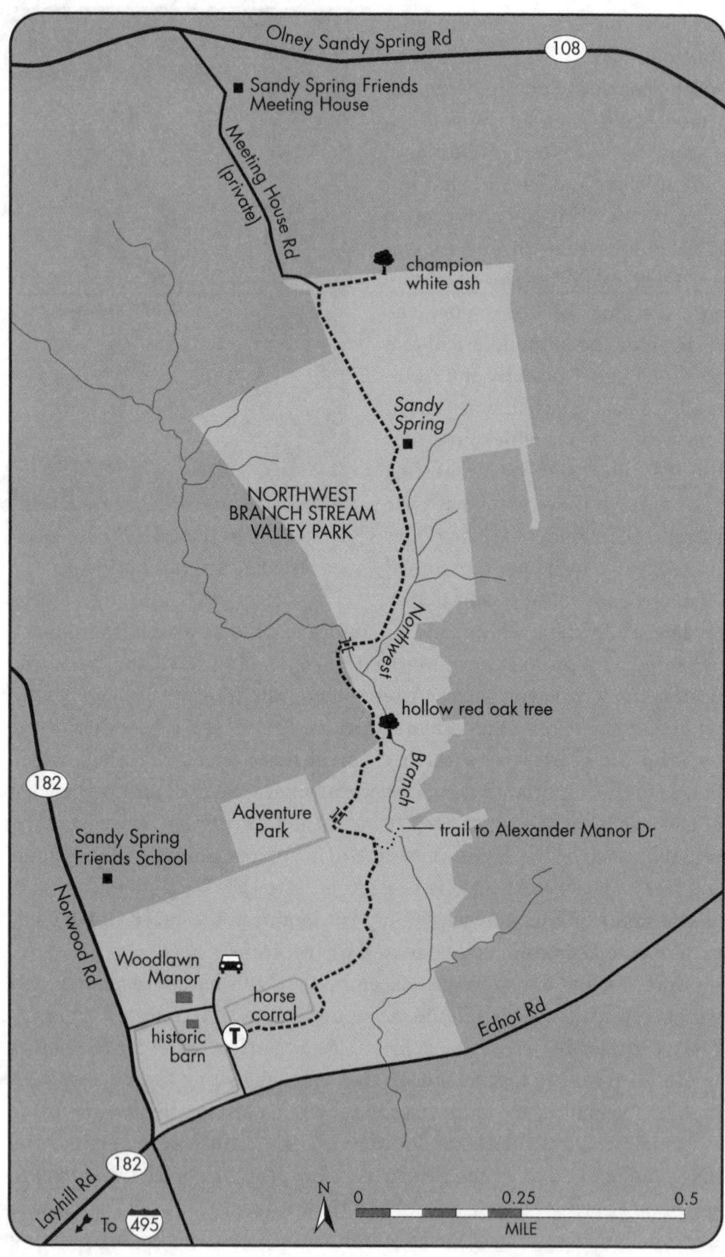
Olney Sandy Spring Rd
108
Sandy Spring Friends Meeting House
Meeting House Rd (private)
champion white ash
Sandy Spring
NORTHWEST BRANCH STREAM VALLEY PARK
Northwest Branch
hollow red oak tree
182
Adventure Park
trail to Alexander Manor Dr
Sandy Spring Friends School
Norwood Rd
Woodlawn Manor
horse corral
historic barn
T
Ednor Rd
182
Layhill Rd
To 495
N
0
0.25
0.5
MILE

trails confused runaways in the past, just as they do many hikers nowadays; therefore, secretive trail blazes were planted to guide slaves.

After the bridge, turn right and walk the wooden puncheon over this wet section of trail. Hike a quarter mile to interpretive location five, "Hollow Tree." At the marker, turn right to view a huge, hollowed red oak. Kids can step inside to pretend to be runaway slaves and gain insight on what it might have been like to be cold, hungry, and fearful of the night and of being captured. From this point, you can backtrack to the marker or walk to the left along Northwest Branch where it intersects the main trail.

The trail ascends a small hill above the stream, then descends to a large bridge over the Northwest Branch, number six on the interpretive guide. There are places to access the stream for some free play: skipping rocks, looking for salamanders and crayfish, and cooling off feet on a hot summer day. In the 1800s, bridges weren't present on trails to help runaways to cross streams—often treacherous and frightening experiences for slaves because most of them didn't know how to swim.

After crossing the bridge, hikers enter a cornfield, location seven on the interpretive guide. Please stick to the trail and dirt road that is blazed with flexible posts labeled "trail." Follow the trail on the edge of the field and woods as it curves to the left and makes a gradual ascent uphill toward the spring. The woods to the right of the trail provided cover for slaves traveling alongside the open field. At the end of the forest-covered stream is Sandy Spring, location eight on the interpretive guide. This spring was the main water source for families living in the area and a meeting spot on the Underground Railroad. Benches among the shade of trees make this an ideal spot for a snack or picnic break. But you must pack your trash out since there are no trash cans.

To visit location nine on the interpretive trail, the champion white ash tree, leave the spring and turn right to follow a tree-lined dirt road 0.2 mile north to a T intersection. At the intersection, turn right and walk a couple hundred feet to the champion tree, which was used as a trail marker for the Underground Railroad.

Turn around here and retrace your steps back to Woodlawn Manor. On the return, follow the trail marker arrows occasionally labeled "Woodlawn." Hiking back allows you and your kids to gain a different perspective of the trail and the experiences runaway slaves had escaping their plantations, slave owners, and the trackers hired to capture them. To enhance this experience for children, hike this trail in the evening or participate in a hike guided by volunteers of Montgomery Parks on Saturday mornings at 10:00 AM during spring, summer, and fall.

RACHEL CARSON GREENWAY TRAIL

BEFORE YOU GO
Map: Available on Montgomery Parks website
Contact: Northwest Branch Stream Valley Park
Nearest city: Silver Spring, MD

ABOUT THE HIKE
Easy/moderate, year-round
Length: 2 miles, out and back
Hiking time: 1½–2 hours
High point/elevation gain: 265 feet/225 feet
Access: Compact soil and rock, not passable for jogging strollers

GETTING THERE

From eastbound I-495 (Capital Beltway), take exit 30 for US 29 north (Colesville Road). Drive 1.4 miles, and turn right into the Washington Suburban Sanitary Commission (WSSC) parking lot (before the gas station and plaza).

From westbound I-495, take exit 29 for US 29 north and University Avenue West. Turn right off the exit ramp. Drive 0.5 mile, and turn right onto US 29 (Colesville Road). Drive 0.8 mile, and turn right into the WSSC parking lot (before the gas station and plaza).

ON THE TRAIL

In Northwest Branch Stream Valley Park, the southern section of the Rachel Carson Greenway Trail, named after the world-renowned environmentalist who lived atop the valley, drops quickly into a peaceful and serene stream valley, leaving behind the busy six-lane road above it. The trail follows the riffling Northwest Branch down and back with various opportunities to stop along its banks to play.

There are two ways to reach the trail along the valley floor: hike to the top of the gorge and then follow the blue blaze trail on compact soil down the gorge to the stream; or, scramble down rocks adjacent to the cascading Northwest Branch. Hikers looking for a challenge may

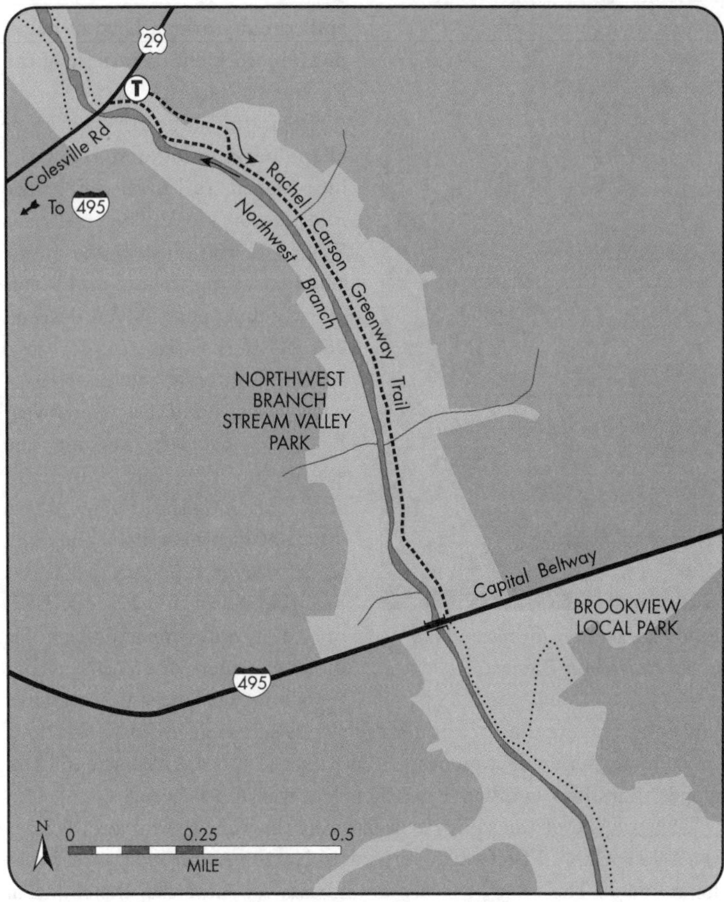

scramble down the rocks into the gorge. However, most people wait until their return trip to climb the barrage of fallen Carolina gneiss that scatters the stream as it falls 150 feet in the length of three football fields. The hike here is described using the blue-blazed trail on compact soil, which provides an alternative and safe route for children to descend to the stream valley floor.

More than a century ago, an old grain mill atop the stream's fall line used the force of the water to grind grain into flour. The mill burned down a long time ago, but the 180-foot concrete dam on the west side of US 29 still stands. Once the water leaves the dam, it continues to

Find big boulders for scrambling along Northwest Branch.

spill rapidly over a bowl of metamorphic rock characteristic of the Piedmont Plateau.

Begin the hike at the far corner of the parking lot, and follow the blue-blazed trail to the left of the information kiosk. The trail rises 75 feet to the crest of the gorge. The houses and condos on the left quickly disappear as you descend 150 feet to the stream valley floor. At the T intersection in front of a trail sign and the Northwest Branch, turn left, keeping the stream on the right. The trail stays flat along the stream. At two different locations along the trail, feeder creeks fall from rocks that line the steep valley walls. Both provide great opportunities for kids to explore the rocks, either to look for creatures like crawfish and salamanders that live under them or to scramble above to test their gross motor skills. The mouths of both creeks have gentle streambank slopes that allow families to get their feet wet and skip rocks.

The silence of the valley is broken at the turnaround point under the I-495 (Capital Beltway) overpass to Northwest Branch, a rest spot for a snack. The busy overpass is high above; therefore, the sound of vehicles on the metal trusses does not interrupt your hike too much. The Rachel Carson Greenway continues south and east, following Northwest Branch into Prince Georges County, but you oftentimes need to use your hands to negotiate the trail's uneven, rocky surface. Within a quarter mile, the people's choice trail meets a paved trail that extends several miles into Prince Georges County as part of the Anacostia Tributary Trail System. Many people use this paved trail for biking.

Once you are hydrated and full, continue back from the I-495 bridge along the Rachel Carson Greenway Trail with Northwest Branch on the left. Along the way, notice the rock outcroppings that jut from valley walls and invite kids to climb them. Tall tulip poplars, red and white oaks, red maples, beech trees, and sycamores dot the stream valley and hold the steep streambank in place.

After you have hiked three-quarters of a mile, the original blue-blazed trail (marked with a trail post) emerges on the right. To bypass the rock scramble, turn right and climb the valley wall for a quarter mile back to the parking lot. For the challenge of climbing the rocks, follow the blue blazes straight ahead to the rocks. People's choice trails may lead feet and minds astray briefly, but they all lead back to the parking lot. It is safer to climb the rocks than to follow one of the steep people's choice trails that have poor traction. This massive bowl of boulders is a hot spot for bouldering (climbing on large rocks without a harness and with shoes and a crashpad to break a potential fall). There are several rocks to climb atop to sit and enjoy the rushing water.

Below and above the boulder field, two small sandy beaches offer an opportunity for kids to use their inquiry skills to discover the mechanics of water flow. Throw in a stick or a tulip poplar bud to learn where its journey ends; you may discover an eddy.

WHEATON REGIONAL PARK

BEFORE YOU GO
Map: Available on Montgomery Parks website
Contact: Wheaton Regional Park
Nearest city: Wheaton, MD

ABOUT THE HIKE
Easy, year-round
Length: 1.6 miles, loop
Hiking time: 1–1½ hours
High point/elevation gain: 456 feet/60 feet
Access: Compact soil, passable for jogging strollers

GETTING THERE

From I-495 (Capital Beltway), take exit 31 for Georgia Avenue north (MD 97) to Wheaton. Drive 3 miles, and turn right onto Randolph Road. Drive 0.3 mile, and turn right onto Glenallan Avenue. Drive 0.7 mile, and turn right into the nature center parking lot. The closest Metro station is Glenmont (Red Line).

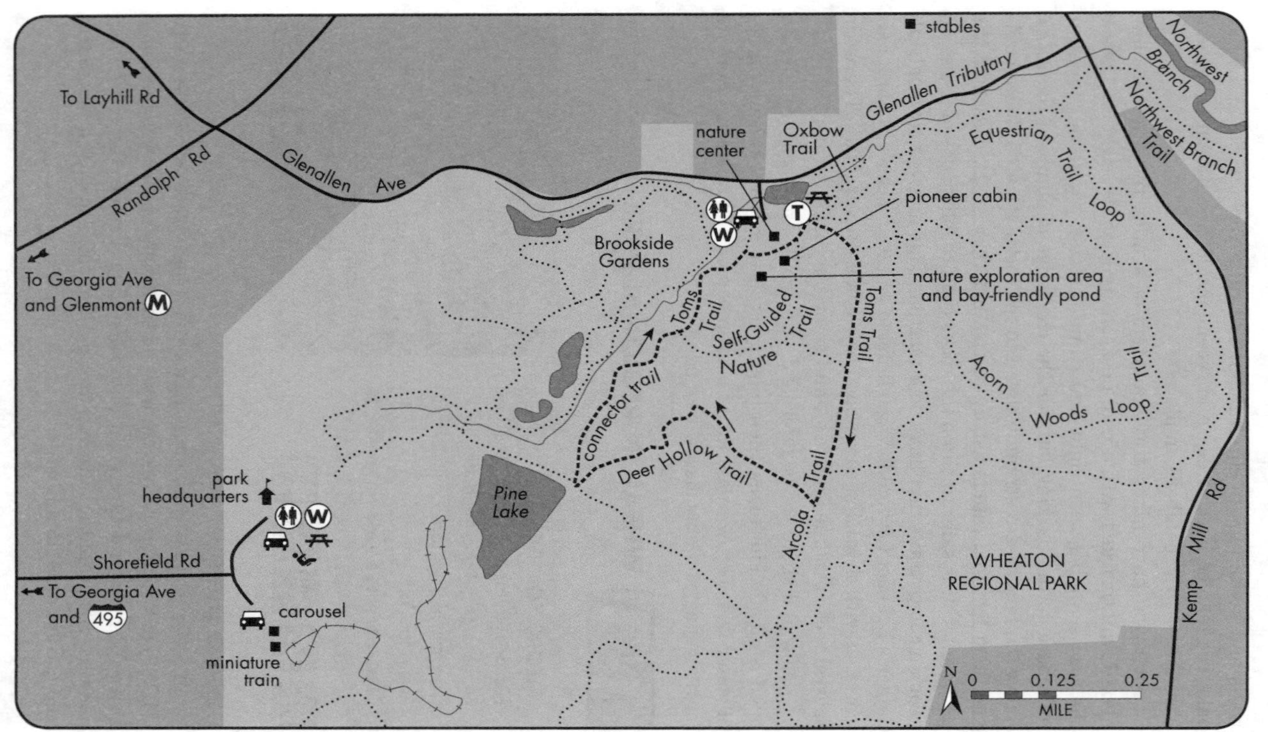
stables
Northwest Branch
Northwest Branch Trail
To Layhill Rd
Glenallen Tributary
Randolph Rd
Glenallen Ave
nature center
Oxbow Trail
Equestrian Trail Loop
pioneer cabin
Brookside Gardens
To Georgia Ave and Glenmont
nature exploration area and bay-friendly pond
Toms Trail
Self-Guided Nature Trail
Toms Trail
Acorn Woods Loop Trail
connector trail
Deer Hollow Trail
Arcola Trail
park headquarters
Pine Lake
Kemp Mill Rd
Shorefield Rd
To Georgia Ave and 495
carousel
miniature train
WHEATON REGIONAL PARK
N
0
0.125
0.25
MILE

ON THE TRAIL

Established in 1960, Wheaton Regional Park was the first regional park in Montgomery County. Today, it is a bastion of recreational activities for all ages and interests, offering trails, a nature center, gardens, an ice skating rink, a tennis bubble, ponds and a lake, a miniature train, an equestrian center, a playground, baseball fields, a carousel, and a dog park. Of the park's 11 miles of trails, 4 miles are paved and 7 miles are dirt, of which a majority traverses under a canopy of large oak trees.

The dirt trails crisscross the northeast section, providing multiple options for loop hikes of a variety of lengths. These trails also connect with the Northwest Branch Trail via a crosswalk on Kemp Mill Road. The 1.6-mile loop described below leads you along wide trails over an undulating landscape behind the nature center and alongside Brookside Gardens. All the trail intersections in Wheaton are posted to point people in the direction of a trail or destination.

The hike begins on Toms Trail. The trailhead is on the east side of the nature center between two split-rail fences. Oxbow Trail is the left fork through a picnic area, and Toms Trail is the right fork. Toms Trail zigzags gently uphill for 0.1 mile before it intersects Acorn Woods Trail. Turn right to continue on Toms Trail. For another 0.2 mile, this trail continues gently uphill until it intersects the Arcola Trail. Turn left and follow it for another 0.2 mile. Just before you turn right on the Deer Hollow Trail, a connector trail to the horse trail loop appears on the left. On both the Toms and Arcola trails, kids may notice large boxes that look like birdhouses nailed high on tree trunks; they are flying squirrel houses.

After hiking 0.2 mile on the Arcola Trail, turn right on the Deer Hollow Trail. Hike a half mile gradually downhill toward Pine Lake. Halfway along the Deer Hollow Trail, the trail S curves and passes over a small wooden bridge to a spring that is usually dry. The Deer Hollow Trail dead-ends at a connector trail from Pine Lake to the nature center. To visit Pine Lake, turn left and walk about 200 yards to its banks; otherwise, complete the loop by turning right on the connector trail to head toward the nature center. This trail is mostly level with a few undulations as it meanders alongside the Glenallan Tributary and Brookside Gardens.

In 0.3 mile, the connector trail intersects the Toms Trail. Turn left and continue heading to the nature center. Before and after this intersection,

Peer into the pioneer cabin.

two people's choice trails appear on the left; although they seem like they provide access to Brookside Gardens, they do not. To access the gardens, hike to the parking lot at the nature center, and enter through

A FLYING SQUIRREL?

Two kinds of flying squirrels live in the United States. The southern flying squirrel makes its home in deciduous forests in states east of the Mississippi River, and the northern flying squirrel lives north of Tennessee and Colorado across the United States and Canada. The nocturnal flying squirrel is the oldest species of squirrel that spends its life in tree canopies. Smaller than gray squirrels, they have brownish-gray fur on their back and white on their belly, large black-ringed eyes, and a flap of skin attached from the ankles of their forelegs to their hind legs, which helps them glide from tree to tree. While in the air, they use their tail to steer.

Their diet consists of nuts and seeds with an occasional insect when the former aren't plentiful. They mate twice a year and create nests in natural tree cavities or old woodpecker holes (or houses built by people). Females give birth to an average of four hairless young that are able to fend for themselves after forty days. Oftentimes during winter, multiple females share a nest; otherwise, they are territorial. The best time to spot a flying squirrel in Wheaton Regional Park is at twilight or at night.

the gate in the chain-link fence. Just before the parking lot, the Toms Trail turns right uphill toward the back of the nature center. Behind the nature center, walk between the split-rail fences to the pioneer cabin and the bay-friendly pond, which displays native wetland plants that benefit the health of the Chesapeake Bay. Cross the driveway to the kiosk to read about the pioneer cabin and smokehouse. The cabin was donated to Montgomery Parks in 1976, which rebuilt the dismantled cabin for demonstration and educational purposes. The Harper family originally built and owned the cabin in Jonesville, Maryland, a town established by freed slaves after the Civil War.

Adjacent to the pioneer cabin on the right is the nature exploration area—a natural playground for kids. Here, kids can pretend to be birds in a nest, follow a chain of logs to test their balancing skills, climb through hollowed-out trunks, make natural music, and play in the sand and garden pits. To return to the parking lot, follow the dirt path back to the pioneer cabin and the driveway. Turn right and walk down the driveway to the east side of the nature center.

WOODEND SANCTUARY

BEFORE YOU GO
Map: Available on the Audubon Naturalist Society (ANS) website or inside the mansion
Contact: Woodend Sanctuary
Nearest city: Chevy Chase, MD

ABOUT THE HIKE
Easy, year-round
Length: 1.1 miles, loop
Hiking time: ½–1 hour
High point/elevation gain: 339 feet/75 feet
Access: Compact soil and mulch; passable for jogging strollers; pets prohibited

GETTING THERE

From I-495, take exit 33 for MD 185 (Connecticut Avenue) south. Drive 0.5 mile, and turn left onto Manor Road. Drive 0.4 mile, then turn right onto Jones Bridge Road. After 0.3 mile, turn left onto Jones Mill Road. The entrance is on the left in 0.2 mile.

ON THE TRAIL

The Audubon Naturalist Society's Woodend Sanctuary is a 40-acre oasis in heavily populated southern Montgomery County. The Wells family gave the land and Georgian-style mansion to the ANS in 1968. Today, both are used for special functions and as an environmental education center for kids and adults. The facility and organization host master naturalist classes for adults and a preschool, camps, and field trips for children. The property is organized to provide many teachable moments about the plants and animals that inhabit this tract of green space in an urban area. The Woodend Sanctuary is a great place for you and your kids to visit nature even if you can spare only a half hour.

The trails at Woodend are not blazed or named. However, they are not difficult to follow because they are concentrated on the southern side of the property. This hike begins behind the mansion and down the driveway toward Brierly Road, the neighborhood street behind Woodend. Three-quarters of the way down the driveway, turn left onto a grass-mowed path skirting the woods and meadow. In the woods on the right is one of two outdoor classrooms constructed by the ANS. Follow

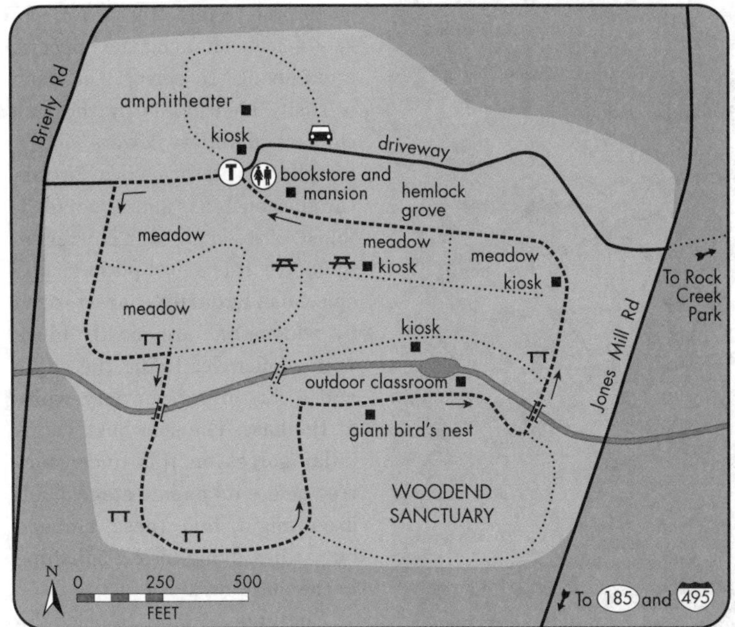

the grass trail as it curves to the left and enters the woods. At the edge of the woods, a trail sign on the right points straight ahead to the pond. After you enter the woods, look for the largest beech tree on the property off the trail on the right side.

The trail crosses a small wooden bridge and comes to a four-way intersection with some benches that look out over another meadow. Turn right and cross a streambed (dry most of the time) and climb up six steps. The trail heads uphill away from the mansion and into the forest, where it circles back in 1000 feet toward the stream and mansion. There are two benches, which were built as Eagle Scout projects, along this section of the trail.

A trail intersects from the right: pass it and continue straight toward the stream. The trail curves right before reaching the stream and dead-ending. Turn right and head away from the bridge with the stream on the left. While turning right, notice a large, old rhododendron. The best time to see this bush in bloom is May. A few hundred feet ahead on the right is a human-sized bird's nest used for nature play and to educate kids about birds during field trips and camp.

The Audubon Naturalist Society mansion at Woodend Sanctuary

In mid- to late March, you can spot spicebush along the opposite streambank. In spring, the bush is easily identifiable by the tiny clusters of yellow flowers closely attached to its branches. In fall, the spicebush has small red, inedible berries, single or in clusters of up to five. It is a host plant for the spicebush butterfly, characterized by wings that are mostly black with semicircles lining the edges and a dusting of powdery white at the base. The spicebush caterpillar gorges on this understory tree before its pupate stage. Children might find these hatched butterflies flying in the sunshine in the meadows.

Continue hiking along the stream until you reach the pond. The ANS uses this stream to teach adults and kids about testing and understanding water quality and its impacts on stream inhabitants like fish and macroinvertebrates by using chemical tests of pH, turbidity, nitrates, temperature, and dissolved oxygen. Students collect, identify, and inventory the stream's macroinvertebrates. These bug larvae and aquatic worms indicate the health of the stream; some can survive only in unpolluted water. The pond is used to study the life cycle of amphibians. They lay their eggs and metamorphose in the pond until they reach the adult stage, where some remain aquatic and others become terrestrial, like the northern dusky salamander.

Pass the pond and turn left over the third bridge to the stream. Upon reaching a three-way intersection with benches, continue straight toward the kiosk at the edge of the woods, adjacent to the driveway. At the kiosk, turn left and choose the middle path through the meadow toward the mansion. Even though this meadow is hot during summer, it is the best place to see tons of butterfly action. Look closely and you may spot a monarch caterpillar on the plentiful milkweed growing in this meadow. With its alternating black, white, and lime green stripes, it can't be missed. This 1-mile hike ends at the front of the mansion.

Before you leave, enjoy a picnic lunch or snack on one of the picnic tables on the west side of the mansion (Woodend is a pack-in, pack-out sanctuary). In addition, visit the bookstore to grab some bird seed, a feeder, or the latest nature-inspired children's book.

13 CABIN JOHN TRAIL: MACARTHUR BOULEVARD

BEFORE YOU GO
Map: Available on Montgomery Parks website
Contact: Cabin John Local and Stream Valley Parks
Nearest city: Bethesda, MD

ABOUT THE HIKE
Moderate, year-round
Length: 2.4 miles, out and back
Hiking time: 1½–2 hours
High point/elevation gain: 236 feet/220 feet
Access: Compact soil, not passable for jogging strollers

GETTING THERE

From Maryland, take I-495 (Capital Beltway) to exit 39 for MD 190 (River Road). Turn right on River Road, and drive 1.3 miles. Turn right on Wilson Lane (MD 188), and drive 0.9 mile. Turn right on MacArthur Boulevard, and look for Cabin John Local Park in 0.3 mile on the right.

From Virginia, take I-495 (Capital Beltway) to exit 41 for Clara Barton Parkway. Drive 1.2 miles, and exit for Cabin John Local Park. Turn left off the exit ramp. Turn right on MacArthur Boulevard, and look for Cabin John Local Park on the left.

ON THE TRAIL

The entire Cabin John Trail, starting at the Chesapeake & Ohio (C&O) Canal and ending at Goya Drive, is 9 miles. Major roads such as Democracy Boulevard bisect the trail. Most of this 9-mile-long trail is open to hikers, bikers, and equestrians. However, this 1.2-mile section (2.4 miles out and back) from MacArthur Boulevard to Seven Locks Road is restricted to hikers because it has steep ridges and sidehill drop-offs into Cabin John Stream.

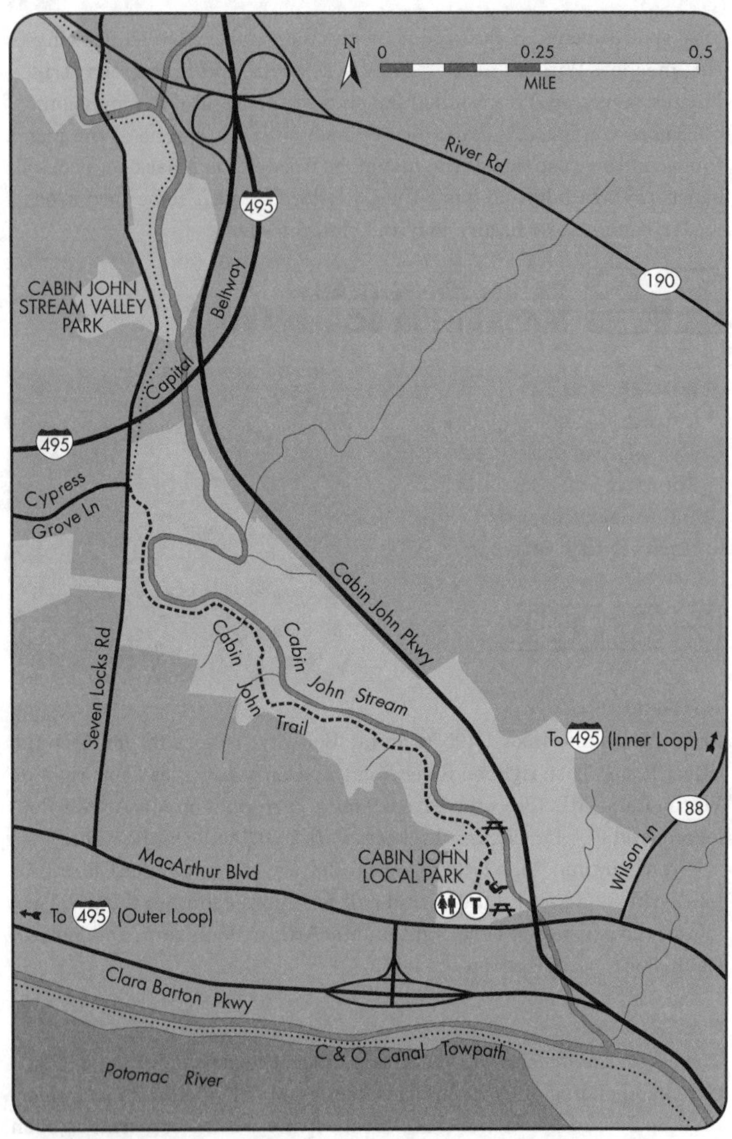

Montgomery Parks has designed the MacArthur Boulevard section of the Cabin John Trail as one of the county's "best natural areas"—parcels of parkland that have unique landscapes or geologic formations, a high biodiversity of plants and animals, and healthy aquatic and forest ecosystems or wetlands. This section boasts a large variety of spring ephemerals—wildflowers such as wild geraniums, jack-in-the-pulpits, Solomon's seal, spring beauties, bloodroot, Virginia bluebells, trout lilies, and mayapples. These flowers are best seen in bloom during April. Overall, this section of the Cabin John Trail is a slice of wilderness within miles of the District of Columbia border.

The trailhead is on the forest's edge adjacent to the playground. To begin this out-and-back hike, descend the steep bluff toward the Cabin John Stream. Sixty steps lead down the bluff to a dry streambed that can be crossed on two rocks. It is wet during rainstorms when water flows off the bluff on the path of least resistance to the stream. Turn left at the Y intersection, and follow the blue double blaze back up the bluff. Two people's choice trails veer right toward the stream. The first one leads to a picnic table at a curve in the stream. The water deposits rocks along the inside of this bend, and kids could hang out here forever creating adventures on the rocky streambank.

At the top of the bluff, a neighborhood trail enters from the left. Pass it and follow the blue double blaze as the trail curves to the right and stays above the stream. About 0.3 mile into the hike, descend a set of wooden steps back toward the stream's edge. There are many places to access the stream to play along its banks. Just beyond the base of the steps is a large riffle followed by artificial streambank stabilization. Above the riffle is a sandy bank perfect for playing a game of tic-tac-toe with a stick. Pass a stream-retaining wall and then walk through densely packed bamboo.

HOLDING UP A STREAM: HUMAN INTERVENTION

Local or state governments install streambank stabilization, such as the rock and cement wall you will see along the trail, to improve the stream's water quality, reduce its sediment build up, improve its habitat for animals, maintain the integrity of its channel, prevent it from meandering, and to stabilize the steep streambank. The land use within its buffer zone can strongly affect a stream. A buffer zone with a lot of impervious surfaces increases the runoff, thus increasing the amount of water and its speed, which in turn, changes the stream's hydrology (the water that flows through its natural channel).

Two hikers soak up the sun in the middle of Cabin John Stream.

Past the edge of the bamboo, a people's choice trail to the right leads to the stream. Continuing on the Cabin John Trail, cross a small feeder stream to follow the undulations of the trail above the stream. Hike with caution on this section because the trail is narrow and drops steeply into the stream.

After 0.75 mile, the trail divides around some trees to quickly rejoin and descend toward an intersection with a divided feeder stream. A few rocks help keep your feet dry as you step across. The trail then heads back to the edge of Cabin John Stream on a small floodplain. You can access the stream in different locations: straight ahead on the floodplain or after the trail curves sharply left. A small rockbar creates an eddy here, and just off the rockbar is a truck-sized boulder. Kids can access this boulder by walking up the Cabin John Trail 50 feet from the people's choice trail and following another one over stream debris to be king or queen of the rock.

After returning to the Cabin John Trail from the rockbar, make a right to travel north. Climb over a large boulder in the trail tread, then rise on the ridge above the stream. About a mile into the hike, look up on

BAMBOO: PANDAS LOVE IT, BUT OUR FORESTS DO NOT

A highly invasive plant often used as a natural privacy barrier in yards, bamboo is a grass and grows to its full height and diameter within sixty days of a cane erupting from the soil. It falls into two growing categories: running or clumping. Running bamboo emerges from the soil by shoots from runners growing in lines. Clump bamboo grows from a singular spot in the soil creating a vertical cascade of bamboo leaves. Bamboo's density provides a cavelike feeling when you hike through it, but it can crowd out native species with its prolific spread.

the ridge to find large boulders 50 feet off the trail, another place along the trail to discover adventurous play. For the next 0.1 mile, the trail follows the undulating contour of the land. At one point in this area, it narrows again and drops steeply on the outside edge to the stream below. The trail dips to cross a feeder stream and rises steeply before descending to be level with the stream again. At 1.1 miles into the hike, the trail crosses another floodplain before a Y intersection. At the blue double blaze, turn left and follow the trail uphill toward Seven Locks Road, reached in less than 0.2 mile. Seven Locks Road is the turnaround point for this hike.

If you want to continue on the Cabin John Trail, it follows the edge of Seven Locks for a couple tenths of a mile before ducking back into the woods along the edge of the road. Close to the intersection with River Road, the trail crosses Seven Locks and follows the stream in the woods. The section between Seven Locks and River Road is 1.3 miles.

After hiking this urban wilderness trail, enjoy a picnic lunch and playtime back at the playground with tables. This is a great playground in the heat of summer because the large canopy provides a lot of shade. Don't forget that you have to climb 60 steps on a steep incline before resting in the shade of the picnic tables.

CABIN JOHN TRAIL: RIVER ROAD

BEFORE YOU GO
Map: Available on Montgomery Parks website
Contact: Cabin John Stream Valley Park
Nearest city: Bethesda, MD

ABOUT THE HIKE
Easy/moderate, year-round
Length: 2.4 miles, out and back
Hiking time: 1½–2 hours
High point/elevation gain: 279 feet/110 feet
Access: Compact soil, passable for jogging strollers

GETTING THERE

From I-495 (Capital Beltway), take exit 39 for River Road (MD 190). Drive north 0.7 mile past a firehouse. Look for the dirt parking area on the right side of the road before you cross the bridge over the Cabin John Stream.

ON THE TRAIL

The 9-mile Cabin John Trail stretches from the Chesapeake & Ohio (C&O) Canal in Cabin John Stream Valley Park to Goya Boulevard in Rockville. Most of the trail is multiuse, shared by hikers, bikers, and equestrians. This 2.4-mile out-and-back hike along the Cabin John Stream is restricted to hikers and bikers. The trail is shaded and has about 100 feet of elevation change spread out over the first quarter mile and the last 0.1 mile before the turnaround point at Bradley Boulevard. Most of the hike is flat and traverses through the floodplain adjacent to the stream. Due to this, the trail can be muddy in places. This section of the Cabin John Trail offers a glimpse of native plant growth in our urban and suburban deciduous forests.

The hike begins at a dirt parking lot on River Road that holds approximately five cars. A sign marks the trailhead and the trail is blazed in blue. The first 100 feet of the trail is on asphalt, and then it turns to

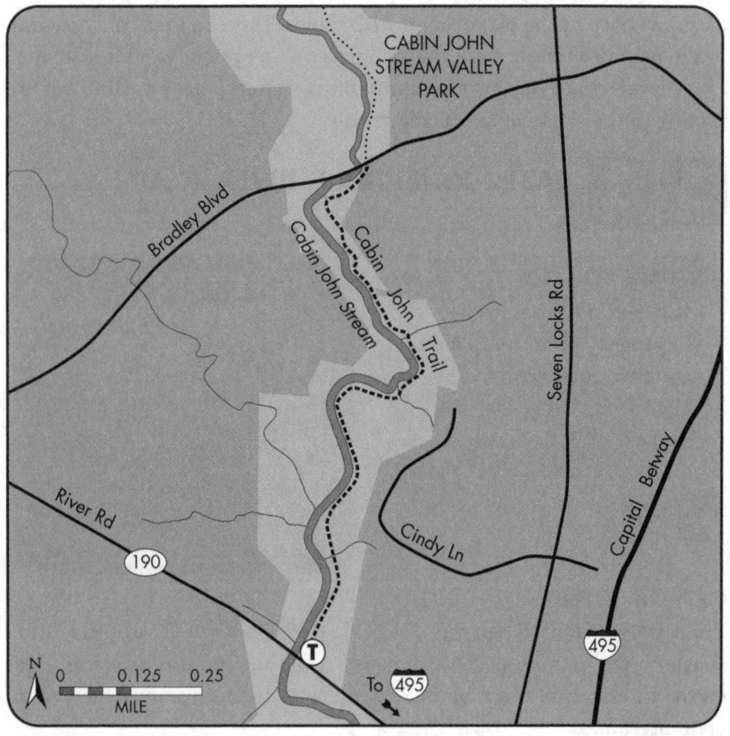

gravel and compact soil in the first quarter mile. The stone helps prevent sediment erosion along the trail and into the stream. Within 100 yards of the parking lot, the trail rises up a gentle hill to a plateau before descending again; it crosses a mostly dry feeder stream and then heads back uphill on its steepest grade.

Near the crest of the hill, a people's choice trail leading to Cindy Lane in the adjacent neighborhood intersects from the right. Two more people's choice trails intersect the Cabin John Trail on the right, both also allowing access to Cindy Lane. After passing the first people's choice trail, descend the ridge toward the stream. For most of the next mile, the trail runs next or close to the stream, allowing multiple opportunities to play alongside or in it.

Reaching the stream's edge, walk just above it with the ridge walls rising steeply on the right of the trail. The next 0.3 mile is a prime example of a Piedmont Plateau deciduous forest with few invasive plants. This area has dry soil, lots of rock, and steep ridges. The dominant plant in this area of the trail is the mountain laurel, which grows well in this habitat.

On the floodplain along the stream, invasive plants like multifloral rose have drowned out native plants. The rich, moist soil provides an excellent habitat for invasive plants to take hold and flourish. However, invasive plants are detrimental to the ecosystem that they intrude upon. They overpower native plants, reduce food sources for animals, change landscapes and soil composition, rob native plants of nutrients and pollinators, genetically change native plant composition, and reduce the biodiversity of an ecosystem. Swaths of bamboo, garlic mustard, stinging nettle, bush honeysuckle, and many more species have taken over large areas of land in the floodplain in the Cabin John

Hiking the Cabin John Trail

Stream valley. On the other hand, the steep slopes close to the stream are inhabitable for most of these invasive plants.

After you hike for a half mile, the steep ridge gives way to the floodplain. Just before the floodplain, the trail curves to the left. Notice a low area off to the right covered in skunk cabbage.

At 0.7 mile, the trail intersects with a feeder stream; cross it on a couple of large rocks. Two people's choice trails intersect the trail after you cross the stream: one on the right and the other straight ahead. Turn left and follow the blue blazes. Shortly after the left turn, find a great place to access the stream where a rockbar that juts out at a riffle; it makes for a great place to play in the water. However, it is important to note that the stream's channel changes constantly due to the amount of stormwater that enters it after heavy rains. Therefore, this large rockbar may disappear or expand. After leaving the rockbar, turn left and continue north on the trail.

The next 0.4 mile may be wet and muddy while you hike through the floodplain. Hikers have widened and divided the trail by placing large sticks and logs in the trail tread in an attempt to gain a few inches of higher ground and keep their feet mud-free. But as the soil erodes from floodwater, the trail gets wider, killing more vegetation, which in turn creates more erosion—a vicious cycle. Mud is a durable surface, but plants aren't. Show those muddy shoes with pride.

For the last 0.1 mile, the Cabin John Trail rises gently in elevation as it comes closer to the park boundary and private property. Just before Bradley Boulevard, come to a bridge over a feeder stream, the turnaround point. Another section of the Cabin John Trail continues across Bradley Boulevard, where you can hike 1.8 miles to Democracy Boulevard. Or hike 1.2 miles back to the parking lot at River Road.

A STINKY PLANT: SKUNK CABBAGE

Often the first green plant seen in the forest, skunk cabbage grows along streams, ponds, wetlands, and vernal pools. The plant never dies but hibernates just beneath the soil, producing its own heat to remain alive. The spathe, a purple sheath, rises aboveground in early spring, as early as the end of February. If it snows, the plant can melt the snow around the spathe. Before the large green leaves appear, the spathe reveals a spadix, its flower. The plant gets its name from the odor it emits when broken or bruised. The smell attracts insects to pollinate the flower.

LOCUST GROVE NATURE CENTER

BEFORE YOU GO
Map: Available outside the nature center or on Montgomery Parks website
Contact: Cabin John Regional Park
Nearest city: Bethesda, MD

ABOUT THE HIKE
Easy/moderate, year-round
Length: 1.4 miles, loop
Hiking time: 1 hour
High point/elevation gain: 312 feet/62 feet
Access: Compact soil, passable for jogging strollers

GETTING THERE

From I-495 (Capital Beltway) in Maryland, take exit 36 for MD 187 (Old Georgetown Road). Turn right off the exit ramp. Drive 0.9 mile, and turn left onto Democracy Boulevard. Drive 1.8 miles. The Cabin John Regional Park and nature center parking lot is on the right.

From I-495 (Capital Beltway) in Virginia, stay left where I-270 and I-495 split. Take exit 1 for Democracy Boulevard west. Keep left on the exit ramp. Turn left onto Democracy Boulevard, and drive 0.8 mile. The Cabin John Regional Park nature center parking lot is on the right.

ON THE TRAIL

One of four Montgomery County nature centers, the Locust Grove Nature Center is in the southwestern part of the county in Cabin John Regional Park. This park offers residents playing fields, playgrounds, an indoor ice skating rink, tennis courts, a children's train, a nature center, and paved and compact soil trails. At the southern end of the park on Democracy Boulevard, the nature center offers a wonderland of exploration opportunities: a wildlife observation deck, a butterfly naturalist garden, an indoor oak tree exhibit, live animals (such as resident corn and black snakes), and the outdoor natural playground. Before enjoying the natural playground, take this 1.4-mile hike through a meadow, among tall tulip poplars, and along the Cabin John Stream.

From the parking lot, walk over the bridge toward the nature center. Before reaching the center entrance, turn right and head up the steps on the Upland Meadow Trail, marked by a trail post. To the left of the

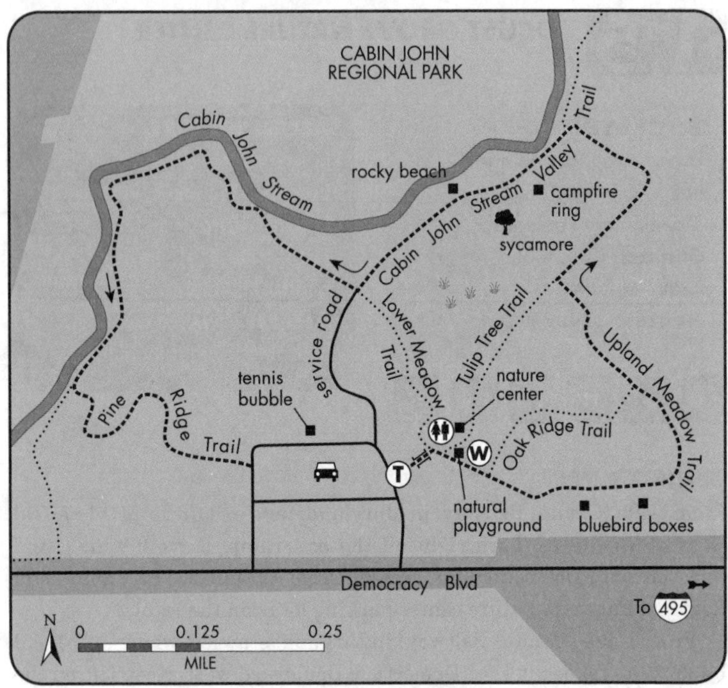

trail are the natural playground and the butterfly garden. Pass the Oak Ridge Trail on the left and a picnic pavilion straight ahead. For the next 0.1 mile, walk through a small meadow habitat. A few bluebird boxes are placed at the edge of the forest. Then the Upland Meadow Trail curves to the left and enters the forest as it descends the ridge toward the stream. The Oak Ridge Trail connects with the Upland Meadow Trail on the left.

Come to a T intersection with the Tulip Tree Trail. This trail is aptly named because many tulip poplars tower over both this trail and most of the Upland Meadow Trail. Some of the poplars are more than a century old and still standing strong, providing animals and humans with extraordinary benefits: food and shelter, a windbreak, a filter for air pollution, erosion control, oxygen, streambank stabilization, shade, a filter for soil, noise pollution control, and a carbon sink. Turn right on the Tulip Tree Trail even though it feels counterintuitive to walk away from the stream. After crossing a small bridge over a feeder stream, the trail curves to the left and back toward the stream. Before the Tulip Tree

Balancing on a fallen tree over the Cabin John Stream

Trail reaches the Cabin John Stream Trail, it cuts right to maintain a perpendicular line to the slope. Where the Tulip Tree dead-ends into the Cabin John Stream Valley Trail, turn left.

The Cabin John Stream Valley Trail is an 8.8-mile compact soil trail with a trailhead on MacArthur Boulevard at its southern tip and on Goya Drive at its northern tip. From MacArthur Boulevard to River Road, the trail is restricted to hikers because steep slopes make it unsafe and unsustainable for horses and mountain bikers. North of River Road, the topography allows for sustainable use by mountain bikers. Locust Grove's ample parking makes it a great staging area for mountain biking on this portion of the Cabin John Stream Valley Trail.

While hiking south along the Cabin John Stream Valley Trail, there are many places to stop and access the stream for water fun. The best place is just after the large campfire ring and benches. Here, a large stone beach provides ample opportunity to skip rocks. Before reaching this rock beach, stop and admire the 200-year-old sycamore tree that stands behind the campfire ring. This tree is worth seeing during all four seasons. On a sunny winter day, its stark white limbs contrast brightly with the azure sky. Because of its prominence in the meadow, you might wonder whether it is the largest sycamore in Montgomery County, but according to the Registry of Champion Trees of Montgomery County, the largest known sycamore in the county is in McKee-Beshers Wildlife Management Area in Poolsville. That sycamore stands 143 feet with a trunk circumference of 243 inches. The specimen in Cabin John Regional Park stands 85 feet with a trunk circumference of 144 inches.

A champion tree is defined as a tree that has the largest combined trunk circumference, tree height, and average crown spread for its species.

After having fun at the rocky beach, return on the Cabin John Stream Valley Trail to the intersection with the service road straight ahead and the Lower Meadow Trail to the left. Turn right after the small wooden bridge to continue on the Cabin John Stream Valley Trail. The trail follows the stream with a few access points. For the most part, the trail sits 15 to 20 feet above the stream. Occasionally, floodwaters wash out trees along the streambanks, and they fall across the stream and bridge the banks. Sometimes these trees are easily accessible to kids who can traverse their large trunks on hands and knees, providing endless gross motor skill development and challenge.

After hiking approximately a half mile on this section of the Cabin John Stream Valley Trail, turn left and hike up the Pine Ridge Trail toward the tennis bubble. Cross the parking lot to reach the nature center. Don't forget to visit the natural playground to dig in the sandpit, climb aboard carved bears, jump from stump to stump, and build a rock tower or fort. This playground is fenced in, so moms and dads don't have to worry about wandering children. The trails and outdoor experiences at the Locust Grove Nature Center provide endless hours of fun for kids.

FORD MINE TRAIL

BEFORE YOU GO
Map: Available at the visitor center and on the park's website
Contact: Chesapeake and Ohio Canal National Historical Park (charges a fee)
Nearest city: Potomac, MD

ABOUT THE HIKE
Moderate/difficult, year-round
Length: 2.7 miles, loop and spur
Hiking time: 2–2½ hours
High point/elevation gain: 338 feet/285 feet
Access: Compact soil, passable for jogging strollers

GETTING THERE

From I-495 (Capital Beltway), take exit 41 for Clara Barton Parkway west toward Carderock. Drive 1.8 miles, and turn left onto MacArthur

Boulevard. Drive 2 miles to the intersection with Falls Road, and stay left on MacArthur Boulevard. Drive 1 mile to the park entrance. The trailhead is located at the end of the parking lot.

ON THE TRAIL

The Chesapeake and Ohio Canal National Historical Park boasts the 184-mile towpath that connects Cumberland, Maryland, to Washington, DC, providing a natural buffer zone for the Potomac River and a great

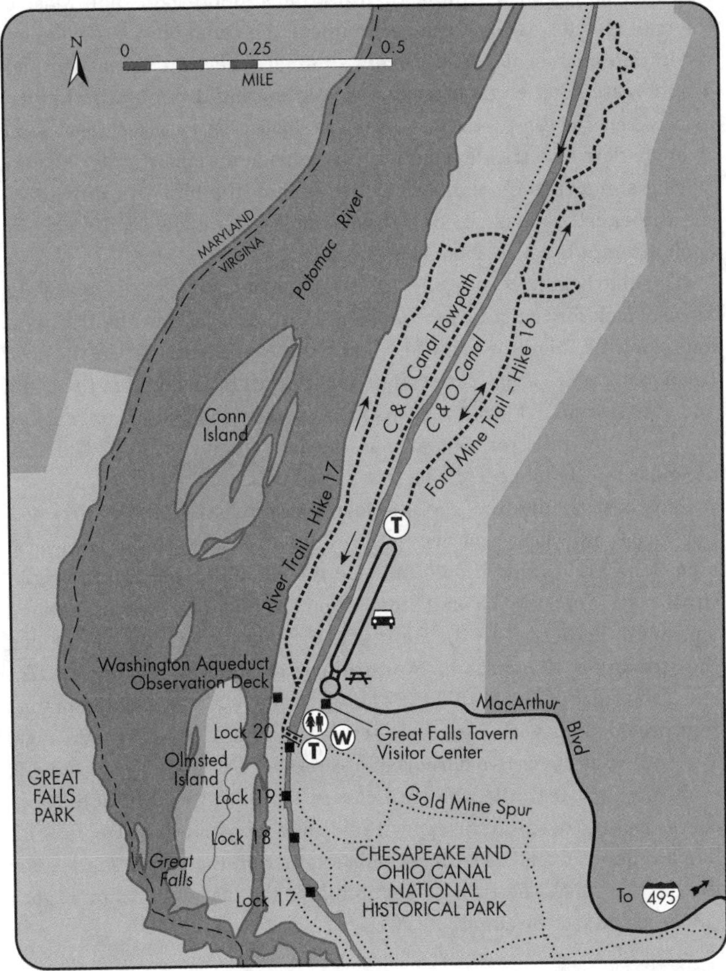

recreational destination. At various points along the towpath, you can find good areas for hiking with your kids: for example, along the Paw Paw Tunnel in Green Ridge State Forest and close to DC at the Great Falls Tavern. The Great Falls area of the C&O Canal National Historical Park offers about 15 miles of trails.

The blue-blazed Ford Mine Trail is a peaceful but adventurous hike through upland forest and along the canal away from the park's most popular trails. It follows a 0.6-mile out-and-back segment to a 1.5-mile loop that starts on the bluff, then descends along the canal. Most of the trail is wide, except for a section near the canal on the loop where vegetation encroaches on it during summer. The trail passes through deep forest, along rock outcroppings, and up and down bluffs that are intersected by three streams that the loop crosses six times. Some streams flow at a trickle, while others provide an opportunity for play. During summer, the neighboring houses atop the bluff are difficult to see through the forest. Look for box turtles along the trail; however, don't attempt to touch them.

The hike begins at the end of the parking lot opposite the Great Falls Tavern; look for the trail post labeled "Ford Mine." From the trail post and sidewalk, hike toward the canal bank over stones set in the trail tread along a wet area. The trail then curves right, away from the canal and over two small feeder streams on bridges. In the last 0.2 mile before the loop, the trail crosses two more feeder streams on logs. The trail ascends slightly to meet the loop at a trail post.

It is best to hike the 1.5-mile loop counterclockwise. The first section is 0.9 mile long and above the canal on bluffs. At the trail post, hike straight, heading uphill and past a rock outcropping on the right. Cross a stream on rocks, and stay left on the blue-blazed trail, passing a people's choice trail on the right. The trail curves left and stays along the stream for 100 yards before turning right and away from it. Hike along the sidehill of a bluff for 0.2 mile, passing a few rock outcroppings that provide kids with a good gross motor skill and climbing challenge. The trail winds over two berms before crossing a mostly dry streambed.

In the next 0.1 mile, the trail curves left to switchback uphill and curves right to descend the opposite side and cross another stream. Just like a roller coaster, the trail ascends another bluff on switchbacks. For the next 0.3 mile, the trail heads uphill for the last time before it goes downhill toward the canal.

Beware! Box turtle crossing

At the bottom of the bluff, the trail turns left at the trail post. For the next 0.6 mile, it follows the canal. Shortly after the turn, the trail tread is rocky just before it crosses a feeder stream. Cross three more streams—the trail can be wet and muddy in areas—before the loop concludes. The last stream has the largest flow and can be crossed on a fallen log or on rocks. Either way, this last stream's riffles and pools provide a great place for some playtime in water, and before the stream crossing, two large boulders sitting on the edge of the canal offer a great respite in the shade for watching the canal.

After your break at this last stream on the loop, hike uphill to the trail's intersection with the spur. Turn right, head slightly downhill, and hike 0.6 mile and across four streams back to the parking lot. Before leaving the park, you can walk to the historical tavern and the seasonal snack bar.

BOX TURTLES

Eastern box turtles are a common reptile species in our region, but they have good camouflage and a timid nature. Most often they are spotted because hikers come upon them moving slowly across the trail. Their best defense mechanism is to enclose their head, tail, legs, and feet inside their shell. This hard shell protects adult turtles from predators; however, juveniles are prey for skunks, raccoons, and snakes because they are small and the hinge on their shells has not developed to enclose them completely.

Box turtles are omnivores, eating both plants and animals, such as insects, salamanders, frogs, snails, and slugs. Young turtles eat more animals while they are growing because their bodies are consuming more energy, but as they get older, they become herbivores, eating more plants. Box turtles can live to be a century old.

RIVER TRAIL

BEFORE YOU GO
Map: Available at the visitor center and on the park's website
Contact: Chesapeake and Ohio Canal National Historical Park (charges a fee)
Nearest city: Potomac, MD

ABOUT THE HIKE
Easy, year-round
Length: 2.4 miles, loop
Hiking time: 1–1½ hours
High point/elevation gain: 197 feet/70 feet
Access: Compact soil and cinder, passable for jogging strollers

GETTING THERE

From I-495 (Capital Beltway), take exit 41 for Clara Barton Parkway west toward Carderock. Drive 1.8 miles, and turn left onto MacArthur Boulevard. Drive 2 miles to the intersection with Falls Road, and stay left on MacArthur Boulevard. Drive 1 mile to the park entrance.

ON THE TRAIL

The Chesapeake and Ohio Canal National Historical Park at Great Falls offers some of the best family-friendly hikes in the Washington area. From the challenging rock scramble on the Billy Goat Trail: Section A (see Hike 19) to the gentle, jogging-stroller-passable hike on the River Trail, you and your kids can spend multiple weekends enjoying nature along the Potomac River.

A loop hike, the River Trail travels 1 mile on compact soil adjacent to the calm waters of the Potomac River just upstream from where the river crashes 60 feet over the falls, and returns to Great Falls Tavern on the crushed stone towpath along the C&O Canal.

From the Great Falls Tavern, cross the pedestrian bridge at Lock 20. (If it is not open due to boat tours on the canal, then walk southeast toward the second bridge over the canal at Lock 19.) Turn right and head northeast up the C&O Canal Towpath to the River Trail trailhead, which is past the Washington Aqueduct Observation Deck. Turn left on the blue-blazed trail to walk toward the Potomac River. Hike a short distance, down a few steps, and over a rock puncheon to reach the Potomac's edge.

Even though the river looks placid and calm, it has a deadly current and undertow. Within a few hundred feet, millions of gallons of water plunge over metamorphic rock as the Piedmont Plateau gives way to the Atlantic Coastal Plain. Wading in the river, even just to get your feet wet, is not recommended. However, this spot provides a great launchpad for throwing rocks or watching a stick move swiftly toward the falls.

The trail turns right and follows the river northeast. The River Trail traverses a floodplain, which means that it is wet and muddy in locations and that vernal pools dot the woods. Low areas in the land that provide a temporary place for water to collect, vernal pools are valuable habitats for amphibians and fairy shrimp.

As you and your family hike the River Trail, you will likely notice that its best features are its location next to the water and its many large trees, such as sycamores, some maples, and oaks. The paw paw tree dominates the understory with its big lime green leaves that provide a natural barrier from the bustling towpath a quarter mile inland. Many sycamore trees stretch their trunks and crowns out over the Potomac. These and many large snags, or fallen trees, litter the ground, providing an incredible natural playground to jump, balance, crawl, and shimmy on. The circumferences of some of these large sycamore tree trunks are wider than the armspans of two adults hugging the trunk. Most of these specimen trees are alive, but a few of the ones that have died now provide niches for animals in their hollows.

Stop to climb a sycamore tree along the River Trail.

After hiking almost a mile along the Potomac, the trail turns right at the blue double blaze to connect back to the towpath 0.2 mile ahead. The trail follows a feeder stream that flows into the river. Upon reaching the towpath,

FAIRY SHRIMP

Fairy shrimp are crustaceans on the threatened species list that live their life in vernal pools. They hatch from eggs in early winter and mature within forty-one days. By May, the females have laid eggs that adhere to the dry bottom of the vernal pool during summer. Once moisture returns to the pool, the eggs hatch and begin their life cycle. An essential component to the woodland ecosystem, fairy shrimp eat algae and plankton and are prey for birds. Habitat destruction and human recreation threaten the fairy shrimp's vernal pool habitat.

turn right and hike a little more than a mile southwest back to the Great Falls Tavern. While walking along the canal, look for eastern painted turtles sunning themselves on rocks or dead limbs, the northern water snake (nonpoisonous), and fish. Before leaving the park, check out the museum and bookstore in the tavern, or grab an ice cream at the refreshment stand. There are picnic tables next to the refreshment stand for enjoying a picnic lunch or dinner.

GOLD MINE TRAIL

BEFORE YOU GO
Map: Available at the visitor center and on the park's website
Contact: Chesapeake and Ohio Canal National Historical Park (charges a fee)
Nearest city: Potomac, MD

ABOUT THE HIKE
Moderate, year-round
Length: 3.8 miles, loop
Hiking time: 2½–3 hours
High point/elevation gain: 397 feet/226 feet
Access: Compact soil, crushed stone, and raised wooden boardwalk; not passable for jogging strollers

GETTING THERE

From I-495 (Capital Beltway), take exit 41 for Clara Barton Parkway west toward Carderock. Drive 1.8 miles, and turn left onto MacArthur Boulevard. Drive 2 miles to the intersection with Falls Road. Stay left on MacArthur Boulevard, and drive 1 mile to the park entrance.

ON THE TRAIL

The Chesapeake and Ohio Canal National Historical Park and Great Falls Park in Virginia boast many great family-friendly hikes along the Potomac River. This hike along part of the Gold Mine Loop takes you on top of the ridges above the canal and Potomac River and back down to Olmsted Island to view Great Falls. The Gold Mine Loop is named after the ruins of the Maryland Mine, a historic site at the corner of MacArthur Boulevard and Falls Road. A Union Army soldier discovered gold in the area during the Civil War, and subsequently, numerous gold mines dotted the landscape around the falls. You can visit the ruins by hiking 0.3 mile out and back on the Falls Road Spur, which is off the Gold Mine Loop.

The Gold Mine Spur trailhead post is beyond the Great Falls Tavern and at the base of the ridge. Turn left and enter the blue-blazed trail to walk uphill. The first 0.3 mile is the steepest uphill portion. Beech trees populate this area of the park; they are many of the young trees that make up the understory. As you hike farther along the trail, tulip poplars and oak trees populate the canopy. Chestnut and post, white, and red oaks are the predominant species. Within 0.2 mile, the Lock 19 Spur intersects the Gold Mine Spur. Continue straight and up steps where a double blaze appears ahead; go left.

The trail levels out on top of a berm where trolley tracks were housed in the early 1900s; this trolley helped people from Washington, DC, escape city life for the quiet of nature at Great Falls. Previously, the canal passenger boats transported people to the solitude of the rocks along the river, where they could enjoy a good meal at the tavern and perhaps a night's stay in the bunkrooms for 25 cents. If a couple was married, they paid 50 cents and, with proof of their marriage, they could stay in the third-floor honeymoon room. The 14-mile trip took six to eight hours by canal boat; the trolley sped up the trip, allowing people to visit for one day.

The short walk on the trolley berm leads to a tunnel made of 20-foot banks covered with trees and vegetation. At the end of the tunnel of soil and vegetation, the trail turns right at two double blazes. Hikers sometimes mistakenly go straight here because of a people's choice trail, but it leads to MacArthur Boulevard. After climbing more than 300 feet in elevation, the trail descends gently on the back side of the ridge. For the next mile, ascend and descend rolling hills with an elevation change of no more than 75 feet.

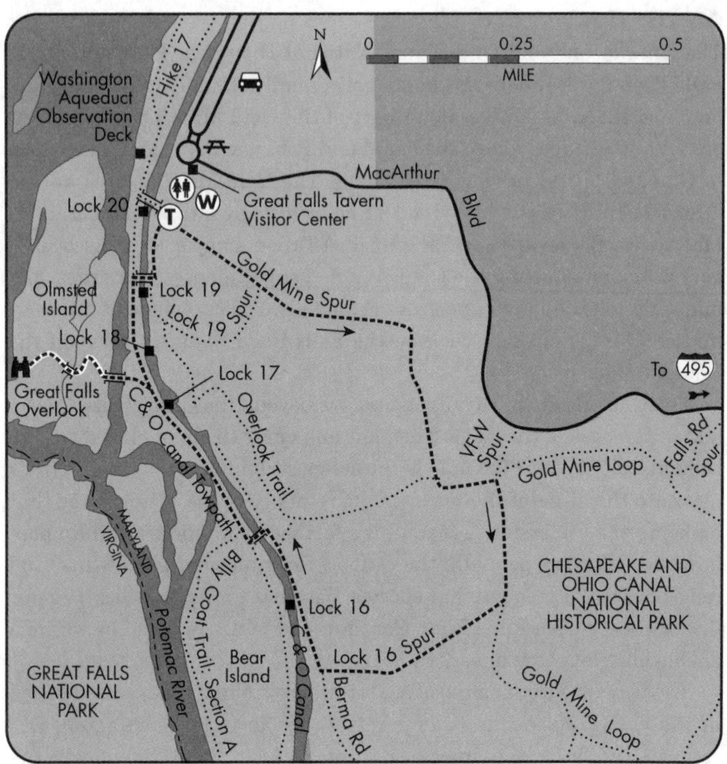

Within 0.2 mile, a trail post appears at a trail intersection. The Overlook Trail is on the right, which connects to the Lock 19 Spur and the tavern, but your Gold Mine Spur continues straight. For the next 0.2 mile, the trail zigzags uphill. Pay attention to the blazes and double blazes to follow the trail to the next intersection with the VFW Spur and the Gold Mine Loop. Turn right onto the Gold Mine Loop and hike 0.2 mile to the Lock 16 Spur trail post. You might play a game of "I Spy" for tree hollows with your kids on this section. Many trees along this section have hollows, which form when the tree's heartwood is compromised. Birds, reptiles, amphibians, and mammals use the hollows for shelter.

Turn right onto the Lock 16 Spur. This yellow-blazed trail descends the ridge to the Berma Road above the canal. The Lock 16 Spur has the rockiest tread and is steep for the last 0.1 mile. Upon reaching Berma

Road, turn right on this wide, gravel road and follow it until you reach the stop gate (a wooden shed that sits on a wooden bridge over the canal). Pass the Overlook Spur on the right that ascends the ridge. Turn left onto the bridge, and head northwest on the C&O Canal Towpath.

Shortly after descending the stairs, pass the turn off for Section A of the Billy Goat Trail (see Hike 19) on Bear Island. Keep going approximately 0.3 mile to the trail to the Great Falls Overlook on Olmsted Island. Just before this junction, to the left of the towpath, is a people's choice trail down to a sandy area along the Potomac River.

Olmsted Island is one of the many islands in the middle of the Potomac River. More than 1 million years ago, this area was a floodplain, but during the last ice age, the Atlantic Coastal Plain fell 1000 feet. The exposed metamorphic bedrock created islands, gorges, and waterfalls along the fast-moving Potomac's path to the Atlantic Ocean. Olmsted Island has a unique bedrock river terrace forest ecosystem. The dominant tree on the island is the post oak due to its ability to survive in drought conditions. The ground is covered mainly in wild oats, a member of the grass family.

Great Falls Tavern

The hike to the overlook is 0.6 mile out and back on a raised boardwalk that protects the island's unique ecosystem. The boardwalk complies with the American Disabilities Act (ADA), but bikers, scooters, roller bladers, and dogs are prohibited. Stop on the bridge to the island for a perfect example of the force and power of water on a landscape. The water is mesmerizing to watch. At the end of the boardwalk, a large wooden deck built atop the bedrock provides ample space to take photos, play, and listen to the roar of the waterfall. The water drops 60 feet here and another 85 feet before reaching the Key Bridge in Georgetown.

Walk back on the boardwalk toward the towpath, and turn left toward the Great Falls Tavern. Pass Lock 18 on the canal, and take the first bridge to the tavern at Lock 19. Often the bridge at Lock 20 (directly in front of the tavern) is closed on weekends because the National Park Service offers boat rides on the canal. For a fee, you can take a one-hour interpretive boat ride on the canal to learn about its primary purpose in the 1800s, how mules pulled the canal boats, and how the locks work to transport boats down 600 feet of elevation from Cumberland, Maryland, to Washington, DC.

BILLY GOAT TRAIL: SECTION A

BEFORE YOU GO
Map: Available at the visitor center and on the park's website
Contact: Chesapeake and Ohio Canal National Historical Park (charges a fee)
Nearest city: Potomac, MD

ABOUT THE HIKE
Difficult, year-round
Length: 3.7 miles, loop and spur
Hiking time: 3–4 hours
High point/elevation gain: 207 feet/154 feet
Access: Rock, compact soil, and crushed stone; not passable for jogging strollers

GETTING THERE

From I-495 (Capital Beltway), take exit 41 for Clara Barton Parkway west toward Carderock. Drive 1.8 miles, and turn left onto MacArthur Boulevard. Drive 2 miles to the intersection with Falls Road. Stay left on MacArthur Boulevard, and drive 1 mile to the park entrance.

ON THE TRAIL

Section A of the Billy Goat Trail is the most popular and well-known hike in Washington, DC, for good reasons. Its location on the high rocky cliffs above the Potomac River makes it very scenic. Furthermore, the landscape on both sides of the Potomac River between Great Falls and

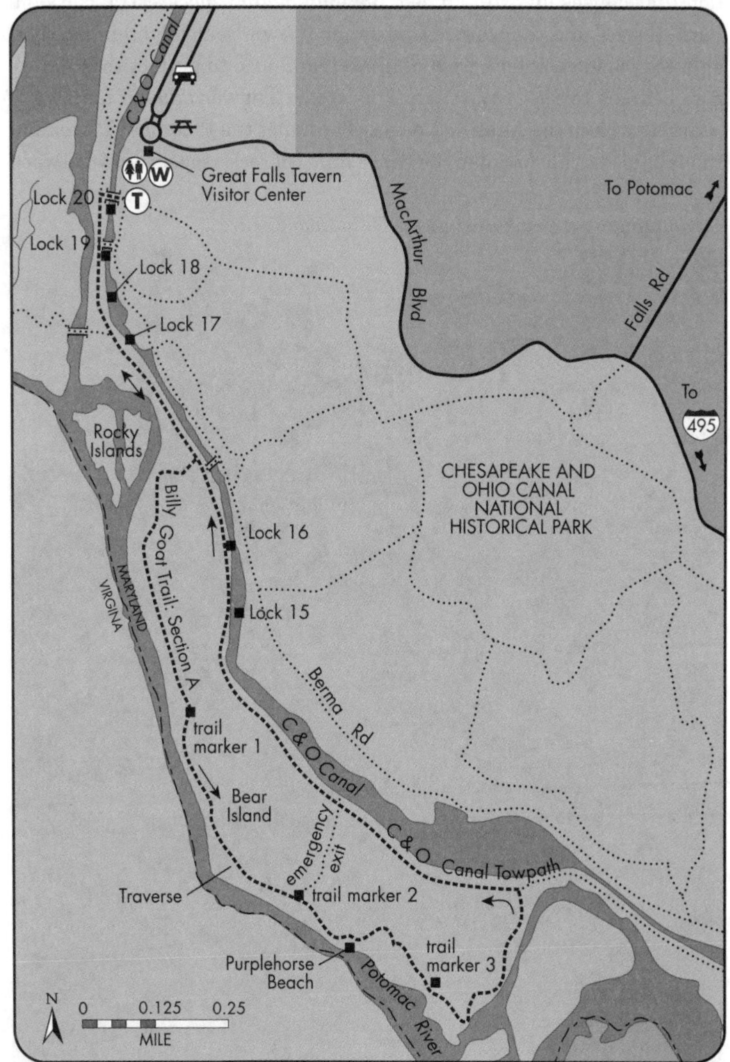

Carderock is a playscape for adults and big kids, with hiking and scrambling on the Billy Goat Trails, mountain biking on the Chesapeake and Ohio (C&O) Canal Towpath, kayaking on the Potomac River, and rock climbing on the cliffs of the Mather Gorge.

This section of the Billy Goat Trail is on Bear Island, a unique ecosystem that houses fifty threatened and endangered species. The National Park Service and the Nature Conservancy own Bear Island in partnership to provide a safe recreational area and also to protect the island's rare bedrock terrace ecosystem. This ecosystem was created millions of years ago when the Atlantic Coastal Plain met the Piedmont Plateau at the fall line in the Potomac Gorge, 15 miles of rocky topography between

Scrambling up the rock wall on the Billy Goat Trail

Great Falls and Georgetown. Along the fall line, the sandy soil of the coastal plain intersperses with the metamorphic rock of the plateau. The fall line's geology and its continual flooding provide a rich and special environment for a variety of plant and animal species that do not live anywhere else.

The National Park Service recommends that children be at least eight years old to hike this trail due to sections of strenuous and difficult rock scrambling that require good balance and physical fitness. They recommend that hikers, both adults and children, wear study shoes with good tread; flip-flops, sandals, and tennis shoes are not advisable because they may cause you to slip and fall—the sandy soil acts like little roller balls on rocks underneath shoes. Bring plenty of water due to the physical demands of the hike and the trail's exposure to sun. Because the trail is prone to flooding, the National Park Service sometimes closes it for hiker safety and to protect the island's fragile environment.

Even though the trail poses challenges and potential limitations for you and your kids, seeing the views of the Mather Gorge from atop impressive rock formations is worth the preparation and trek. Along the trail, you will hike through a variety of habitats, such as barren pine growing from soil in rock crevices, potholes in the bedrock, prairies of river oats, rock walls, sand beaches, and vernal pools.

The hike commences at the Great Falls Tavern. From the tavern, cross the C&O Canal at Lock 20, and turn left to hike south on the towpath. Hike the towpath for a half mile past Locks 19, 18, and 17, and the trail to the Great Falls Overlook. Section A of the Billy Goat Trail begins on the right, just before the stop gate (a wooden shed that sits on a bridge atop the canal). This bridge connects the towpath with Berma Road, a compact dirt road that continues south for 2 miles above the canal to the Cropley parking lot.

The Billy Goat Trail tread is compact soil for a couple hundred feet before large rocks poke out of the surface of the earth. For the next half mile, the trail is a combination of soil and rocks that you have to step over. You and your kids will occasionally need to grab a tree or the edge of a rock for balance. The trail's blue blazes appear often on trees and boulders to help you stay on the trail. Barriers have been placed along the trail in this section to keep hikers from creating shortcuts, which cause a lot of damage to the fragile plant ecology.

After hiking a half mile on the trail, reach trail marker 1, which indicates several things: the towpath is in 1.2 miles, an emergency trail exit is in 0.4 mile, and a warning that the trail becomes strenuous, requiring balance and the use of both hands. From the trail marker, climb up on the rock to experience a different ecosystem on a cliff above the Potomac River. This area is known as Pothole Alley due to the potholes found in the bedrock. A long time ago, the Potomac rose above these cliffs. The turbulence of the water over the rocks caused a vortex effect underwater where grains of sand eroded the rock's surface and created potholes. Some of the potholes are filled with water, which sustains life. Geologists believe that potholes the size of a Volkswagen Bug exist in the river along the fall line. Swimming in this area of the Potomac is very dangerous due to these potholes—the water swirling in them can suck people under. Hiking this section requires balance and the use of your hands, and sometimes you may even need to scoot. However, this area provides the most stunning views of the Mather Gorge.

Climb off the bedrock terrace overlooking the Potomac and back into an area of tree-covered rocks. Within a short distance, meet the river's edge in front of a 40-foot wall known as the Traverse, which the trail ascends. It is the most challenging part of the trail but also the most rewarding for kids. You don't need any rock climbing equipment, but you do need to carefully choose where to place both your hands and feet on the wall. The trickiest placements are toward the top of the wall where the rock faces are longer and the crevices are farther apart. For safety, you should hike behind kids on this wall to help support and spot them. At the top, the trail levels off a bit and enters some trees; the tread is a mixture of soil and rocks that require some scrambling.

Before reaching Purplehorse Beach, you will come to trail marker 2, indicating the emergency exit to the towpath. The towpath is a couple hundred feet to the left. The Billy Goat Trail continues straight for another 0.75 mile before it dead-ends into the towpath. Ahead on the trail is a rock scrambling area where you must use your hands and feet to climb up and down large mounds of bedrock. Between the two bedrock mounds is Purplehorse Beach, which looks like an ideal place to get wet in the Potomac, but the river is still very dangerous here. Purplehorse Beach is covered with shells from invasive Asiatic clams.

After you scramble across the second mound of bedrock, the trail weaves between vernal pools. These permanent pools are created by the water's inability to seep through the bedrock. They are a vital breeding ground for the wood frog. The third pool has a constant flow of water from the C&O Canal and then drains into the Potomac. A single log

CLAMS IN FRESHWATER?

Asiatic clams are an invasive mollusk brought to the Pacific Northwest in the late 1930s by Chinese immigrants as a food source. Biologists believe that the clam larvae were spread throughout the United States via birds' feet. This clam is highly adaptive to many environments. Its larvae spread by floating in water, whereas those of the native clam species are transported via the gills of specific host fish. Furthermore, the Asiatic clam can burrow in any surface, but native clams need a specific substrate. Asiatic clams are plentiful along the Potomac riverbanks and can be found in many of the tributary streams of the Chesapeake Bay.

bridge here makes crossing it easier. Turn right and hike through some trees up the rocks and then scale the back side. Ahead is this hike's last overlook of the Potomac. From this exposed spot, you might see kayakers playing in the Maryland Chutes, practicing their whitewater maneuvers. On top of the bluff on the Virginia side is the private Madeira School. Below this bluff, the Difficult Run enters the Potomac River.

After the overlook, the trail curves sharply to the left to another sandy beach along the Potomac. Leave the beach for a roller coaster last section of the trail before it reaches the towpath. The trail descends and ascends three short, steep hills, crossing two low areas that may be filled with water, depending on the river's height. On the final ascent, look for a double blaze on the left, and climb a wall of rock. At the top, the trail curves to the right where it meets the towpath within a couple hundred yards.

The return hike to the tavern is 1.5 miles. Turn left and hike northwest, keeping the canal on your right. This widest part of the canal where the water fills the bedrock terrace is a perfect place to spot great blue herons standing on the rocky edges watching the water for a meal. In 0.2 mile, cross the spillway bridge that helps prevent flooding in the canal. Within 0.4 mile, the emergency exit trail off the Billy Goat appears on the left. In 0.7 mile, pass Lock 15 and then 16 shortly thereafter.

At 1 mile, hike under the stop gate—the shed that sits atop the bridge over the canal. Before returning to the tavern, pass the Section A trailhead, Lock 17, the Great Falls Overlook on Olmsted Island, and

Locks 18 and 19. To access the tavern, restrooms, refreshment stand, and parking lot, cross the bridge over the canal either at Lock 19 or 20. On weekends from spring to fall, the bridge at Lock 20 is often closed to pedestrians because rangers give tours on the old canal boat. The area around the tavern is often very crowded on weekends during spring and fall because the natural beauty of this adventurous playscape attracts people from around the world.

BILLY GOAT TRAIL: SECTION B

BEFORE YOU GO
Map: Available at the visitor center and on the park's website
Contact: Chesapeake and Ohio Canal National Historical Park (charges a fee)
Nearest city: Potomac, MD

ABOUT THE HIKE
Moderate, year-round
Length: 2.6 miles, loop
Hiking time: 1½–2 hours
High point/elevation gain: 236 feet/144 feet
Access: Compact soil and crushed stone, not passable for jogging strollers

GETTING THERE

From I-495 (Capital Beltway), take exit 41 for Clara Barton Parkway west and Carderock. Drive 1.8 miles, and turn left on MacArthur Boulevard. Drive 1 mile, and look for the Cropley parking lot on the left across from Old Anglers Inn.

ON THE TRAIL

Section B of the Billy Goat Trail is one of three trails with that name that follow the Potomac River from mile marker 14 along the canal to mile 10 in the Chesapeake and Ohio Canal National Historical Park. Each of the Billy Goat Trails is accessible via the towpath; they follow the river and then loop back to the towpath. All three trails traverse the metamorphic rock that dominates this area of the riverbank as the river crosses the fall line and the land transitions from the Piedmont Plateau to the Atlantic Coastal Plain. Section B is a combination of what families can experience on the other two sections. Section A (Hike 19) is

Hikers explore rocks jutting out into the Potomac River.

the most difficult with a lot of rock scrambling; whereas, the trail in Section C (Hike 22) is mostly soil with very little, easy rock scrambling. Section B is a mix of both soil and rock scrambling.

Section B, a blue-blazed 1.6-mile trail, follows the riverbank, passing four large islands in the Potomac: Offutt, Hermit, Herzog, and Vaso. There are a few areas along the trail where you must scramble across rocks, but they are not difficult, unlike some found on Section A. The trail makes one stream crossing on rocks, which is manageable unless there has been a rainstorm within the past twenty-four hours. The trail ends at the towpath 1 mile from the parking lot at Cropley.

The trailhead is at the end of the lower parking lot next to some large signs. Walk over the bridge to the canal, and turn left on the towpath. On the right an access road steeply descends to the Potomac; a lot of kayakers and emergency vehicles use it. Pass this road and walk 0.1 mile to the Billy Goat trailhead, which is marked by a trail sign. Turn right onto the blue-blazed trail. For 0.3 mile, the trail stays above the Potomac, and you may have a sneak peek of the river through the heavy canopy. The trail is rocky in a few places before it descends to meet the banks of the river where it curves left. Pass the people's choice trail that heads for the water here.

At 0.5 mile, the trail veers right around a large slab of rock that juts out to the river. You have a choice at this junction. A people's choice trail on the left that climbs this rock slab and then immediately scrambles down on the opposite side provides a fun challenge for young kids. At the top of the slab, look right and head down the rocks toward the river. The blue blazes appear again on the trees near the riverbank. If you don't want to climb the rock slab, then you can follow the blue blazes on the rocks and trees around the slab to the right adjacent to the river. *Warning*: When the river is high, the only way to continue on the trail is by climbing the slab.

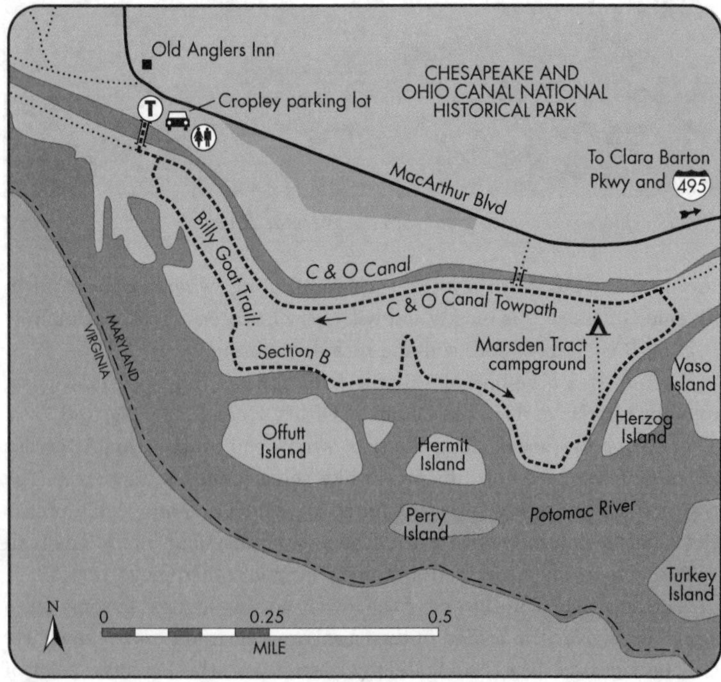

COLD-BLOODED ANIMALS

Turtles are cold-blooded animals, which means that their body temperature matches that of the surrounding environment. They are active in hot environments and sluggish when it is cold. The warm environment creates a chemical reaction in their muscles that causes them to move. Warm-blooded animals need many calories to maintain an even body temperature for survival; whereas, cold-blooded animals convert more calories to building body mass.

On the opposite side of the slab, a beach that comes into view is a great place to hang out and play along the river. Park rangers advise against swimming in the Potomac due to its swift currents.

For most of the remainder of the hike, the trail is about 10 to 15 feet above the river due to heavy erosion during flooding. After the beach, the trail curves left away from the river along a feeder stream. At 0.9 mile into the hike, cross the stream on rocks. The trail turns right after crossing the stream. A people's choice trail on the left leads 0.1 mile back to the towpath.

The trail follows the feeder stream back to the river's edge where it curves left and follows the river for the next 0.8 mile. In 0.2 mile from the stream, pass a people's choice trail on the left, at which point the trail curves right onto a peninsula. The trail here is rocky and requires some scrambling; follow the blue blazes on the rocks. At the point of this peninsula, the trail turns left over a rock, requiring hikers to climb down and onto a soil-covered trail. Just beyond is a second beach for some playtime.

At 1 mile into the hike is the trailhead for the Marsden Tract, a campground for groups (available only by reservation). A signpost here indicates that there is 0.6 mile left to reach the towpath. Shortly after the signpost, pass huge boulders on the left that many people use for rock climbing. The rest of the trail follows the river closely until it turns left at a double blaze where you need to hike a rocky bluff to reach the towpath via some rock steps.

At the towpath, turn left and hike northwest 1 mile back to the parking lot at Cropley. Along the way, play "I Spy" the turtles in the canal with the kids. The many fallen logs in the canal provide perfect ramps for turtles to climb and sun themselves to increase their body temperature.

In 0.2 mile, a trail to the Marsden Tract from the towpath is on the left. In another 0.1 mile, pass a bridge over the canal leading to a trailhead at MacArthur Boulevard. Continue hiking straight along the canal. At 0.5 mile, a people's choice trail on the left is a shortcut from the Billy Goat Trail to the towpath at the stream crossing. The hike ends in a half mile where the towpath meets the bridge over the canal and returns to the Cropley parking lot.

BERMA ROAD TO C&O CANAL TOWPATH

BEFORE YOU GO
Map: Available at the visitor center and on the park's website
Contact: Chesapeake and Ohio Canal National Historical Park (charges a fee)
Nearest city: Potomac, MD

ABOUT THE HIKE
Easy, year-round
Length: 3 miles, loop
Hiking time: 1½–2 hours
High point/elevation gain: 249 feet/125 feet
Access: Crushed stone, passable for jogging strollers

GETTING THERE

From I-495 (Capital Beltway), take exit 41 for Clara Barton Parkway west and Carderock. Drive 1.8 miles, and turn left on MacArthur Boulevard. Drive 1 mile. The Cropley parking lot is on the left across from Old Anglers Inn.

ON THE TRAIL

Berma Road and the towpath are part of the 184-mile trail system in Chesapeake and Ohio Canal National Historical Park. Both are located in the Great Falls region of the park. An old trolley rail bed, the Berma Road was used in the early 1900s by residents in Washington, DC, who wanted to escape to the country for respite and recreation. Today, it is a multiuse trail connecting the Cropley parking lot to three compact soil trails and the towpath along the C&O Canal via the stop gate. Berma Road is a wide, shady, and level 1.4-mile trail made of crushed stone. Note that the Cropley parking lot is a very busy place on the weekends,

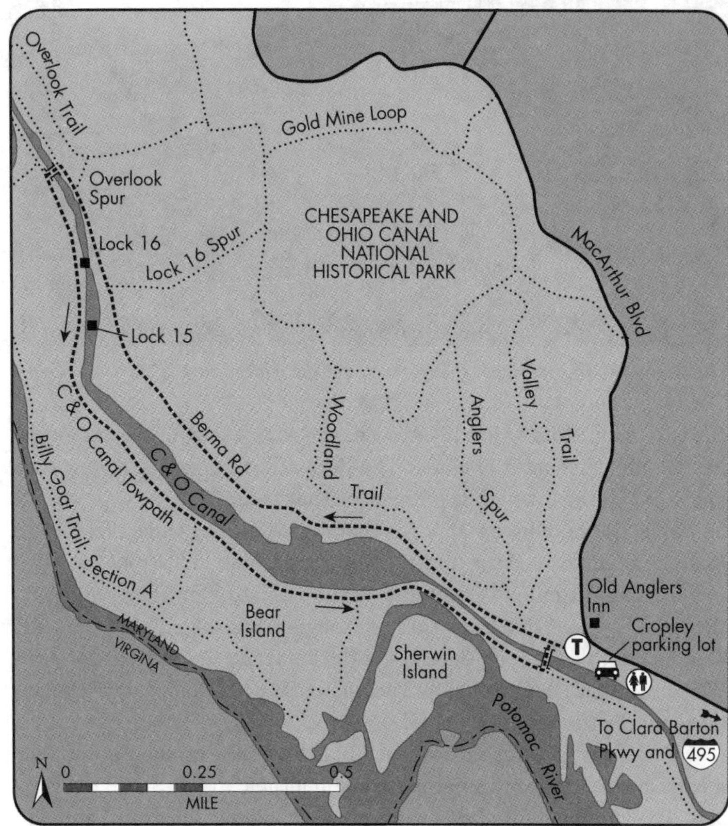

attracting hikers to multiple trailheads, bikers to the towpath, and kayakers to the Potomac River. Its capacity is approximately fifty cars, and parking is prohibited along MacArthur Boulevard. On weekends with gorgeous weather, plan to hike early or late to avoid the midday crowds.

This 3-mile loop hike connects the Berma Road and the C&O Canal Towpath, providing families with a level and wide trail to hike. The Berma Road is the shady portion of the hike, while the towpath can be sunny in the morning and shadier as the afternoon progresses. Both trails are made of crushed stone, making it easy to push a jogging stroller along them. The only obstacle for strollers along the hike is a descent along stairs at the stop gate (the bridge over the canal connecting

The Berma Road and towpath offer views of the widest part of the C&O Canal.

the two trails). The entire hike passes the widest part of the canal, giving the illusion that it is a lake. The Berma Road provides a view from above, while the towpath is adjacent to the canal.

Begin the hike by passing the metal gate on the wide, dirt Berma Road located between the upper and lower parking lots. From the parking lot, hike 0.1 mile to a fenced-in area (protecting pressure valves for the sewer system that runs through the park) to the right of the trail. Just before this fence on the right is the trailhead for Anglers Spur, the Woodland Trail, and the Valley Trail. There is no trail sign, but a yellow blaze marks the beginning of all three trails.

From the Anglers Spur trailhead, hike for 1 mile on the Berma Road along sloped ridges and adjacent to metamorphic rock faces on the right side. The tree canopy is large with species of redbud, dogwood, and paw paw trees in its understory. In April, the many redbud trees that line the road are in bloom. At 0.2 mile from Anglers Spur, the widest part of the C&O Canal comes into view off to the left. You will continue to see this view for another 0.2 mile.

At 1.1 miles into the hike, the Lock 16 Spur trailhead appears on the right. It is marked by a trail post and ascends the ridge quickly. Continue straight on the Berma Road, and pass a historic lock house in 0.1 mile on the left and the Overlook Spur on the right in another 0.1 mile. Shortly thereafter, turn left onto the bridge, otherwise known as the stop gate, over the canal. At the end, turn left down the stairs to access the C&O Canal Towpath along the canal. The towpath feels and looks level, but descends in elevation as the land transitions over the fall line from the Piedmont Plateau to the Atlantic Coastal Plain.

Within 100 yards of leaving the stop gate, a people's choice trail appears on the right, and a vehicle access road over the canal appears on the left. There are some riffles in the canal here that are fun for playing and throwing rocks with kids. Continue down the towpath past Locks 16 and 15. Between these two locks, there are a few vernal pools in the bedrock where fish swim and turtles hang out, and frogs can be heard but not seen. Furthermore, you can observe the juxtaposition of cattails, a wetland plant, growing alongside the vernal pools, while lamb's ears grows in the rock crags.

After Lock 15, cross a long wooden bridge. At 0.8 mile from the stop gate, the shortcut (emergency exit trail) from Section A of the Billy Goat Trail (see Hike 19) appears on the right. Continue past it. Hike 0.3 mile over another long bridge and past the trailhead for Section A. This 0.3-mile section of the towpath passes alongside the widest part of the canal, which looks like a lake. Often, hikers and bikers on the towpath can observe people paddle boarding, canoeing, or kayaking this area of the canal. It can be accessed via the bridge near the Cropley parking lot.

The towpath rounds a corner to the right and finishes in 0.4 mile at the bridge over the canal. Cross left on the bridge, and walk back to the parking lot.

BILLY GOAT TRAIL: SECTION C

BEFORE YOU GO
Map: Available at the visitor center and on the park's website
Contact: Chesapeake and Ohio Canal National Historical Park (charges a fee)
Nearest city: Potomac, MD

ABOUT THE HIKE
Easy/moderate, year-round
Length: 2.5 miles, loop
Hiking time: 1½–2 hours
High point/elevation gain: 155 feet/118 feet
Access: Compact soil and crushed stone, not passable for jogging strollers

GETTING THERE

From I-495 (Capital Beltway), take exit 41 for Clara Barton Parkway west and Carderock. Drive 0.9 mile, and take the exit for Carderock and

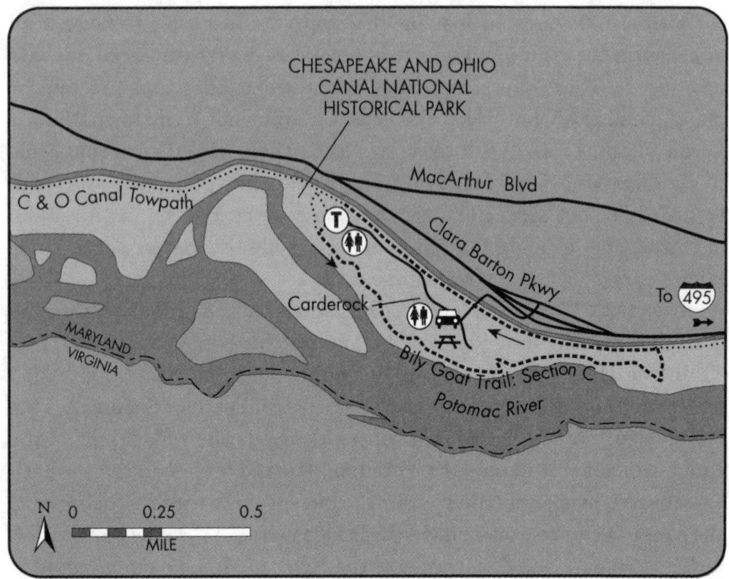

the Naval Surface Warfare Center. Turn left off the exit ramp toward Carderock. Within 100 yards, turn right toward Carderock. Drive 0.25 mile, and turn right at a stop sign. Drive to the last parking lot.

ON THE TRAIL

Section C of the Billy Goat Trail sits in the shadows of its sister trails up the Potomac River. While Section A on Bear Island is the most popular hike in Washington, DC, Section C at Carderock offers captivating scenery in forested slopes along the river. It provides kids younger than eight an opportunity to hike and play among the metamorphic rock outcrops along the trail. You may also see rock climbers using the rock faces as a playground.

The trailhead is adjacent to the large sign and restroom. Hike past both onto a raised boardwalk over a low area in the terrain that is often wet during spring. At the end of the boardwalk, follow the blue blazes to the left with a large metamorphic slab on the right. Have fun climbing this slab and watch rock climbers from atop it. Kids will likely be fascinated by watching climbers mount the rock and inch their way up to its top. If you choose to watch, use safety precautions and have your child lay on his or her stomach to peer over the edge. Holding their feet or legs can be an added safety measure. Make sure, though, that children stay clear of the belay lines attached to trees at the top. These lines keep climbers safe. Also clearly explain to your kids the danger of throwing anything from the top. Even a small object can severely injure a climber or hiker below. To watch rock climbers from below, turn right at the end of the boardwalk that leads to the base of the slab.

Taking a break next to a small waterfall

After watching the climbers or doing your own scrambling on the metamorphic points, follow the blue blazes south with the Potomac River on the right. The first half mile of the trail stays high above the river, dipping once to an area that can be wet during and after heavy rains. As you crest this small ravine, look for pencil-pointed tree stumps, evidence of beaver activity. Before you descend to the river, a people's choice trail to the cliff's edge lets hikers view Scotts Run Nature Preserve across the river and Stubblefield Falls in the Potomac.

For the next mile, the trail follows the river along its shore with different points of access to play along its edge. Swimming in the Potomac River along any access points on the Maryland or Virginia sides in the metropolitan region is inadvisable due to swift currents. The first access point is just after the first bridge crossing.

Two people's choice trails shortly before and at the second bridge exit the Billy Goat Trail to the left and lead to the Carderock picnic area. Continue looking for blue blazes to follow the Billy Goat Trail across the long bridge over a feeder stream.

At three different points on this flat section, you need to scramble over rocks, but none of these sections are difficult. The first time is after the first bridge on the river's edge. The second time occurs after the second bridge, 0.75 mile into the flat section. Shortly thereafter, scramble over rocks at a stream crossing. Look up at the small waterfall while you are crossing. Within a few hundred feet of the stream crossing, there is a quiet eddy that is great for enjoying a picnic, throwing rocks or sticks, and climbing on the rocks and downed trees. This is also a perfect place to let your dog swim because it is sheltered from the rapids by a peninsula. Climb over the third set of rocks, and follow the blue double blazes left and up the gentle hill to the towpath.

At the Chesapeake & Ohio (C&O) Canal Towpath, turn left and hike northwest to complete the loop, gaining the greatest elevation in this section. Despite being 184 miles long from Washington, DC, to Cumberland, Maryland, the towpath gains only 600 feet of elevation. However, the largest elevation gain, 125 feet, occurs within the first 10 miles from Washington, DC, 80 feet of which occurs during the last mile of this hike.

While this section of the C&O Canal Towpath is less scenic, it is an easy walk to end the hike. Hikers share the path with bikers, who occasionally whiz past at a good speed. Play "I Spy" a biker with your kids to encourage them to pay attention while hiking the path. Turn left at a very wide opening in the trees to return to the parking lot.

MUDDY BRANCH GREENWAY TRAIL

BEFORE YOU GO
Map: Available on Montgomery Parks website
Contact: Muddy Branch Stream Valley Park
Nearest city: Darnstown, MD

ABOUT THE HIKE
Moderate, year-round (best in spring)
Length: 3.2 miles, out and back
Hiking time: 2–2½ hours
High point/elevation gain: 413 feet/272 feet
Access: Compact soil, passable for jogging strollers

GETTING THERE

From I-495 (Capital Beltway), take exit 39 for MD 190 (River Road). Turn left onto MD 190, and drive 9.5 miles (through Potomac Village). Park in the Blockhouse Point Conservation Park lot on the left, which is across the street from the trailhead.

ON THE TRAIL

The Muddy Branch Greenway Trail is a 9-mile multiuse trail from the Chesapeake & Ohio (C&O) Canal in Blockhouse Point Conservation Park to Darnstown Road (MD 28) through Muddy Branch Stream Valley Park. The trail was constructed to accommodate mountain bikers, hikers, and equestrians. It follows Muddy Branch a majority of its 9-mile length, undulating up and down the stream's ridges and passing through meadows, upland forests, and vernal pools.

This 3.2-mile out-and-back hike on the southwesternmost section of the Muddy Branch Trail from River to Esworthy roads in the Muddy Branch Stream Valley Park traverses ridgetop forests, skirts floodplains and meadows, and brushes past vernal pools and Muddy Branch. The best season to hike this trail is early spring. Even though the lush green of summer is nonexistent, you and your kids can observe the early signs of spring ephemerals and wetland plants. In addition, the vernal pools in the stream's floodplain are rich with the reproduction of amphibians.

Begin the hike by crossing River Road from the Blockhouse Point Conservation Park's parking lot. The trailhead, marked by a sign post,

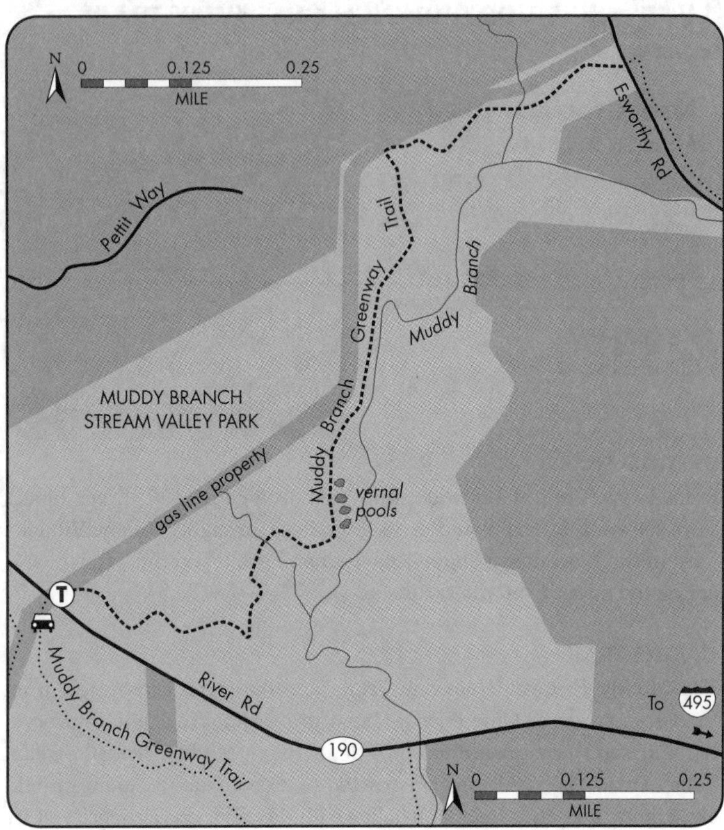

is to the right of the clearing. This gap is due to the construction of gas lines. The trail weaves close to this property multiple times and onto it toward the turnaround. Enter the forest and follow the trail as it curves to the right to parallel River Road for 0.3 mile. The trail then curves left and moves away from the road. A people's choice trail intersects it at this curve. Watch for the Japanese stilt grass that blankets the forest floor here, preventing any native plant species from propagating. Deer heavily browse the forest in this area, and they have eaten most of the native ground cover, saplings, and bushes, leaving only large canopy trees and stilt grass.

The trail makes a few small zigzags and then two switchbacks to gently descend the ridge toward a small feeder stream. At the bottom, cross the narrow stream at a half mile into the hike. Little kids will have a fun time playing in the stream and getting wet during summer. There are no rocks to use to cross it, so offering them a hand may be helpful. The trail then butts up against a ridge wall and turns right to follow it with the floodplain on the right. Sunlight hits the floodplain here, and in summer, you may see Joe Pye weed growing in the meadow. Joe Pye weed grows four to six feet tall with long, slender leaves with pointed tips. It blooms from July to September with pinkish-purple clusters of flowers at the top of each tall stem. The flowers provide a lot of nectar and therefore attract monarch butterflies and many varieties of swallowtail butterflies.

Vernal pools along the Muddy Branch Greenway Trail

The trail curves left and continues to follow the base of the ridge. Within 100 yards of the curve, pass a series of vernal pools with shallow black water just off the right side of the trail. During spring, you may spot a variety of frogs and their egg masses here. However, it is important to be silent because frogs easily sense the presence of animals and humans. After the vernal pools, the trail stays level and follows the edge of the floodplain until it reaches an opening in the forest cover. The trail skirts the meadow of the gas line property. This spot is another great place to look uphill and observe butterflies and dragonflies feasting on the blooms of Joe Pye weed.

After this small clearing, the trail begins to gently climb the ridge wall where it meets the Muddy Branch streambank at about a mile into the hike. Here, there are some large flat rocks on the streambank where you can sit and share a snack or play in the riffles of Muddy Branch. After returning to the trail, continue hiking uphill, veering away from the stream, for almost 0.2 mile to the top of the ridge. The trail follows the ridgetop before descending slightly back toward the meadow.

For the last 0.4 mile, the trail weaves back and forth from the edge of the meadows to the cover of the forest, following the natural undulations of the landscape. The trail crosses another feeder stream 0.2 mile from Esworthy Road. This stream crossing is shallow but wider than the first one. There are no rocks to use to cross the stream, but a few people's choice trails to the right lead to a narrower crossing. Once you are across, the trail enters the meadow for 100 yards where in the summer you will hike among daisies, black-eyed Susans, and Joe Pye weed. From the stream crossing to Esworthy Road, the trail ascends through the meadow and then back into the woods.

Esworthy Road is the turnaround point for this section of the Muddy Branch Greenway Trail. While it might sound like a good idea to drop off a car on Esworthy Road before your hike so that you don't have to hike back, there is not a parking lot on this road and it lacks a shoulder on either side to safely park a car. Hiking out and back offers you and your kids a different perspective of the natural beauty and landscape; maybe you will catch a glimpse on the way back of something you did not observe on the journey out.

BLOCKHOUSE POINT

BEFORE YOU GO
Map: Available on Montgomery Parks website
Contact: Blockhouse Point Conservation Park
Nearest city: Darnstown, MD

ABOUT THE HIKE
Moderate/difficult, year-round
Length: 3 miles, loop and spur
Hiking time: 2–2½ hours
High point/elevation gain: 436 feet/253 feet
Access: Compact soil, passable for jogging strollers

GETTING THERE

From I-495 (Capital Beltway), take exit 39 for MD 190 (River Road). Turn left onto MD 190, and drive 10 miles (through Potomac Village). Pass the main parking lot for Blockhouse Point Conservation Park, and park in the small five-car parking lot on the left at the intersection with Pettit Way.

ON THE TRAIL

Blockhouse Point Conservation Park is 630 acres of rich upland forest along the Potomac River. This park is designated by Montgomery Parks as a "best natural area" because of the rare and threatened species it supports, the diversity of plant and animal life in the undisturbed forest, and the schist bluffs that tower over the Chesapeake and Ohio (C&O) Canal. Furthermore, the park was named after three blockhouses that were constructed on the bluff during the Civil War as protected bunkers for Union soldiers as they kept watch over Confederate action across

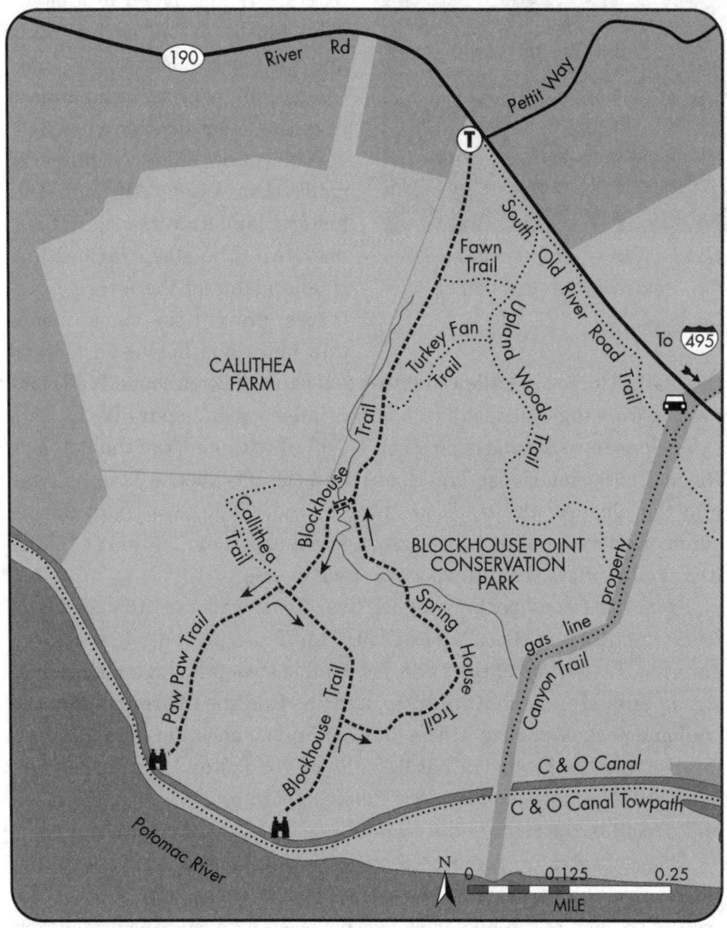

Catch views of the Potomac River from two rocky overlooks along the trail.

the river. In 1861, a large Union encampment was established in the floodplain of the Muddy Branch along the Potomac. The Massachusetts infantries were the main ones who camped here to guard the towpath along the C&O Canal and the Potomac River crossing. In 1864, a Confederate regiment led by Colonel John Mosby destroyed the camp and the blockhouses when Union troops left to protect the capital from Confederate attack.

The park offers 7 miles of trails that wander through this historic land and its rich natural resources. The steep ravines and fragile plants of the forested ecosystem prevent the use of mountain bikes and horses on most of the trails. Horses are allowed only at the end of Blockhouse Trail, connecting from the Callithea Trail. This 3-mile loop-and-spur hike has two extensions to rock outcroppings on the bluff with views of the Potomac River. The Spring House Trail loops with the Blockhouse Trail halfway into the hike. All the trails are blue blazed. Hiking this park during summer offers families a lush, green forest experience; however, hiking it in winter offers the best views of the Potomac.

From the second parking lot on River Road, walk past the kiosk and fence to enter the Blockhouse Trail. This fence prevents horses from entering this section of the park. The trail is straight with an occasional zigzag around large mature trees, and the Callithea Farm borders the trail and park on the right. The first half mile makes a gradual descent, intersecting the Fawn Trail at 0.2 mile on the left and the Turkey Fan Trail at 0.4 mile also on the left. Between both intersections, the creek appears off to the right of the trail in a heavily eroded creekbed.

At the bridge over the creek, the Spring House Trail enters the Blockhouse Trail from the left—you will complete the circuit from this trail at the end of the hike. For now, however, hike over the bridge. You can access the creek at the end of the bridge on the left before heading uphill for 0.3 mile. At the signpost at the top of the ridge, the Blockhouse Trail turns left. However, to visit the Potomac overlook, turn right toward the Callithea Trail and then left on the Paw Paw Trail. The trail is named after the thick growth of paw paw trees under the canopy trees here. A native understory tree that lives well on dry ridges and bluffs, paw paws dominate the canopy understory along the rocky bluffs of the Potomac River. Due to the dense forest here and in other sections of the park, ferns blanket the ground. Three common ferns inhabit this park and many eastern US forests: Christmas tree, maidenhair, and New York. Christmas tree ferns have thicker stems and leathery leaves. Maidenhair ferns are small and delicate with thin purple stems; they often grow in rock crags. New York ferns, the most common, provide a rich kelly green carpet over a shady forest floor. The ones along the Paw Paw Trail are mainly New York ferns.

To reach the rock outcropping at the end of the Paw Paw Trail, hike steeply down the edge of the bluff for a quarter mile, paying attention to the broken schist on the tread that acts like little roller balls. The outcropping provides a couple of great seats for taking photos, observing the spectacular view, and resting. To return to the Blockhouse Trail, hike back on the Paw Paw Trail, and turn right at the end. The signpost marking the Blockhouse Trail appears within 100 yards; continue straight on the Blockhouse Trail, following it as it curves right, heading back toward the river. In this section of the Blockhouse Trail, you will notice many mountain laurel bushes, which bloom in May. Furthermore, this area is where the three namesake blockhouses existed during the Civil War. All that remains are pits in the ground. The Montgomery Parks archaeology department leads interpretive hikes upon special request.

At 0.3 mile from the Paw Paw Trail, the Spring House Trail intersects on the left. Continue on the Blockhouse Trail to the overlook by following the blue blazes down the edge of the bluff to the end of the trail.

After the Spring House Trail intersection, the forest canopy opens on the left where hundreds of swamp chestnut oak saplings are fighting each other in a race to reach the sky. This park is one of the few areas in Montgomery County where an abundance of these swamp chestnut oak and shagbark hickory trees live. The chestnut oak can be identified by its wide, oval leaves with shallow, rounded lobes. Out of the hundreds competing to be big canopy trees, only about 1 percent will survive and mature.

From the overlook, hike back 0.1 mile to make a right onto the Spring House Trail. The trail rises uphill for 100 yards to level off. Following a rolling contour, it zigzags on the edge of the ridge. The trail makes a final curve to the left and descends the ridge sidehill where it crosses the creek at the bottom of the ridge. The bridge and Blockhouse Trail are 0.2 mile ahead. Once you reach them, turn right onto the Blockhouse Trail, and hike a half mile slightly uphill back to the parking lot.

SUGARLOAF MOUNTAIN PARK

BEFORE YOU GO
Map: Available at East and West View trailheads and on the park's website
Contact: Sugarloaf Mountain Park
Nearest city: Dickerson, MD

ABOUT THE HIKE
Difficult, year-round
Length: 2 miles, loop
Hiking time: 2–2½ hours
High point/elevation gain: 1282 feet/410 feet
Access: Compact soil and rocks, not passable for jogging strollers

GETTING THERE

From I-495 (Capital Beltway), take the exit for I-270. Drive 19 miles, and take exit 22 for MD 109. After 0.2 mile, turn right onto Old Hundred Road (MD 109). Drive 3 miles, and turn right onto Comus Road. Follow it 2.4 miles, and turn right onto Sugarloaf Mountain Drive (not Sugarloaf Mountain Road). Following signs for West View, switchback up the mountain 1.5 miles to the trailhead at the West View parking area.

ON THE TRAIL

The summit of Sugarloaf Mountain is 1282 feet in elevation, and the park named for it boasts 17 miles of trails, the longest of which is the 7-mile Yellow Trail, a multiuse trail for hikers, mountain bikers (from Memorial Day to Labor Day), and equestrians. The Yellow Trail trailhead is at the base of the mountain, while a majority of the park's trails can be reached from trailheads at the East View and West View parking areas. The West View parking area is the busiest because it offers a short but steep route to the top of Sugarloaf Mountain.

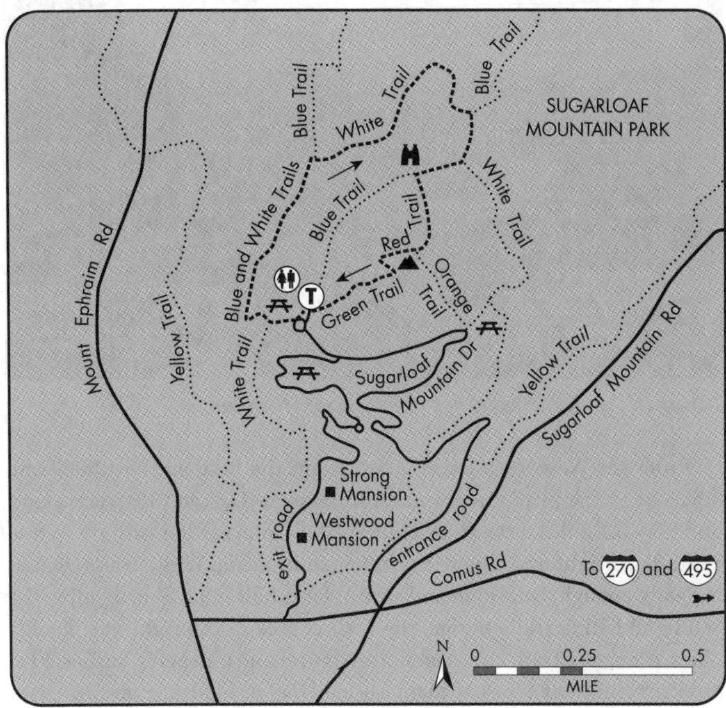

Stronghold Incorporated and its board of trustees maintain the 3000-acre property. Gordon and Louise Strong created Stronghold Incorporated as a land trust in 1946 to preserve the land on the mountain after their deaths. The Strong Mansion is not available for daily public use but can be reserved for functions.

This 2-mile hike mainly follows the Blue and White trails and then finishes on the steep Red and Green trails. They are all well marked with blazes and signs posted at many intersections. The trail tread is rocky in most places and follows the rolling nature of the two main ridges that stem from the mountain. There are many rock outcroppings along the hike and at the summit of the mountain to provide extra adventure for kids. The two highlights of the hike are the views from McCormack Overlook and the summit of Sugarloaf Mountain. The 250 feet of elevation gained in 0.25 mile on the Red Trail will get your heart pumping, but the view from the top is worth it. Half of the Green Trail is stone steps, while the other half is rocky tread.

Taking in the view from the top of Sugarloaf Mountain

From the West View parking lot, begin the hike on the Blue Trail, adjacent to the picnic tables and roundabout. Descend the rock steps, and hike 0.1 mile on the Blue Trail until its intersection with the White Trail. Turn right and follow the conjoined Blue and White trails (blazed logically enough, both blue and white) for a half mile. Shortly after the White and Blue trails merge, the trail curves to the right at a double blaze. Along the trail, notice mountain laurel and blueberry bushes. Five hundred different types of plant species live around and on Sugarloaf Mountain. Red and white oak trees dominate the tree canopy, but you can also see black birch, black gum, eastern hemlock, and tulip poplars.

The conjoined Blue and White trails split at an intersection 0.6 mile from the hike's start. The Blue Trail forks left, while you continue on the White Trail to the right. For the next 0.3 mile, the trail rolls up and down to make a steep ascent up a short ridge where a people's choice trail forks left; follow the white arrow and blaze straight ahead. The White Trail curves right uphill and then levels off on top of the ridge before descending the back side toward the Blue Trail.

At the intersection with the Blue Trail, turn right. The Blue and White trails conjoin again here for the next 0.1 mile. Notice the carpet of ferns and new, densely packed stand of tulip poplars. Less than a decade ago, this area became open and sunny after a storm knocked down several trees. However, natural succession is occurring, and tulip poplars have taken hold. Fast growers who need a lot of sunlight, they are racing each other to rule the sky in this area. Only 1 percent of them survive to grow into tall, large canopy trees.

At the fork, hike right uphill 0.1 mile on the Blue Trail to the McCormack Overlook and the intersection with the Red Trail. The overlook is an open area of jutting rocks that faces north; it is a great spot to rest, have a snack, or play on the rock points and faces. When you are finished at the overlook, turn left on the Red Trail, and ascend the steep trail a quarter mile to the summit of Sugarloaf Mountain. Halfway up, the Orange Trail intersects from the left; bypass it and continue on the Red Trail to the top.

Sugarloaf is a monadnock, a type of mountain or ridge created when all the land around it erodes. Quartzite, a metamorphic rock, is the dominant rock that makes up Sugarloaf. It took 14 million years for land to erode and create this mountain. Its exposed quartzite top provides some good views, in particular to the southwest where you can see the Dickerson Power Plant along the Potomac River. The summit does not provide 360-degree views owing to the stunted oaks that have grown among the cracks in the rocks. The rocks on the summit are an excellent natural playground for both rock scrambling and technical rock climbing.

To descend Sugarloaf, look for green blazes, and follow them along the rock at the top to where the trail curves right and descends stone steps on the steepest section of the mountain. At the bottom of the steps, hike an additional 0.2 mile on rocky trail tread back to the West View parking lot.

BUCKLODGE FOREST CONSERVATION PARK

BEFORE YOU GO
Map: Available from the Montgomery Parks website
Contact: Bucklodge Forest Conservation Park
Nearest city: Poolsville, MD

ABOUT THE HIKE
Easy/moderate, year-round
Length: 2.6 miles, loop
Hiking time: 1½–2 hours
High point/elevation gain: 626 feet/75 feet
Access: Compact soil, passable for jogging strollers

GETTING THERE

From I-495 (Capital Beltway), take the exit for I-270. Drive 14.5 miles and take exit 18 for MD 121 north (Clarksburg Road). Turn right onto

MD 121 (Clarksburg Road). Drive 0.5 mile, and turn left onto MD 355 (Frederick Road). Drive 1.2 miles, and turn left onto Comus Road. Drive 1.4 miles, and turn left onto Slidell Road. Drive 0.8 mile. The parking lot is on the right.

ON THE TRAIL

Bucklodge Forest Conservation Park in upper Montgomery County provides families with a quiet and peaceful hike during which you can observe forest succession and will have a chance to see deer, hawks, box turtles, wood frogs, and many species of woodpeckers. The forest physically changes along this trail, particularly in the northern and western sections. The start of this hike in the park's northern section is dominated by new tree growth, while the northwest corner (off-trail) provides the best display of the oldest growth in the forest.

From the trailhead in the parking lot, hike 0.1 mile to the Bucklodge Loop Trail. (Ignore the first trail on the right at the trailhead as it connects to equestrian trails on private property.) At the signpost indicating the loop, turn right to walk this loop counterclockwise.

Along the northern section of the loop, the trees are the youngest in the forest with an average trunk diameter of between 2 and 6 inches. The layers of a mature forest (ground cover plants like spring ephemerals, woody shrubs like spicebush, understory trees like redbuds, and mature canopy trees like tulip poplars) have not been well established. Some ferns have established roots; however, large patches of ground are covered with leaf litter devoid of plants. The young trees are all racing each other toward the sun; each one wants to be the first to provide its entire crown with sunlight. The more sunlight a tree's leaves receive, the more food the leaves produce for the tree. These densely packed, energetic trees block sunlight from reaching the ground and prohibit the next layers of the forest from growing. Furthermore, the overpopulation of white-tailed deer in Montgomery County has exacerbated the problem. They heavily browse the forest ground cover and shrubbery, which creates an imbalance in the natural succession of a forest habitat.

From the trailhead, the Bucklodge Loop Trail meanders north, west, and eventually south within the first half mile. In this section, the forest changes twice: from new growth to a more mature forest of oaks, then to maturing forest that is dominated by tulip poplars. At the northwest corner of the loop, the trees suddenly become 16- to 20-inch-diameter oaks and you can observe the layers of a successive forest habitat.

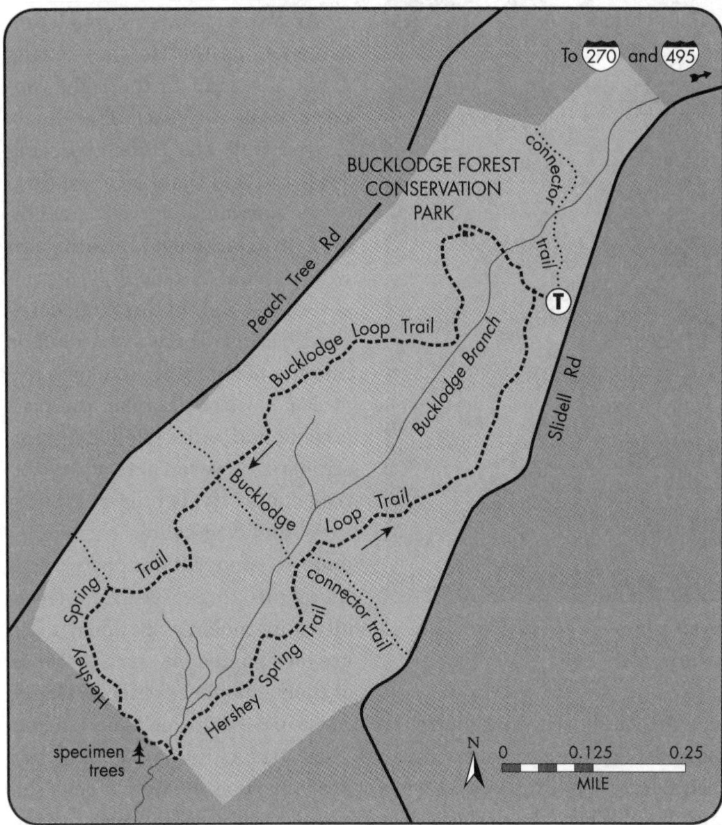

Unfortunately, Japanese bush honeysuckle, an invasive plant, dominates the woody bush layer in Bucklodge.

As you leave the mature oaks, a stand of immature tulip poplars and pine appears along the trail. After hiking 1 mile, come to a four-way intersection; continue straight on the Hershey Spring Trail. To shorten your hike, turn left on the Bucklodge Loop Trail. The trail on the right leads out of the park to Peach Tree Road.

Past the intersection, the tall tulip poplars provide a cathedral-like feeling. Their crowns reach high into the sky with their trunks resembling skyscrapers. The tulip poplar dominates the southwestern corner of this hike with an occasional black cherry, black locust, or red maple thrown into the mix.

Hiking through the cathedral-like tulip poplars

At the southwest corner, continue left on the Hershey Spring Trail. The trail to the right connects again to Peach Tree Road. As you walk the Hershey Spring Trail, the tread gets soggy because of the surrounding wetlands created by Bucklodge Branch. You will encounter muddy spots on several sections of this trail, deepened because there are a greater number of horses than hikers.

For most of the hike, the trail is wide and accessible for jogging strollers. However, here where the trail abuts private property, it narrows and vegetation encroaches upon it. Along this property line, there are three specimen trees, all tulip poplars. Specimen trees are designated as such because of their uniqueness in size, shape, age, or beauty within a particular landscape. The three tulip poplars located here are specimens because their trunks are wider than two feet. Locate the three largest trees spaced apart on the right side of the trail here. When you find one, hug it (as long as it doesn't have poison ivy growing up its trunk!).

To stay on the Hershey Spring Trail, turn left at a Y intersection where two blue blazes appear, one on each side of the trail. Many people have made the mistake of following the people's choice trail straight. Within a couple hundred yards, cross Bucklodge Branch, which is often dry during summer. After crossing, turn left at the trail intersection, and continue to follow the blue blazes on the Hershey Spring Trail. Bucklodge Branch is directly on the left. The last mile of the hike is dominated by maturing tulip poplars and oaks. The forest along the remainder of the hike displays forest succession with invasive herbaceous plants and woody shrubs dominating the first two layers of the forest ecosystem.

The trail intersection with the Bucklodge Loop Trail is a half mile

THE GRAFFITI TREE

Beech trees have very smooth, light gray bark with oval sawtooth-edged leaves and a pointed tip. Saplings can tolerate shade during their early, slow-growing years: however, they prefer full sun. Characteristic of old-growth forest, beech trees live more than a century and play a valuable role in the forest ecosystem. Black bears feed on the beechnut, which falls from the tree in autumn; it provides them essential nutrition before they hibernate. Often called the graffiti tree because of how easy it is for people to carve its thin bark, beech trees are highly susceptible to disease due to these incisions.

after you cross Bucklodge Branch; continue straight to leave the Hershey Spring Trail and enter a large stand of beech trees on the Bucklodge Loop Trail.

The last half mile of the hike climbs gently. At the Bucklodge Loop sign, turn right and hike a few hundred yards to the parking lot.

TURKEY HILL LOOP

BEFORE YOU GO
Map: Available on the Montgomery Parks website
Contact: Black Hill Regional Park
Nearest city: Boyds, MD

ABOUT THE HIKE
Easy/moderate, year-round
Length: 1.2 miles, loop and spur
Hiking time: 1–1½ hours
High point/elevation gain: 502 feet/95 feet
Access: Large gravel, asphalt, and compact soil; passable for jogging strollers

GETTING THERE

From I-495 (Capital Beltway), take the exit for I-270. Drive 14.5 miles, and take exit 18 for MD 121 (Clarksburg Road). Turn left onto MD 121 toward Boyds. Drive 1.7 miles, and take a slight right onto West Old Baltimore Road. Drive 0.7 mile, and turn left onto Ten Mile Creek Road. There is no parking lot at the trailhead, and Ten Mile Creek is a short, narrow country road with one private residence. A few cars will fit on the right side of the road before the gate marking the trailhead.

ON THE TRAIL

Black Hill Regional Park is located in upper Montgomery County west of I-270. The park surrounds most of Little Seneca Lake, which was created by damming Little Seneca Creek and its two tributaries, Ten Mile Creek and Cabin Branch. The park offers fishing, picnicking, hiking, canoeing and kayaking, biking, and a nature center. Turkey Hill Loop is located in a remote western section of the main park where Ten Mile Creek creates one of the four legs of Little Seneca Lake. It is the first of three connected loops along the western edge of the lake. This 1.2-mile spur-and-loop hike crosses Ten Mile Creek and then meanders above the lake, with a few access points to it, and along the forested ridge. The wide trail begins on asphalt, changing to large gravel through a small wetland at the source of the lake, and is finally grass covered. The trail is not blazed, but there are signs at the intersections. This very quiet, serene trail will make you feel like you are in the wilderness.

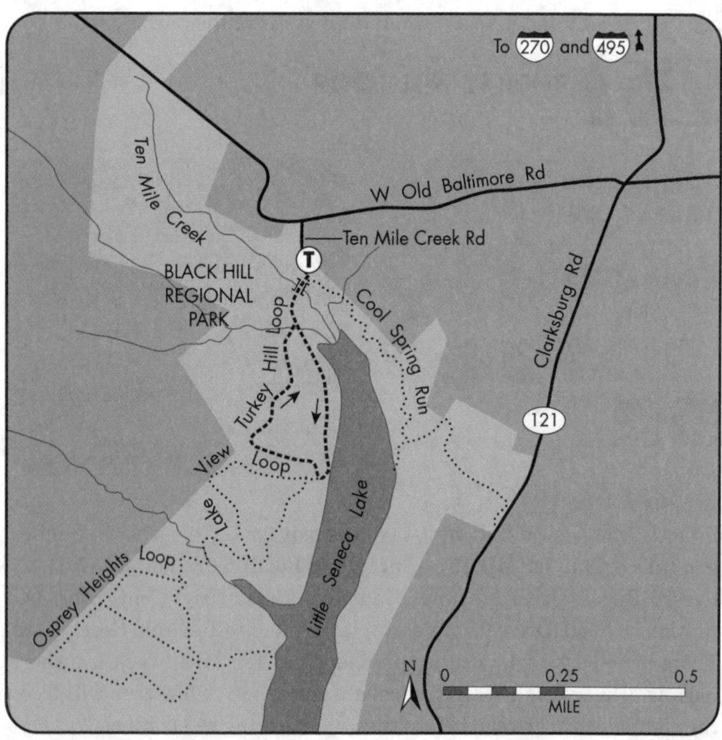

A trail sign marks the beginning of the hike on the opposite side of the gate near the parking area. Hike downhill on the paved road to Ten Mile Creek. In 0.1 mile, at the bottom of the hill, Cool Spring Run intersects from the left; continue straight to the bridge. To the right of the bridge, there is access to the streambanks and rockbars along Ten Mile Creek.

Ten Mile Creek is the healthiest stream in Montgomery County because of the high biodiversity of the creatures and plants living in and along the stream and its wide, forested buffer zones, which provide pervious surfaces that filter and prevent stormwater runoff. In the 1960s, the Maryland National Capital Park and Planning Commission began buying land around Little Seneca Creek to preserve its watershed and forested land. The creek drains into Little Seneca Lake, which was built and dammed in 1983 to provide the region with a secondary water supply after the Potomac River. Little Seneca Lake is 505 acres within the 2000-plus acres of Black Hill Regional Park.

Hike across the bridge over Ten Mile Creek and onto a large gravel trail that runs through the floodplain adjacent to the creek. On the right side of the trail, there are vernal pools, a great place to listen to mating amphibians in the spring. In 0.1 mile, the Turkey Hill Loop begins; continue straight and hike the loop clockwise. The trail remains wide and grass covered for most of the 0.8-mile loop, which is a more of a triangle than a circle. The first leg along the lake travels 0.3 mile uphill overlooking the lake and then drops back down next to the lake in the last

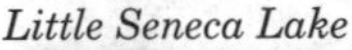

Little Seneca Lake

0.1 mile. There are a few spots to fish in this area, along with a small, shallow rocky area in the lake—perfect for wading or throwing rocks—before the trail curves right to intersect with the Lake View Loop 50 feet after the curve. The Turkey Hill Loop continues on the right. To extend your hike, proceed left on the Lake View Loop, hiking either clockwise or counterclockwise (neither of which is described here). The Lake View Loop adds an additional 0.75 mile to your hike. For an even longer hike, the Osprey Heights Loop, an additional 1.4 miles, connects with the Lake View Loop and is the last loop along this section of Little Seneca Lake.

The second leg of the Turkey Hill Loop travels 0.2 mile uphill, then curves right. The beginning of the third leg is the steepest uphill portion of the hike. Then the trail levels off for more than 0.1 mile before a sign appears, indicating a steep descent to the end of the loop. There is little on this hike that impedes a jogging stroller; however, this steep descent can present a challenge.

At the bottom of the hill, turn left to hike back toward Ten Mile Creek, over the gravel and bridge, past Cool Spring Run, and uphill on the paved road to the trailhead gate.

LAKE NEEDWOOD

BEFORE YOU GO
Map: Available on Montgomery Parks website
Contact: Rock Creek Regional Park
Nearest city: Rockville, MD

ABOUT THE HIKE
Easy/moderate, year-round
Length: 2.2 miles, loop and spur
Hiking time: 1½–2 hours
High point/elevation gain: 449 feet/160 feet
Access: Compact soil, passable for jogging strollers

GETTING THERE

From I-495 (Capital Beltway), take exit 31 for MD 97 (Georgia Avenue) north toward Wheaton. Drive 7 miles, and turn left onto Norbeck Road (MD 28). Take the first right onto Muncaster Mill Road (MD 115). Drive 2 miles, and turn left onto Avery Road. After 0.4 mile, turn right onto Needwood Lake Drive. Follow the signs to the boathouse.

ON THE TRAIL

In the Washington, DC, region, there are two parks named Rock Creek. Rock Creek National Park is in the District of Columbia and has been owned and operated by the National Park Service since 1890. Rock Creek Regional Park is in Montgomery County and is owned and operated by Montgomery Parks. Both parks are buffer zones for Rock Creek and provide ample recreational opportunities for area residents: biking, hiking, fishing, picnicking, kayaking, canoeing, golfing, and horseback riding. Both parks also have nature centers, which provide educational opportunities for families.

Lake Needwood offers 7 miles of trails around its 75-acre dammed lake. This 2.2-mile hike along the west side of Lake Needwood loops through upland forests. The trails are blue-blazed, and every trail intersection is clearly marked with signed posts. The hike is mostly shady, except for a section over the dam on the south side and a sliver of a meadow where gas lines are buried. The wide, partially gravel trail

Hiking through a little meadow next to Lake Needwood

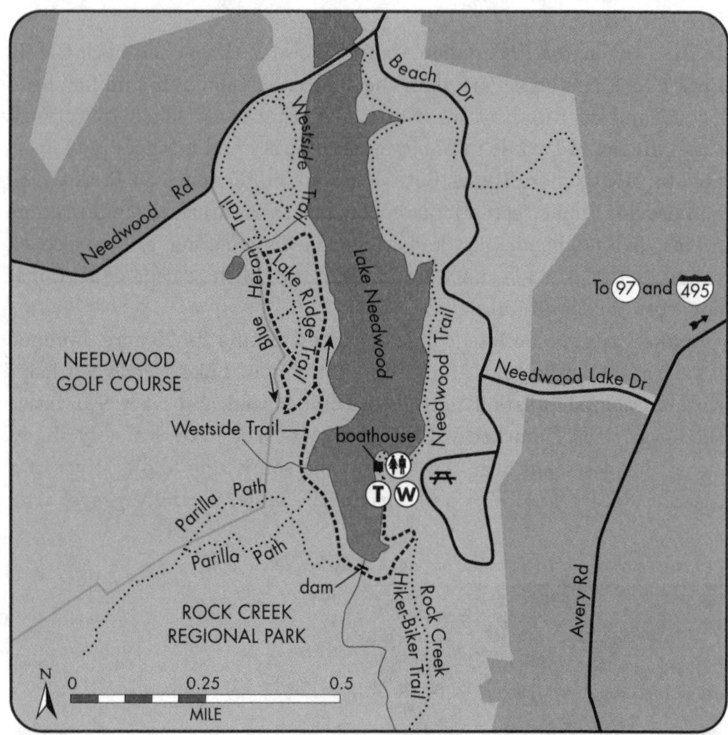

follows the undulations of the land above the lake. For a majority of the hike, it is not adjacent to the lake's edge, but there are multiple opportunities to visit the lake via people's choice trails.

Start the hike from the western side of the boathouse, where the Needwood Trail follows the lake south. For 0.1 mile, the trail passes benches and picnic tables tucked under trees. It then curves left over a boat ramp; just short of the parking lot make a 160-degree right turn onto the gravel trail that leads uphill to the dam. Cross the dam and take in the view of the lake from high above. The dam was constructed in 1965 to prevent flooding, catch sediment from upstream erosion, and provide recreation for county residents.

After you cross the dam, the Parilla Path intersects the Westside Trail from the left. The Westside Trail veers to the right, enters the woods, and follows the lake's western shore. Continue on the Westside Trail 0.2 mile to a second intersection with the Parilla Path. Staying on the Westside Trail, you will then descend slightly to pass a people's choice trail to the lake. A small feeder stream trickles through a culvert here; during heavy rains, the culvert overflows and the trail can be wet. The trail ascends to a narrow meadow where you can spot many wildflowers, butterflies, dragonflies, bees, and birds. At 0.7 mile, at the edge of the meadow and forest, the Westside Trail continues past the unmarked Blue Heron Trail on the left.

The Westside Trail continues for another 0.3 mile, passing a people's choice trail halfway on both the left and right before it curves sharply left. In 0.1 mile, this trail intersects the Blue Heron Trail. In a clearing straight ahead is a small pond with trees on its opposite side. Here you can observe geese, ducks, and blue herons in the pond and may hear frogs among the cattails. From the trail intersection, make a 90-degree left turn, and follow the Blue Heron Trail uphill.

At 1.2 miles, you reach the first junction with the Lake Ridge Trail; continue straight on the Blue Heron Trail past an unmarked trail that connects the Blue Heron and Lake Ridge trails. In 0.2 mile, there is another junction with the Lake Ridge Trail. The Blue Heron Trail continues right and then curves left following the edge of the Needwood Golf Course for approximately 100 feet. Just before the Blue Heron Trail curves left into the meadow, look for a patch of wineberry on the right.

A FRUITY INVASIVE PLANT

The invasive wineberry with origins in China grows aggressively in thickets, smothering native ground plants. Its berries are edible, and it is often mistaken for raspberry. While the wineberry stalk is covered thickly with both fine and large thorns, raspberries have regularly placed large thorns. Wineberries are ripe for picking around the beginning of July.

Hike in the meadow along the forest edge for 0.1 mile until the Blue Heron Trail dead-ends into the Westside Trail. Turn right and follow the Westside back along the lake, past the two Parilla Path junctions, and over the dam. At the parking lot, make a 160-degree left turn onto the Needwood Trail and follow it back along the lake's edge to the boathouse.

When you are planning your visit to Lake Needwood, allow enough time to picnic either under the trees or under the pavilion at the boathouse. If you have a free afternoon, hike the trail and then spend time in a paddleboat or canoe on the lake to see it from a different perspective.

LAKE FRANK

BEFORE YOU GO
Map: Available on Montgomery Parks website
Contact: Rock Creek Regional Park
Nearest city: Rockville, MD

ABOUT THE HIKE
Moderate, year-round
Length: 2.5 miles, loop
Hiking time: 1½–2 hours
High point/elevation gain: 423 feet/170 feet
Access: Compact soil, passable for jogging strollers

GETTING THERE

From I-495 (Capital Beltway), take exit 31 for MD 97 (Georgia Avenue) north toward Wheaton. Drive 7 miles, and turn left onto Norbeck Road (MD 28). Take the first right onto Muncaster Mill Road (MD 115). Drive 1.5 miles, and turn left onto Meadowside Lane. Drive to the end of the road, and park in front of the nature center.

ON THE TRAIL

From its source in northern Montgomery County, Rock Creek journeys 33 miles to end at the Potomac River in the District of Columbia. In 1890 the federal government designated some land around the creek as a national park. This park extended its arm from Georgetown to the district's border with Silver Spring, where it becomes Rock Creek Regional Park. The latter was established in the 1930s to provide green space for local residents.

Rock Creek Regional Park occupies a sliver of real estate that provides a protective buffer for the creek and a green space for recreation. This land is at its widest around Lake Frank and its neighbor to the west, Lake Needwood. Created in 1966, Lake Frank is named for Bernard Frank, a local environmentalist and cocreator of the Wilderness Society. The 54-acre lake controls flood waters, reduces the sediment load in Rock Creek, and provides a peaceful place for people and a sanctuary for birds and other wildlife. Swimming, boating, and ice skating are prohibited on the lake, but fishing is allowed with a permit. The area around Lake Frank has 8 miles of trails, which includes a 3.25-mile trail that circumnavigates the lake.

This 2.5-mile hike allows families to experience the best of everything that the area has to offer: a riffling stream, lakeside serenity, great rocks, the Pioneer Farmstead, a nature center, a raptor aviary, a pond, a covered bridge, and the forest.

The hike begins at the end of the parking lot to the left of the nature center and right of the kiosk. The cinder-clad trail forks almost immediately. Turn left to descend a couple of switchbacks and cross two bridges as you head toward the Muncaster Mill Trail. At the bottom, turn right on the Muncaster Mill Trail, keeping the Rock Creek North Branch on the left. Hike 0.1 mile to the first stream access point where there is a rock crossing toward the Lakeside Trail that offers a fun challenge for kids to test their balance skills.

After playing at the rock crossing, return to the Muncaster Mill Trail. Continue straight as you pass the Backbone Trail on the right. Stay to the right when the Muncaster Mill Trail veers away from the stream;

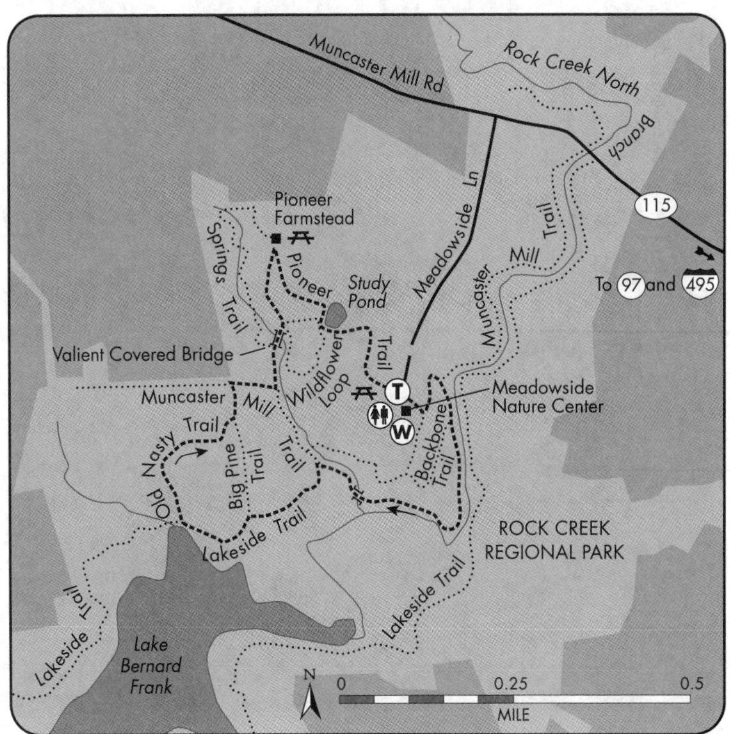

there is a people's choice trail adjacent to the stream. The Muncaster Mill Trail curves back to the stream where large boulders are strewn from the stream up the ridge, waiting for kids to climb them. There is also a long and wide rockbar in the stream in this area. This portion of the Muncaster Mill Trail provides an abundance of rock-themed natural entertainment for kids.

Families using a jogging stroller will have to navigate a large rock slab that sticks up at an awkward angle where the trail turns west and hooks around the ridge. Hike 0.2 mile to a bridge crossing the stream. After the bridge, the Muncaster Mill Trail moves away from the stream's edge where the land flattens to create a floodplain full of vernal pools and wetland plants. The Muncaster Mill Trail intersects the Lakeside Trail within 0.1 mile after the bridge. Turn left onto the Lakeside Trail.

The Valient Covered Bridge

At the beginning of the Lakeside Trail, make a slight detour off the trail to the right up a 20-foot hill to a large patch of pine trees. These congregated pine trees give the forest a different feel—it is almost like being in a cave of green. This pine canopy provides an opportunity to play a game of hide-and-seek on a floor of soft pine needles. There are no ground cover plants here for a couple of reasons: Pine trees create a lot of shade and have many shallow roots that outcompete them for water and nutrients.

Continue on the Lakeside Trail past the intersection with the Big Pine Trail. You will begin to see Lake Frank through the trees. Within a few hundred feet of the intersection, a people's choice trail to the lake's edge appears on the left.

Continue on the Lakeside Trail downhill to a wet area where one of many small feeder streams enters the lake. Cross this wet area on a wooden puncheon, and then make a right onto the Old Nasty Trail. The steepest portion of the hike, the Old Nasty Trail ascends 80 feet in 0.1 mile. The narrow trail may be overgrown in summer. Atop the hill, it curves right and descends a gradual slope for 0.15 mile before dead-ending at the Big Pine Trail. Turn left and walk a few hundred feet to the intersection with the Muncaster Mill Trail. Turn right on the Muncaster Mill Trail, and hike 0.1 mile through a small, forest-edged meadow.

A four-way intersection appears just before a small feeder stream. It feels correct to go straight; however, that route is not a sanctioned trail, so turn left onto the Pioneer Trail, keeping the feeder stream on the right. Within a couple hundred yards, the Valient Covered Bridge appears, and you reach the intersection with the Springs Trail. Rockville High School and the Montgomery County Student Trades Foundation built the covered bridge in memory of a teacher and environmentalist. Stay on the Pioneer Trail, cross the bridge, and walk up the hill to the pioneer farmstead, passing the Wildflower Loop on the right. The wide trail, which used to be a road, hooks to the right and opens up to reveal the farmstead. Roam around to look at the two cabins, a corncrib, a smokehouse, a root cellar, and gardens. There are picnic tables here for families to enjoy.

The Pioneer Trail makes a loop, entering the farmstead on the old dirt road and leaving it on a compact dirt trail behind the smokehouse next to the fenced-in garden. To return to the nature center, continue on the Pioneer Trail for 0.1 mile to the Study Pond. Turn right on the

Pioneer Trail, and walk counterclockwise around the pond to the other side where the trail ascends the meadow hill. At the top of the meadow, pass picnic tables and a campfire ring on the right. Straight ahead is the Meadowside Nature Center and raptor aviary.

Before driving home, spend some time at the natural and cultural history exhibits in the nature center, including climbing through a cave. Behind the nature center is a raptor aviary that takes care of rescued birds such as bald eagles, red-tailed hawks, barred owls, great horned owls, and turkey vultures.

BLUE MASH TRAIL

BEFORE YOU GO
Map: Available from the Montgomery Parks website
Contact: Blue Mash Trail
Nearest city: Olney, MD

ABOUT THE HIKE
Easy, year-round
Length: 2 miles, loop
Hiking time: 1–1½ hours
High point/elevation gain: 535 feet/55 feet
Access: Grass and compact soil, jogging-stroller friendly

GETTING THERE

From I-495 (Capital Beltway), take exit 31 for MD 97 (Georgia Avenue) north toward Wheaton. Drive 11 miles, and turn left onto MD 108 (Olney Laytonsville Road), then turn right onto Zion Road after 2.5 miles. Drive 2 miles. The parking lot is marked and on the left.

ON THE TRAIL

The Blue Mash Trail is located on 545 acres at the closed Oaks Landfill in northern Montgomery County. This hiking-only trail and a separate shared-use trail surround the capped landfill in its buffer zone. Opened in 1982, the landfill stopped receiving waste in 1997 and was capped in 2001. Because of an agreement with area residents, the Department of Public Works and Transportation and Montgomery Parks constructed a network of compact soil trails to create a green space for local residents. The easy Blue Mash Trail is best enjoyed on a blue sky day during spring when you will likely see flowers, birds, and butterflies. This hike is on a wide, mostly grass-covered loop surrounding beautiful

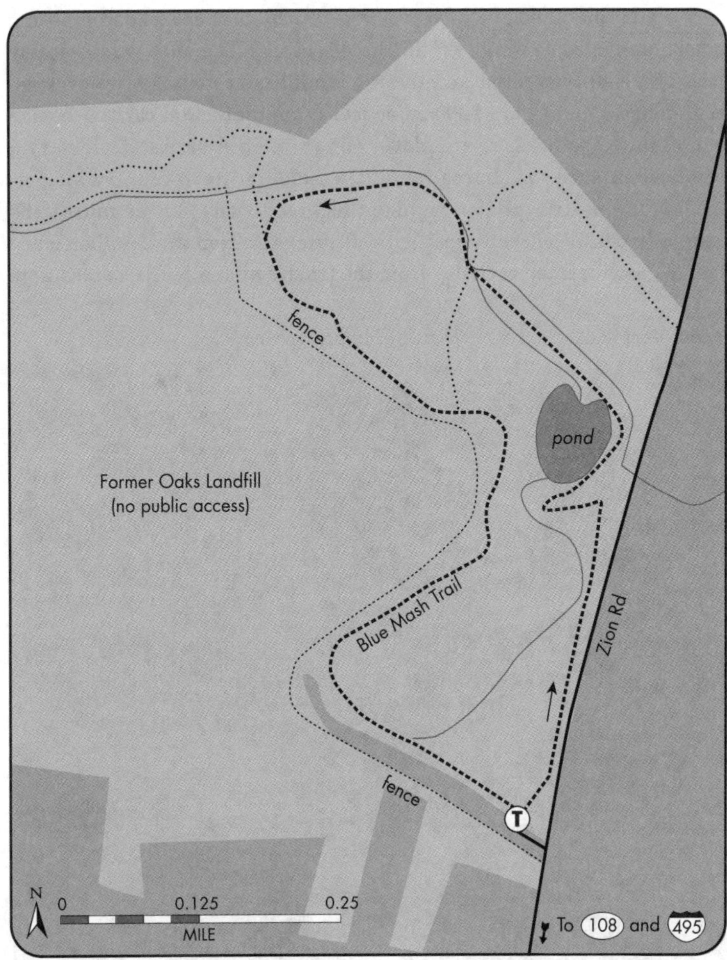

meadows and a large bioretention pond. The trail is not blazed but is marked at the intersections and turns with signs, making for easy navigation.

The Blue Mash Trail is named after the pre-Civil War community of Blue Mash, a settlement made up of freed slaves from the neighboring Riggs Plantation. "Mash" is a colloquial term for "marsh" used by fugitive slaves in the Underground Railroad who used the swamps in the area as places to hide.

Because methane and carbon dioxide are by-products of decomposing trash, many people wonder if this hike is stinky. The answer: absolutely not. The county created an efficient landfill gas management system that collects more than 1000 cubic feet of methane and carbon dioxide per minute. Both gases are blown out through a series of pipes to a candlestick flare that burns them. The smell of fresh country air permeates the nostrils of all who hike this green space. In the future, the county hopes to generate electricity off-property from the 2 million cubic feet of gases created each day from the trash's anaerobic decomposition.

The tunnel of cherry trees is beautiful in any season.

This hike is described counterclockwise. The trailhead is at the northern end of the parking lot, flanked by split-rail fences. Hike for 0.3 mile on a wide, grass-covered trail that parallels Zion Road. This portion of the trail retains water and can be swampy, particularly during rainy times. The trail is bordered by young trees and bushes like witch hazel that have succeeded the meadow. Bluebird houses have been placed along here and throughout the property. Fifty years ago, bluebird populations were threatened; however, their population has rebounded because people have installed houses to increase nesting sites.

At the end of this straight section, a trail sign points hikers to the left over a small stream of water from a series of gulches that run in the landfill's buffer zone to move rainwater away from the capped landfill. A large berm surrounding a bioretention pond looms ahead. Don't follow the people's choice trail straight ahead up the berm; instead, turn left as the trail sign directs, and hike through a row of evergreen trees. Then make a 180-degree turn around the trees, and continue on the berm along the bioretention pond, which is surrounded by a chain link fence and hosts mallards, geese, wood ducks, turtles, and frogs in the warmer months. If you brought a pair of binoculars for the kids, this is a great spot to use them.

Hike two-thirds of the way around the pond, and at 0.75 mile into the hike, enter a tunnel of cherry trees that are beautiful in April. On warm sunny days, this tunnel offers the only full shade on this hike. Leaving the tunnel, the trail intersects a drainage ditch at 1 mile. Straight ahead is a connector trail, restricted to local use, to Zion Road. Turn left and cross the ditch, which is sometimes filled with shoe-deep water. Out of the ditch, turn right at the trail sign, and follow the drainage ditch to the left (going left at the trail sign is a shortcut in the loop). The Blue Mash Trail circles an island of young trees, bushes, and ground cover like crown vetch, which blooms in May.

In a quarter mile, the Blue Mash Trail dead-ends into a chain-link fence. A shared-use trail enters a fern-covered forest on the right; however, follow the Blue Mash Trail to the left with the fence on your right. For the next 0.75 mile, the fence to the enclosed landfill remains on your right. Follow the arrows toward a meadow clearing and a trail intersection.

In the meadow, the shortcut enters the Blue Mash Trail from the left. Turn right to stay on the Blue Mash Trail, and cross the drainage ditch. The trail here skirts the meadow. In July, raspberry and blackberry bushes are ripe with fruit for a trail snack. From spring to fall, find flowers like Joe Pye weed in bloom. It is a favorite plant for many butterflies, such as the monarch, eastern tiger swallowtail, great spangled fritillary, and tawny-edged skipper.

The Blue Mash Trail dead-ends at the driveway to the landfill. Turn left and hike a quarter mile down the driveway toward Zion Road and the parking lot.

RACHEL CARSON CONSERVATION PARK

BEFORE YOU GO
Map: Available on Montgomery Parks website
Contact: Rachel Carson Conservation Park
Nearest city: Laytonsville, MD

ABOUT THE HIKE
Moderate, year-round
Length: 3.5 miles, loop
Hiking time: 2–2½ hours
High point/elevation gain: 591 feet/220 feet
Access: Compact soil, passable for jogging strollers

GETTING THERE

From I-495 (Capital Beltway), take exit 31 for MD 97 (Georgia Avenue) north. Drive 11 miles, and turn left onto MD 108 (Olney Laytonsville Road), then turn right onto Zion Road after 2.5 miles. The park is 3 miles ahead on the right.

ON THE TRAIL

Montgomery County acquired 650 acres of land in Brookville, Maryland, after Rachel Carson's death in 1964 to establish a conservation park in her name. With 6 miles of compact dirt trails for hiking and equestrian use, Rachel Carson Conservation Park boasts four distinct ecosystems: forest, stream, pond, and meadow. The forest ecosystem dominates the park with stands of hickory, tulip poplar, oak, maple, and beech trees. This hike visits all four ecosystems.

The hike begins on the Fox Meadow Loop. You travel only about 200 yards through the meadow for now, but the end of the hike offers a more extensive opportunity to observe the birds, bees, and butterflies that occupy the air above the meadow plant life. Before you turn right on the Rachel Carson Greenway Trail, bluebird boxes stand just above the wildflowers and grasses close to the forest edge. This is prime bluebird habitat.

HOME OF THE BLUEBIRDS

Native to the Mid-Atlantic, bluebirds are important to the ecological balance of the meadow ecosystem. Bluebirds nest in tree cavities near an open field or meadow where their food source of insects and berries is most plentiful. Since their beaks are too weak to drill through a dead tree, they rely on nesting holes made by other bird species. The bluebird population has declined due to a lack of nesting cavities and because nonnative birds, like the house sparrow and starling, use their cavities and destroy their nests. Bluebird boxes have been placed in this meadow and others like it to help increase their population.

After a short jaunt on the Fox Meadow Loop, turn right onto the blue-blazed Rachel Carson Greenway Trail. After entering the forest, read the interpretive sign about the common birds, such as the six different species of woodpeckers, that make these woods their home. The pileated woodpecker with its jackhammer sound that reverberates through the forest is the largest. The woods are open with a large canopy of chestnut oaks and tulip poplars; missing is a thick forest understory. The ground is covered in many places with short blueberry bushes. The invasive plant mile-a-minute has not invaded this section of the park like it has others.

The trail makes a slight ascent to a knoll with a large outcropping of rocks, a natural playground for kids. It then wraps around to the right of the outcropping's base and begins a long, gradual descent to the Hawlings River, now marked by white blazes. The Rachel Carson Greenway Trail intersects the Fern Valley Trail; stay right on the Rachel Carson, which continues to descend to an intersection with the River Otter Trail. Here, you will temporarily leave the Rachel Carson Trail for a half-mile out-and-back on the River Otter Trail to a small pond.

On the River Otter Trail, you will cross the Hawlings River. It is challenging to keep your feet dry, but the river is refreshing in summer if you are wearing hiking sandals. Once you are on the other side, hike up the streambank, and stay left to reach the pond. In July and August, you and your kids can enjoy picking the plentiful raspberries and blackberries along the trail here. Furthermore, during July, the pond is beautifully covered in blooming lilies. Be careful because poison ivy is abundant in this area. When you are done feasting, turn around and head back across the Hawlings River and up the hill to the Rachel Carson Greenway Trail.

Turn right on the Rachel Carson as it weaves away from the river and then back again to follow it for a good distance. This section of the Rachel Carson is starkly different from the trail's beginning. Mile-a-minute, an invasive vine native to Southeast Asia, is suffocating trees, shrubs, and ground cover in this part of the park. The vine asphyxiates all plants in its wake, blocking them from getting enough sunlight for photosynthesis. Furthermore, mile-a-minute has no predators in the ecological food web. Weed Warriors, volunteers with Montgomery Parks, are working hard to eradicate it from this part of the park, as they did along the Fox Meadow Loop.

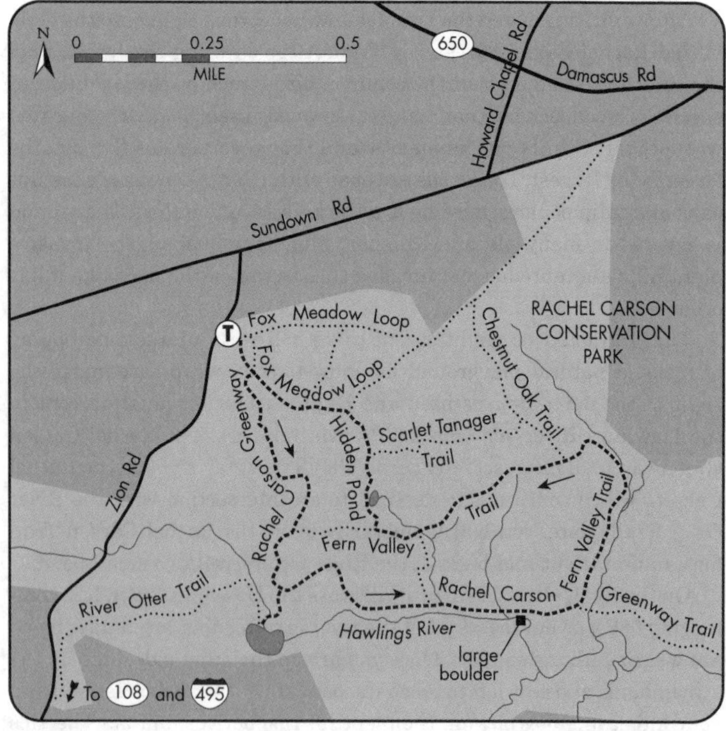

Dogs and kids splash across the Hawlings River.

The Rachel Carson Greenway Trail turns left to follow the Hawlings River for more than a half mile, providing kids many opportunities to play along it. Just after the trail joins the river, for example, a short people's choice trail provides access to skip rocks in the river and hop from boulder to boulder along it. Back on the Rachel Carson, you will pass a ridge wall on the left covered in vegetation with an occasional rock outcropping.

When the Hidden Pond Trail intersects on the left, continue straight on the Rachel Carson along the river. The trail weaves through a soggy area where a small feeder stream carves between two ridges. In this shady, wet area, a carpet of ferns sits knee high. The trail ascends, as does the streambank. In the middle of the Hawlings River here, you will see a truck-sized boulder big enough to seat four people comfortably. Hikers are treated to a rock bathed in sunshine and the peaceful trickle of the river. Mountain laurel is dense here, but there is a 15-foot people's choice trail on the right to access the rock.

After leaving the rock, turn right to stay on the Rachel Carson Greenway Trail. Within 0.2 mile, where the Rachel Carson turns right, continue straight on the Fern Valley Trail. It follows the base of a steep ridge on the left with a Hawlings River feeder stream on the right. Hike a little more than a half mile before the Fern Valley Trail curves left to ascend the ridgeline. Pass the first left (the original trail) that makes a sharp turn up the ridge. This ascent is closed and rerouted at the second left turn. Make the second left turn to stay on the Fern Valley Trail, and follow two switchbacks (the hike's steepest climb) to the top. Once you are on the ridge, stay straight. The closed trail on the left is the old Fern Valley route up the ridge, and on the right is the Chestnut Oak Trail. The trail gradually descends a gentle ramp back to the valley.

Hike over a culvert to the intersection with the Hidden Pond Trail. Stay right and follow the two merged trails for about 0.1 mile. The Fern Valley Trail continues straight, and the Hidden Pond Trail turns right. Turn right and follow the Hidden Pond Trail to the Fox Meadow Loop. A vernal pool appears on the right of the Hidden Pond Trail just after the trails diverge. In spring, the male spring peepers that inhabit this pool loudly call for a mate. The Scarlet Tanager Trail intersects the Hidden Pond Trail on the right within a quarter mile. Pass it and continue straight as the trail ascends out of the woods to the edge of the meadow.

Turn left on the Fox Meadow Loop as it cuts a path through the meadow on the edge of the forest. In the warm sun, birds, dragonflies, and butterflies buzz the grass tips looking for their next meal or a place to camouflage themselves in the meadow foliage. A few paths, including the Rachel Carson Greenway Trail, intersect the Fox Meadow Loop in the meadow; ignore them as the trail gently descends the hill and continues straight back to the parking lot.

PRINCE GEORGES COUNTY

MARSH BOARDWALK AT PISCATAWAY

BEFORE YOU GO
Map: Available at the visitor center and on the park's website
Contact: Piscataway Park
Nearest city: Fort Washington, MD

ABOUT THE HIKE
Easy, year-round
Length: 1 mile, out and back
Hiking time: ½–1 hour
High point/elevation gain: 35 feet/20 feet
Access: Asphalt and boardwalk, jogging-stroller friendly

GETTING THERE

From I-495 (Capital Beltway), take exit 3 for Indian Head Highway (MD 210) south. Drive 10 miles, and turn right onto Livingston Road. Drive 0.1 mile, and turn right onto Biddle Road. Turn left onto Bryan Point Road, and drive 3 miles to the 2800 block. Turn right onto an unmarked, gravel driveway, and drive 0.3 mile to the parking lot. The driveway to the Marsh Boardwalk is before the Accokeek Ecosystem Farm and the National Colonial Farm.

ON THE TRAIL

Piscataway Park was established in 1961 to protect 6 miles of green space along the Potomac River from impinging development. Alice Ferguson, Francis Payne Bolton, and other community members wanted to preserve the green view that George Washington saw each day across the Potomac from Mount Vernon. Today, the National Park Service, Alice Ferguson Foundation, and Accokeek Foundation partner to maintain and preserve the park, and to provide programming to educate individuals and school groups about eighteenth-century tobacco and sustainable farming.

Piscataway Park encompasses Hard Bargain Farm, which is available to school groups by reservation, and Farmington Landing, Marshall

Hall, National Colonial Farm, and Accokeek Ecosystem Farm, all of which are open to the public. The Marsh Boardwalk leads to Mockley Point, where Piscataway Creek empties into the Potomac. The hike on the boardwalk is a great option for families with small children as it is wide and flat with high, narrow-slit railings. There are many benches to rest and climb upon to take a peek at all the animals in the marsh: fish, frogs, turtles, snakes, birds, dragonflies, and lots of butterflies. In addition, kids and parents can watch the boats zoom past on the wide span of the river. The boardwalk has a couple of interpretive signs to educate families about the living shoreline and the tidal ecosystem. An optional dirt road leads to Mockley Point and beyond along Piscataway Creek.

Make sure to schedule enough time to visit the National Colonial Farm at the end of Bryan Point Road. At the farm, children learn how middle-class families raised tobacco for their livelihood in the late 1700s. Interpreters dressed in costume demonstrate candle making, sewing,

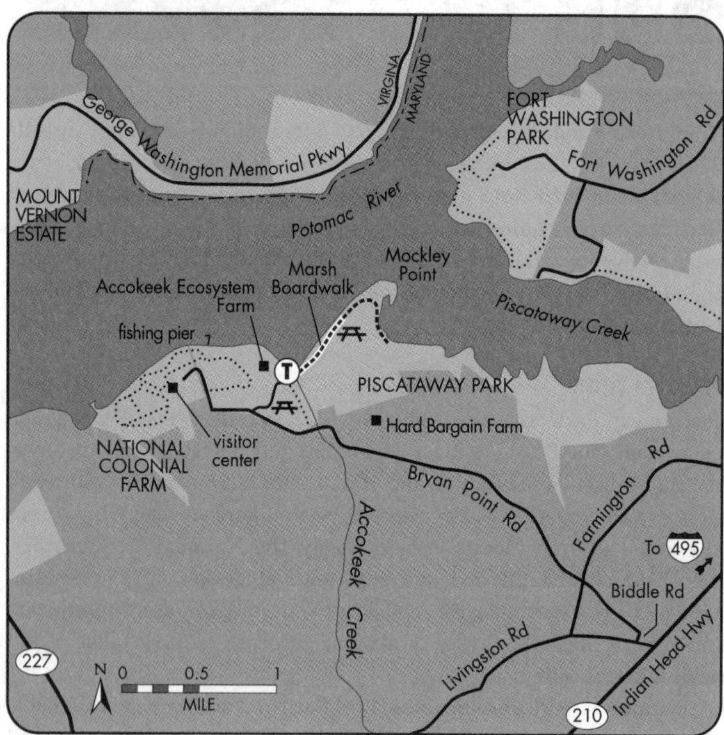

weaving, gardening, dyeing, woodworking, cooking, spinning, and the games children played in this era. A fishing pier provides a direct view of Mount Vernon across the river. A visitor center and restrooms are located at National Colonial Farm; there are none along the Marsh Boardwalk.

A hiker takes a breather on the banks of the Potomac River.

To access the Marsh Boardwalk, follow a paved trail at the end of the parking lot adjacent to the kiosk. There is a picnic table underneath a large black walnut tree and a solar-powered compactable trash can. However, the National Park Service encourages visitors to pack out all their trash. The 0.1-mile path is bordered by trees and grass, and soon meets the boardwalk on the right. Most of the boardwalk was built over vegetation, but two portions span open water, one of which is just after stepping on the boardwalk. When I scouted the trail with my family, we watched an angler cast for largemouth bass and a snake slither across the mouth of Accokeek Creek to hide among the floating vegetation.

After the inlet, continue on the boardwalk along the first of two large bays to read two interpretive signs. The first interpretive sign tells the story of how the National Park Service, Alice Ferguson Foundation, and additional partners spent more than a year reconstructing a half mile of shoreline from Mockley Point to Accokeek Creek and the boardwalk itself. The project was funded by the National Oceanic and Atmospheric Administration under the American Restoration and Recovery Act (otherwise known as stimulus money). Previously, the streambanks in this location were steep and heavily eroded, which affected animal and plant habitat, water quality, and the park's Native American archaeological and cultural sites. Instead of building seawalls and breakers to prevent erosion, the project planners built sills just offshore to break the waves' energy. Sand was backfilled to provide a sloping shoreline, and native vegetation was planted to hold the banks in place, like in a coastal sand dune. The living shoreline allows fish and crabs to spawn along this half-mile, pristine stretch of the Potomac.

The boardwalk passes over a second inlet, where you will see evidence of submerged tree stumps cut by beavers. Just before the bridge, a boardwalk intersects from the right leading back to the wetland forest, and on the left a lower boardwalk allows visitors to observe the living shoreline more closely. Hike the last 0.1 mile on the boardwalk through the wetland forest to reach the end where there are some picnic tables and access to the river.

Either turn around here or extend your hike straight on the dirt road as it follows the river north to Mockley Point. The dirt road, still in the park, continues for another mile around Mockley Point along Piscataway Creek, but it accesses the river and point in a half mile. Within this half mile, you will pass a Native American sweat lodge (please respect the tribe's property; don't touch it or go inside it), a burial plot for Piscataway Chief Turkey Tayac, and dirt Mockley Point Road. The Piscataway Indians have inhabited this park and land from the Anacostia River to southern Maryland for thousands of years. They still live in the area, and this park is their sacred ground.

RIVER TRAIL: FORT WASHINGTON

BEFORE YOU GO
Map: Available at the visitor center and on the park's website
Contact: Fort Washington Park (charges a fee)
Nearest city: Fort Washington, MD

ABOUT THE HIKE
Easy/moderate, year-round
Length: 2.2 miles, out and back
Hiking time: 1–1½ hours
High point/elevation gain: 95 feet/167 feet
Access: Gravel, boardwalk, and compact soil; passable for jogging strollers

GETTING THERE

From I-495 (Capital Beltway), take exit 3 for Indian Head Highway (MD 210) south. Drive 4.4 miles, and turn right onto Fort Washington Road. Drive 1.7 miles to a roundabout, and take the second exit to stay on Fort

The lighthouse at Fort Washington helps boats navigate the Potomac River.

Washington Road. Drive 2.2 miles to the entrance station. Enter the one-way loop, turn right at the lighthouse sign, and drive to the end of the road.

ON THE TRAIL

In the late 1700s, George Washington recommended that a fort be built across the Potomac River from Mount Vernon. However, the fort wasn't constructed until 1809 when tension between the newly formed United States and Great Britain ignited. Fort Warburton, as it was known at first, was purposely demolished in 1814 to prevent the British from taking it over when they invaded Washington, DC, and set fire to the White House, Capitol, and other government buildings. By 1824, it was rebuilt as Fort Washington. Initially constructed with brick, it was fortified in later years with steel and concrete when cannons, rifles, and warships advanced technologically. Before the Civil War, it was the only fort that protected Washington, DC, until the US government built Fort Foote and Battery Rogers along the Potomac in addition to sixty-eight more forts to protect the capital from the Confederates.

Since 1865, control of Fort Washington has alternated between the Department of the Interior and Department of Defense. It has been used as a garrison for many infantry divisions and once housed the Civilian Conservation Corps. For two centuries, Fort Washington's primary purpose was to defend the nation's capital. Today, it is a national park that offers families a great green space for recreation and an incredible historical display detailing the fort's military operations from 1809 to 1946. Exhibits in the visitor center and the fort tell its story.

An underutilized national park in the DC area because it is not well known, this spectacular place provides all the elements necessary for a great family outing: hiking, fishing, picnicking, history, and expansive views along the Potomac River. The hike begins on the river side of the fort. The trail leads you around the fort, along the edge of the peninsula, and past the lighthouse, which is still used for boat navigation. The first 0.75 mile of the trail is wide and gravel, while the remainder of it is boardwalk and compact soil. The unmarked trail follows the riverbank at water's level and from above most of the way with access points for play, but swimming is prohibited. Along Piscataway Creek, the trail enters dense woods filled with many paw paw trees, which give the impression of a rainforest. The primary elevation gain occurs before the turnaround point at Picnic Area D.

The hike begins through two black gates on a paved trail at the end of the parking lot. Within 100 feet, the enormous fort reveals itself behind the hill and tree line. To put the fort into perspective, my son looked like an ant compared to it as he stood on the hill to the left of the trail. A gravel path leading to the top of the fort intersects from the left within 100 yards of the parking lot. The trail turns from paved to gravel at this point.

In another 100 yards, the River Trail intersects from both the left and right. The River Trail follows the water's edge from Swan Creek on the north side of the peninsula to Piscataway Creek on the south side of it. Turn left on the River Trail. The trail heads toward the south side of the fort where it becomes tree covered and shady. You can no longer see the fort when the trail enters the trees. For the next 0.2 mile, the river is on the right with a forest-covered hill on the left.

About 0.4 mile into the hike, the gravel trail ends at a kiosk with information about animals that inhabit the park. Continue on a raised wooden boardwalk for 50 yards to meet a compact soil trail at the end. For 0.1 mile, the trail loses sight of the river's edge as it bisects a tip in the peninsula. However, the trail rejoins the bank, and then it rises above the river as it gains slight elevation in the next 0.1 mile. Cross a bridge at 0.7 mile, and hike another 0.1 mile to pass a people's choice trail and a battery on the right. This battery and seven others were built

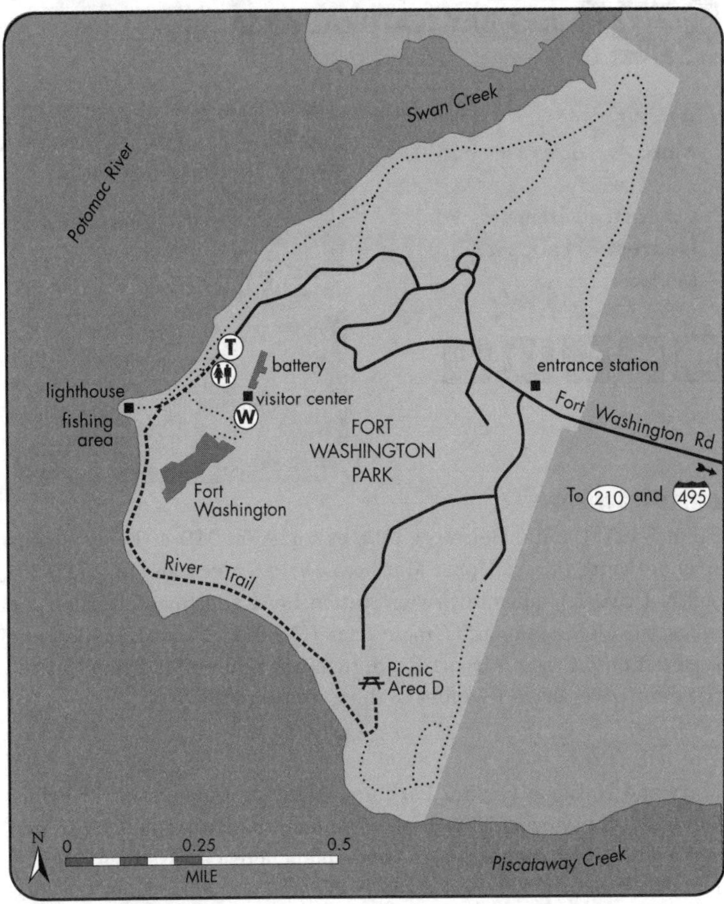

during World War II for training purposes. Hike to the right around it, and then left as the trail curves up and down a short berm.

Within 0.1 mile, pass another people's choice trail at post number four on the right. Continue straight for a short distance to where the trail dead-ends. Hiking to the right leads to a battery. However, turn left and curve right uphill adjacent to the split-rail fence. In 100 yards, the trail switchbacks left and uphill on steps to where it dead-ends at Picnic Area D. Quietly ascend the hill after the switchback to possibly find deer and wild turkeys feeding in the grass. Turn around at the picnic area to retrace your steps 1.1 miles back to the parking lot just beyond the fort.

JUG BAY NATURAL AREA

BEFORE YOU GO
Map: Available at the park visitor center
Contact: Patuxent River Park
Nearest city: Upper Marlboro, MD

ABOUT THE HIKE
Moderate, year-round
Length: 2.5 miles, loop and spur
Hiking time: 1½–2 hours
High point/elevation gain: 75 feet/ 125 feet
Access: Compact soil and boardwalk; not passable for jogging strollers; pets prohibited on Brown Trail

GETTING THERE

From I-495 (Capital Beltway), take exit 11A for MD 4 (Pennsylvania Avenue) south toward Upper Marlboro. Drive 8 miles, and take MD 301 south. Drive 1.7 miles to Croom Station Road and turn left. After 1.6 miles, turn left again onto Croom Road (MD 382). Drive 1.5 miles, and turn left onto Croom Airport Road, then left again after 2 miles at the park entrance. Drive 1.7 miles to the visitor center.

ON THE TRAIL

Maryland National Capital Park and Planning Commission of Prince Georges County owns 7000 acres of land on the Patuxent River to preserve it and its valuable wetland and upland forest ecosystems. Jug Bay Natural Area is 2000 acres within Patuxent River Park. Since the river is an estuary in lower Prince Georges County, it is tidal and brackish. Jug Bay's height depends on the tidal flow of the Atlantic Ocean, which is dictated by the gravitational pull of the moon and sun on the earth as it rotates; it fluctuates 18 inches on average between two daily high and low tides. Because the Patuxent River flows through a wide floodplain at Jug Bay, the channel's width changes dramatically throughout each day. Jug Bay offers an incredible opportunity to observe more than 250 bird species, such as osprey and red-winged blackbirds. Some birds stay here year-round, while others migrate.

Jug Bay has 8 miles of hiking, biking, and equestrian trails. Furthermore, it hosts two canoe and kayak launch points for the 80-mile-long

The overlooks on Jug Bay are great for picture posing and bird-watching.

Patuxent Water Trail. Visitors may rent kayaks and canoes from the visitor center. The park offers educational programming (including a weekly boat trip every Sunday at 2:00 PM), camping, picnicking, fishing, hunting, and two boat ramps. Plus it houses the Patuxent Rural Life Museums, preserved buildings from the late nineteenth and early twentieth centuries depicting rural farm life in southern Prince Georges County.

At the visitor center, you and your kids can visit the small educational exhibit inside and rent canoes and kayaks to see Jug Bay and its marsh from a different viewpoint. There is a mature butterfly garden adjacent to the parking lot. You never know what amazing insects—spiders, preying mantises, bees, butterflies, dragonflies, and much more—you might find in this incredible habitat.

This 2.5-mile loop-and-spur hike takes you through a swamp, to a wetland overlook, and through upland forest. Even though the hike is mostly on level ground, the Brown and Green trails traverse up and down the bluff above the river four times, sometimes on stairs and other times on compact soil. Both trails are well marked with plastic posts at and between each intersection. Much of the Brown Trail is on boardwalk through a swamp and on the edge of the wetland, while the Green Trail is on compact soil on the bluff above the river. Dogs are prohibited on the Brown Trail to protect the delicate swamp.

The hike begins on a dirt road adjacent to the restrooms and across the driveway from the visitor center. In 100 yards, the dirt road leads to the museums. Enjoy the interpretive signs and the hundred-year-old

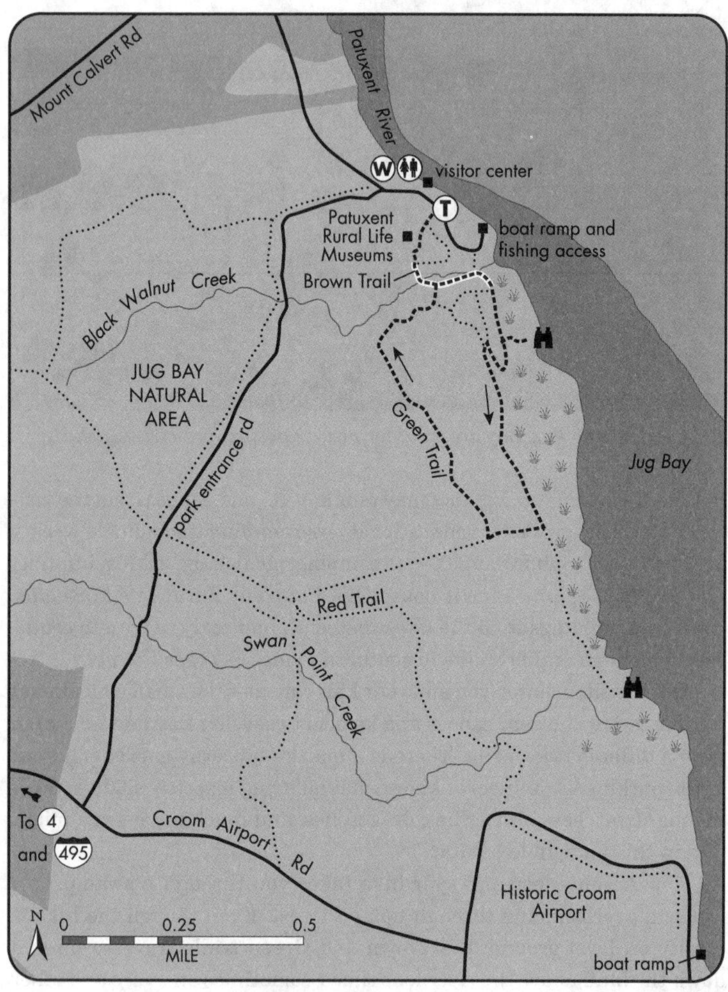

buildings either at the beginning or end of the hike. The most striking is the late nineteenth-century Duckett log cabin that was built on a tenant farm in southern Prince Georges County by a former slave and Union Navy soldier. The trailhead for the Brown Trail is on the right side of the road just after it curves left to the dead-end circle. The trail descends the bluff steeply on steps built into it. At the bottom, the trail curves left and intersects the Brown Trail loop. Turn right and follow the boardwalk through the swamp, which is created by the mouth of Black Walnut Creek as it enters the Patuxent River. Interpretive signs along the Brown Trail educate users about the swamp and its habitat.

At 0.2 mile from the start, pass a set of wooden stairs on the right (your eventual return route), and continue straight on the boardwalk. In 0.1 mile, the boardwalk splits; continue straight out to the edge of the marsh. The boardwalk curves right, and on the inside of it is a bald cypress, an evergreen tree that is native to swamps and grows distinctive "knees." Part of the root system, these knees store carbohydrates and supply oxygen and support for the tree.

After the bald cypress, the Brown Trail stays parallel to the marsh as the trail tread fluctuates between compact soil and boardwalk. The Brown Trail forks at a half mile; continue left along the marsh. For the next 0.2 mile, the trail meanders left and right through the trees where there is evidence of beavers. At 0.7 mile, make a short detour left to the scenic overlook to take in a great view of the marsh and Jug Bay. Look for soaring raptors such as bald eagles, hawks, and osprey. Return to the Brown Trail from the overlook, and turn left. In a short distance, it curves right and ascends the bluff. At the top, the trail makes a dip in a shallow gulch and intersects the Green Trail. This intersection lacks a marker indicating that the Green Trail goes both left and right.

The Green Trail creates a loop with two spurs: one leading to an overlook and the other intersecting with the Red Trail. Turn left on the Green Trail, and hike on a wide, level trail atop the bluff for 0.4 mile until you reach the first spur. You can extend your hike 0.8 mile by continuing straight out and back on this spur of the Green Trail to a scenic overlook on the bluff. If you do not want to take that side trip, then turn right to stay on the Green Trail as it loops. In 0.1 mile, turn right to continue, as the Green Trail loops back to the Brown Trail. At this turn, look on the right side of the trail for a very large old maple tree. How many children does it take to hug this tree?

The last half mile of the Green Trail is level and wide and passes straight through upland forest and some mountain laurel. Turn left onto the Brown Trail, and hike 0.1 mile to the edge of the bluff and down the wooden stairs. There is a wooden platform to the left of the stairs for observing birds in the tree canopy. At the bottom of the stairs, turn left onto the boardwalk, and walk 0.2 mile back on the boardwalk, left up the bluff to the Rural Life Museums, and on the dirt road back to the visitor center.

PATUXENT RESEARCH REFUGE

BEFORE YOU GO
Map: Available at the trailhead and National Wildlife Center and on the refuge's website
Contact: Patuxent Research Refuge and National Wildlife Center
Nearest city: Laurel, MD

ABOUT THE HIKE
Easy, year-round
Length: 1.8 miles, loop and spur
Hiking time: 1–1½ hours
High point/elevation gain: 229 feet/75 feet
Access: Asphalt, compact soil, and boardwalk; passable for jogging strollers

GETTING THERE

From I-495 (Capital Beltway), take exit 22A for Baltimore–Washington Parkway (MD 295) north toward Baltimore. Drive 3.7 miles, and take the Powder Mill Road exit. Turn right onto Powder Mill Road. Drive 1.8 miles, and turn right onto Scarlet Tanager Loop into Patuxent Research Refuge. Drive 1.4 miles to the parking lot.

ON THE TRAIL

President Franklin D. Roosevelt established the Patuxent Research Refuge in 1936. Of the 540 refuges in the United States, it is the only one that conducts research on wildlife (primarily via the US Geological Survey). There are three tracts in the 12,841-acre refuge: the north and south, which offer trails, and the central tract, where research is conducted. The 8000-acre north tract has 20 miles of trails, a small visitor center, and fishing and hunting. The south tract, which this hike explores, has 6 miles of trails, two lakes, an interpretive tram, a fishing pier, and the National Wildlife Visitors Center. The largest in the US Department of the Interior, the center showcases the research that its scientists are conducting. When you take this hike, build in enough time to visit the center's interactive exhibits, which educate visitors about this research. Visitors can also take an interpretive tram ride near Lake Redington.

This 1.8-mile loop hike follows four trails: Goose Pond, Laurel, Valley, and Cash Lake. Each intersection is marked by a trail sign and mileage figure. The shady trails are mostly compact soil with one boardwalk on the Cash Lake Trail. These trails follow the natural undulation of the topography without much elevation gain. You and your kids can extend your hike 0.4 mile on Cash Lake Trail out to the fishing pier and back before continuing on the Valley Trail. Friends of Patuxent created an interpretive guide for this loop, which is available at the trailhead to the Goose Pond Trail. Numbered trail posts correspond with the explanations in the guide.

The hike begins at the Conservation Heritage Loop at the back left corner of the parking lot adjacent to two large signs. Follow this paved trail for 0.1 mile past a bench and three interpretive signs about prominent environmentalists in history and habitat provided by electrical rights-of-way. When it forks, turn left onto a cinder trail at an interpretive sign that describes the discovery hike toward Goose Pond. The trail tread turns to mulch and curves right through a small stand of trees, then opens to Goose Pond and an outdoor education area.

The outdoor education area marks the beginning of the Cash Lake and Laurel trails; follow the Cash Lake Trail to the right, going counterclockwise on the loop. This trail has a good mixture of deciduous and coniferous trees. In 0.1 mile, a side trail on the right leads to a bench

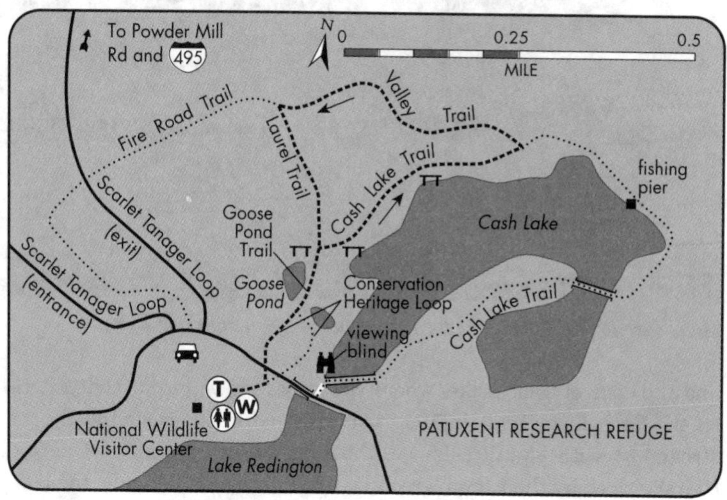

BEAVERS: NATURE'S ENGINEERS

Beaver lodges are often built on the edges of ponds and lakes. The lodge in Cash Lake is two layers: intertwined logs and sticks packed with mud on the top layer and then a cavity dug into the soil to accommodate a male, female, and their kits. The entrance and exit of the lodge is a canal through the bank into the water.

Make sure to peek inside the former beaver lodge along Cash Lake.

and the edge of Cash Lake, where you may observe bird activity. Back on the Cash Lake Trail, in 100 yards cross a bridge over a mostly dry streambed with skunk cabbage, the first flowering plants of spring characterized by their large green leaves. In the next 0.2 mile, the trail meanders left and right a few times out to a point where there is a bench and a people's choice trail on the right. The trail curves left and passes a former beaver lodge. By stepping closer to the lodge, kids can see inside it.

The intersection with the Valley Trail appears 0.1 mile after the beaver lodge. You may choose to add 0.4 mile out and back to the fishing pier by going straight at this intersection. On sunny days, a canopy cover provides some shade. On the pier, observe the osprey that make their nest on the wooden platforms in Cash Lake. These raptors can be observed in many areas along large bodies of water like the rivers of the Chesapeake Bay. Fishing is by permit only.

To continue the main hike, turn left onto the Valley Trail. The trail meanders right and left and gently up and down as it follows the natural ripples of the land. The dense forest surrounding it displays healthy layers of ground cover, understory, and canopy vegetation with minimal invasive species. Keep an eye out for tree snags (standing dead trees) with woodpecker holes. Woodpeckers seek out snags to feed on the bugs that live in them and to create nesting cavities.

Reach the Laurel Trail in 0.6 mile. At the three-way intersection with the Valley, Laurel, and Fire Road trails, turn left onto the Laurel Trail, and hike 0.4 mile as it meanders back to Goose Pond. Just before you reach Goose Pond, an interpretive sign explains forest fragmentation and its impact on some species of birds.

At the outdoor education area, follow the sign straight ahead past Goose Pond to the Conservation Heritage Loop. At the end of the Goose Pond Trail, turn right onto the paved loop back to the parking lot. If you want to extend your hike, turn left at the end of the Conservation Heritage Loop and follow the wide, paved path to the floating bridge at the end of Cash Lake. If you are quiet, you will hear carpenter and green frogs among the aquatic plants.

TRAIL MEANDERS

Why does a trail meander? Trail planners and builders construct trails that meander left and right to provide a more interesting experience through the ecosystem instead of a straight line; designing a meandering trail also allows planners to avoid plants or trees that a trail may negatively impact and to improve its sustainability by reducing erosion.

GREENBELT PARK: AZALEA TRAIL

BEFORE YOU GO
Map: Available at the park headquarters and on the park's website
Contact: Greenbelt Park
Nearest city: Greenbelt, MD

ABOUT THE HIKE
Easy, year-round
Length: 1.2 miles, loop
Hiking time: 1 hour
High point/elevation gain: 220 feet/82 feet
Access: Compact soil, passable for jogging strollers

GETTING THERE

From I-495 (Capital Beltway), take exit 23 for MD 201 (Kenilworth Avenue) south toward Bladensburg. Drive 0.5 mile, and turn left onto Greenbelt Road (MD 193). Drive 0.3 mile, and turn right into the park. At the stop sign, turn right to the Sweetgum picnic area. This hike is accessible via a 3-mile walk from the College Park Metro station on the Green Line.

ON THE TRAIL

Greenbelt Park was created in 1950 when President Harry Truman transferred 1100 acres of land from the Public Housing Authority to the National Park Service. Today, it is a green space gem in a densely populated area of suburban Washington, DC. Families can enjoy three picnic areas, a campground with 174 campsites, 9 miles of trails, scheduled nature events, and the Junior Ranger program. The 5-mile Perimeter Trail, the longest loop in the park, follows the park boundary. The Azalea Trail connects all three picnic areas: Sweetgum, Laurel, and Holly, each of which is named after a species of tree or bush that resides along the trail. It boasts one other benefit besides its beautiful natural setting: twenty fitness stations along a quarter of its length.

The hike begins at the Sweetgum picnic area. A large sign on the driveway into Sweetgum marks the trailhead; you will hike the white-blazed Azalea Trail counterclockwise. The trail slopes gently downhill for the first 0.1 mile. This first section is the closest to the road and the noisiest due to the heavy traffic on Kenilworth Avenue and Greenbelt

Road. After that stretch, the trail becomes quiet. The sweetgum tree dominates the canopy in the first 0.2 mile of the Azalea Trail.

Several of the fitness stations, featuring stretching and calisthenic exercises, sit along the beginning of the trail. About 0.2 mile into the hike, the fitness stations continue on a trail that veers left to connect to the large grassy field where you began. You will see more of the fitness stations again in the last 0.1 mile of the Azalea Trail between the Holly and Sweetgum picnic areas.

Exercise stations along the Azalea Trail

After the fitness trail veers to the left, the Azalea Trail levels off to follow North Branch Still Creek. Between mile markers 0.2 and 0.4, there are a few places to access the creek for some playtime. A half mile into the hike, the trail curves left and over a bridge crossing a feeder creek, then curves left again. In the next 0.1 mile (in addition to other places in the park), you can observe young and mature American holly trees.

At 0.6 mile, the trail ascends the landscape before reaching the driveway to the Laurel picnic area. Cross the driveway, and continue on the Azalea Trail on the opposite side. The trail is close to the Baltimore-

SWEETGUM

Sweetgum trees can reach heights of 100 feet and live for up to four centuries. They are a pioneer species, and their saplings are highly competitive, fast growers that can be a dominant species in sunny, low-lying areas. Sweetgum fruit is easy to identify because when it releases its seeds, the fruit is a medium brown ball, smaller than a golf ball, with prickly points. It looks like a medieval ball and chain. The fruit is pointed to protect the seeds from predators, like squirrels, chipmunks, and birds.

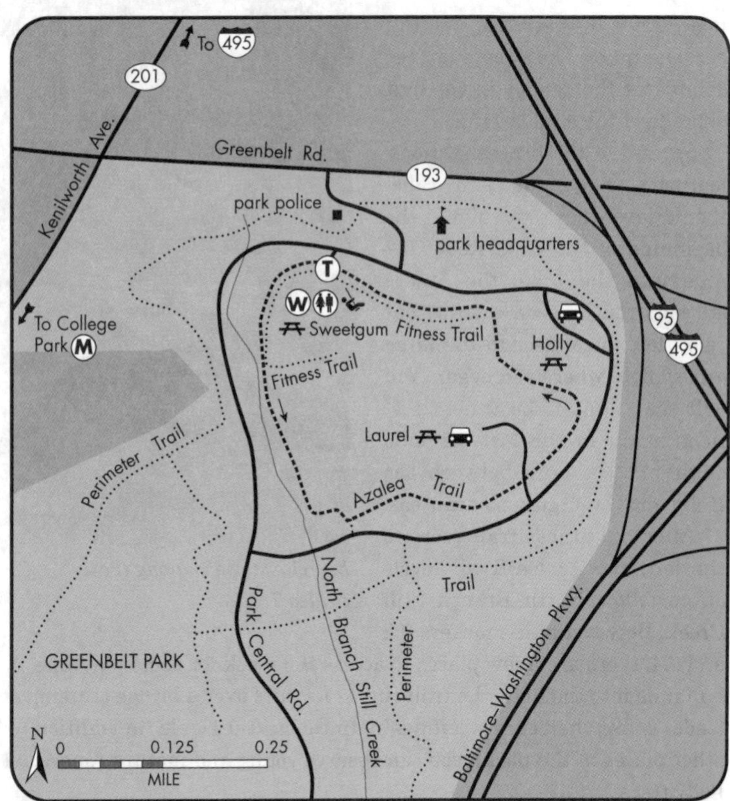

MORE THAN AN ORNAMENTAL TREE

American holly is easy to identify in our region because it is evergreen. The waxy leaves are oval with small sawtooth points, each of which has a thorn. This understory tree, growing on average 40 feet tall, is native to the Mid-Atlantic region. Its red berries are an important food source for birds and mammals like deer and raccoons. Songbirds depend on the red berries in winter when food is scarce.

Washington Parkway for a period of time, and so you may hear the rush of cars. The trail curves to the left and follows the rolling topography. Notice a mixture of deciduous and conifer trees at 0.8 mile into the hike.

The conifers give this stretch a cozy feeling. While hiking, you can point out to your kids tree hollows near the base of trunks. Playing a game of "I Spy" while hiking is a great way to engage kids; you never know what they might spy inside a tree hollow.

The Azalea Trail approaches the driveway to the Holly picnic area; however, it makes a hard left turn and does not cross it. A trail sign points left toward the Sweetgum picnic area. Here is the beginning of the fitness trail, with more stretching and calisthenic activities. Hike 0.1 mile to the wood's edge. The fitness stations continue to the left along the edge of the field, but cross the field toward the parking lot to complete the hike. Enjoy the picnic tables and two playgrounds before you leave the park.

LAKE ARTEMESIA

BEFORE YOU GO
Map: None available online or at the park
Contact: Prince Georges County Department of Parks and Recreation/Lake Artemesia
Nearest city: College Park, MD

ABOUT THE HIKE
Easy, year-round
Length: 1.4 miles, loop
Hiking time: 1–1½ hours
High point/elevation gain: 108 feet/35 feet
Access: Asphalt, jogging-stroller friendly

GETTING THERE

From I-495 (Capital Beltway), take exit 23 for MD 201 (Kenilworth Avenue) south toward Bladensburg. Drive 0.4 mile, and turn right onto Kenilworth Road. Drive 0.2 mile, and turn right onto Greenbelt Road. After 1 mile, turn right onto Branchville Road which becomes Ballew Avenue after a hard left. Drive 0.7 mile, and turn left into the parking lot on the corner of Ballew Avenue (55th Avenue) and Berwyn Road. To get to this park via Metro, take the Green Line, get off at the College Park station, and walk east on Paint Branch Parkway to the Northeast Branch Trail.

ON THE TRAIL

On the other side of the railroad tracks from the University of Maryland is an oasis of nature within the suburban jungle of Prince Georges County. In 1976, the Washington Metropolitan Area Transit Authority (Metro) constructed this park and 38-acre lake in return for taking sand

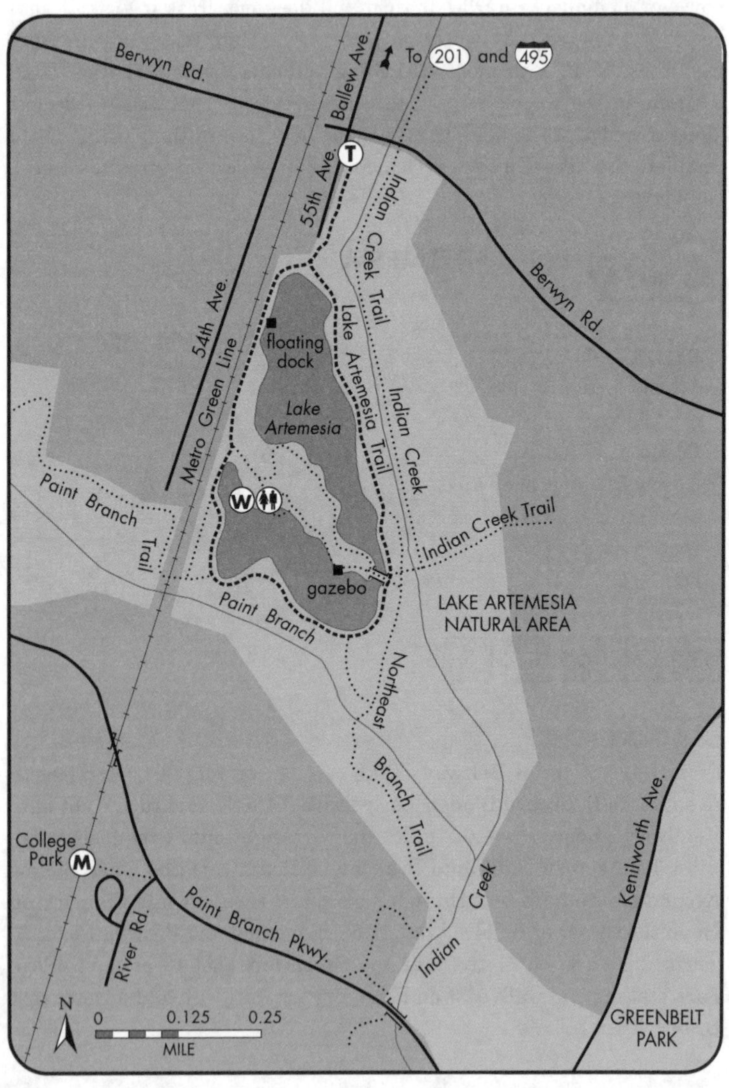

Lake Artemesia

and gravel from this location to build the neighboring tracks and Greenbelt Metro station, the last station on the Green Line. Named after Artemesia Dref, who donated ten lots for green space in 1972, this park is an incredible gift to the neighboring communities of Berwyn Heights and College Park and an island of refuge for migrating and native birds.

Inside the gated park, the paved trail circles the two fingerlike lakes that are connected by an inlet. Linking the outside 1.4-mile loop is an extension via a bridge onto a peninsula furnished with bathrooms, a floating dock, a raised gazebo to observe waterfowl, and a stage with grassy steps perfect for summertime concerts. In addition to these amenities, many benches are scattered along the water for watching blue herons, egrets, and red-winged blackbirds, as well as snapping and eastern painted turtles, and listening to bullfrogs and green frogs. Across the trail from the restrooms is a mowed trail that allows individuals to look for birds and butterflies in a beautiful meadow filled with thistles, Joe Pye weed, and milkweed.

It doesn't matter whether you hike the trail clockwise or counterclockwise; the experience is similar. Dotting the entire circuit are benches, seven gazebos, and nine interpretive signs about the animal species found around or in the lake and about the history of the park. When walking the trail counterclockwise, hikers reach a handicapped-accessible floating dock within 0.3 mile. The Paint Branch Trail is a half mile farther at the southwest corner of the park. In the southeast corner, the Northeast Branch Trail can be accessed via four different trailheads.

If you are hiking the trail counterclockwise, you can extend your hike by another 0.8 mile if you add in the Indian Creek Trail. Just after you round the southern tip of the lake, watch for the trail sign to the Indian Creek Trail on your right after the bridge over Indian Creek. Turn right. When the Indian Creek Trail intersects Berwyn Road, take a left to return to the parking lot. The Lake Artemesia Trail also connects to two different bike trails: Paint Branch and Northeast Branch trails. From here, a hiker or biker can travel many miles on the Anacostia Tributary Trail System, which includes Sligo Creek, Northwest Branch, Northeast Branch, and Paint Branch.

CALVERT CLIFFS STATE PARK: RED TRAIL

BEFORE YOU GO
Map: Available at the entrance station for a small fee and on the park's website
Contact: Calvert Cliffs State Park (charges a fee)
Nearest city: Lusby, MD

ABOUT THE HIKE
Moderate, year-round
Length: 3.6 miles, out and back
Hiking time: 2–2½ hours
High point/elevation gain: 90 feet/90 feet
Access: Compact soil and boardwalk, passable for jogging strollers

GETTING THERE

From I-495 (Capital Beltway), take exit 11A for MD 4 (Pennsylvania Avenue) south toward Upper Marlboro. Drive 45.5 miles, and turn left at County Route 765 (Hg Trueman Road) and the sign for the park. Drive 300 feet to enter the park straight ahead.

ON THE TRAIL

Calvert Cliffs State Park is a unique place in southern Maryland, known for its shoreline cliffs along the Chesapeake Bay where you and your kids can pretend to be archaeologists and search for fossils. The cliffs were created 15 million years ago at the end of the Miocene epoch when the ocean receded over southern Maryland and the cliffs, once underwater, were exposed. The bones of prehistoric land and sea animals were then also exposed on the walls of the cliffs and in the sand. Today, you can sift for shark teeth and fossils on the beach (not on the cliffs, as they give way easily). The park has more than 1000 acres of upland forests, freshwater marsh, and beaches along the Chesapeake Bay. It offers 13 miles of trails, a picnic area, playground, and youth group camping area.

The Red Trail (appropriately marked with red blazes) is the shortest hike to reach the beaches and cliffs along the bay. This 1.8-mile hike that descends 90 feet in elevation is mostly shaded and follows Grays

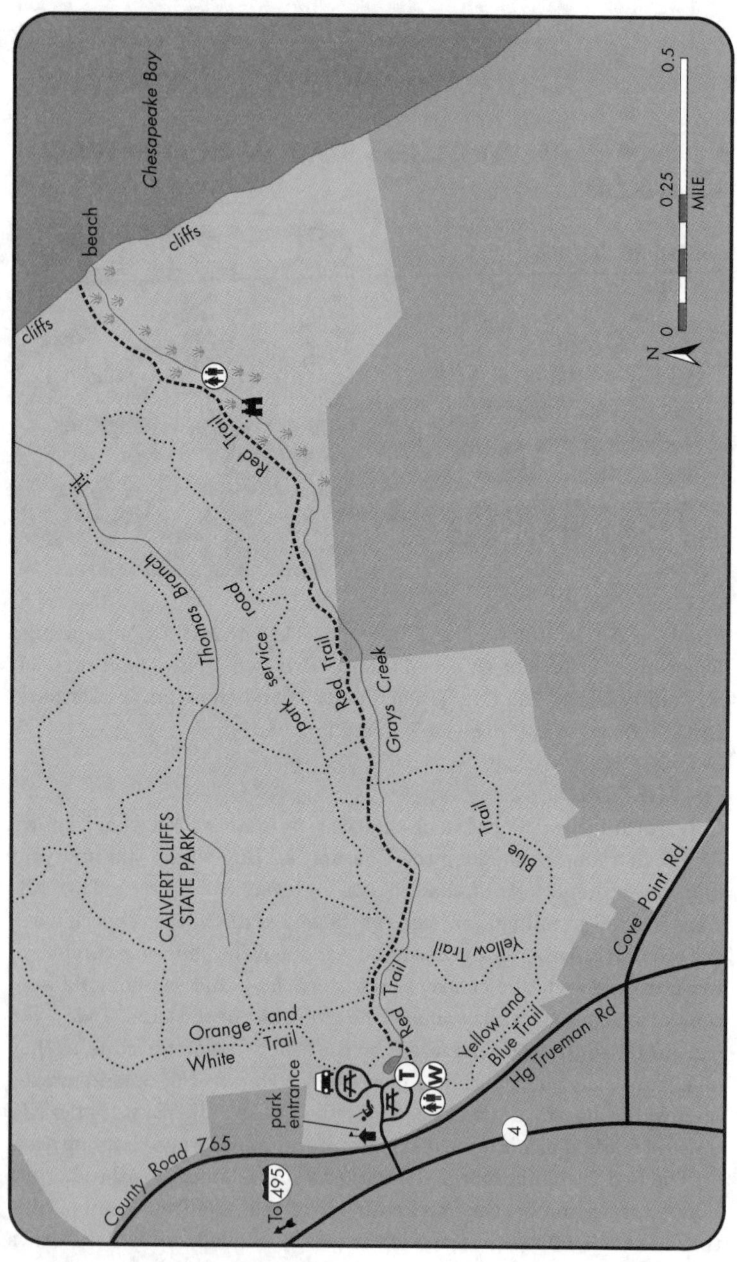
Chesapeake Bay
beach
cliffs
cliffs
Red Trail
Thomas Branch
park service road
Red Trail
Grays Creek
Blue Trail
CALVERT CLIFFS STATE PARK
Yellow Trail
Red Trail
Orange and White Trail
Yellow and Blue Trail
park entrance
Hg Trueman Rd
Cove Point Rd.
County Road 765
To 495
4
0
0.25
0.5
MILE
N

Creek to Chesapeake Bay. The well-signed trail is easy to follow. Furthermore, it has benches and mile markers. You will hike past a pond at the beginning, through a lush upland forest, and past a large marsh at the mouth of Grays Creek.

The trailhead for the Red Trail is near the restrooms and adjacent to a small parking area on the one-way loop. The beginning has mulch, but that quickly gives way to a boardwalk that follows the pond's edge before ending on the other side. Here, the trail intersects an informal trail from another parking lot on the left; turn right and follow the sand-filled trail tread downhill to its intersection with the service road in 0.15 mile. The trail sign points right to continue on the Red Trail, otherwise known as the Cliff Trail. The Red Trail and service road merge for 0.1 mile until the Red Trail splits off to the right and follows next to the creek.

In the next 0.1 mile, cross two bridges before the intersection with the Yellow Trail on the right. Near this intersection a fun chair carved into the base of a fallen tree trunk gives the impression of sitting on a throne with a root-ball sticking straight up behind you. In the next 0.2 mile, the trail descends gently downhill as it curves to the left and crosses a bridge. The forest is lush with an understory of mountain laurel and blueberry bushes. The best time to pick them is July. Unlike the commercial variety, wild blueberries are small but concentrated with intense flavor.

Before the 0.6-mile marker, the trail traverses a boardwalk in a wet area and passes an unsigned trail connector to the service road on the left. At 0.6 mile, pass the Blue Trail on the right. This trail climbs up a 70-foot ridge in the upland forest to connect with the Yellow Trail. Continue straight on the Red Trail to walk on another boardwalk and pass another unsigned trail connector on the left. At 0.9 mile, the marsh appears on the right. There are a few benches here and some signs telling hikers not to enter the marsh. Before the 1.1-mile marker, the last unsigned trail connector to the service road intersects the Red Trail from the left.

Kids head toward the beach on the boardwalk.

In the next 0.1 mile, the marsh widens and comes into full view for the next 0.4 mile. This is a great area to observe birds and look for beavers, frogs, snakes, and turtles. Along the wetland, the trail crosses bridges and boardwalks and passes a few benches. The marsh drains over a wall of rocks in Grays Creek at 1.6 miles (there is a porta-potty here). Hike the last 0.2 mile to the beach, where there are a few picnic tables and a kiosk. The beach in front of the cliffs is often closed because the cliffs erode and have landslides. However, there is plenty of beach to explore to the right in front of the wetland area of Grays Creek. About 100 yards down the beach, Grays Creek empties into the Chesapeake Bay. Swimming is allowed in the bay, but be aware that stinging nettles, a type of jellyfish, are present in the water from about mid-June until mid-fall.

When you have soaked in enough sun and sand on the beach, hike back up the Red Trail 1.8 miles to the restrooms and parking lot. If your kids haven't had enough fun in the sand, then perhaps they can play on the recycled tire playground.

CYPRESS KNEE NATURE TRAIL

BEFORE YOU GO
Map: Available at the nature center
Contact: Battle Creek Cypress Swamp Sanctuary
Nearest city: Prince Frederick, MD

ABOUT THE HIKE
Easy, year-round
Length: 0.25 mile, loop
Hiking time: ½ hour
High point/elevation gain: 49 feet/20 feet
Access: Compact soil and boardwalk, not passable for jogging strollers

GETTING THERE

From I-495 (Capital Beltway), take exit 11A for MD 4 (Pennsylvania Avenue) south toward Upper Marlboro. Drive 34 miles, and turn right onto Sixes Road (MD 506). Drive 2 miles, and turn left onto Grays Road. Drive 0.3 mile, and turn right into the park driveway.

ON THE TRAIL

Bald cypress swamps are found in only two Maryland parks: Pocomoke, east of the Chesapeake Bay, and Battle Creek, west of the bay and the closest to Washington, DC. Furthermore, Battle Creek in Calvert County has the distinction of being one of the northernmost cypress swamps in the world. Even though this hike is short, it is well worth a visit to peer into this ecosystem, which is unusual for the DC area. In addition, the nature center at Battle Creek Cypress Swamp Sanctuary offers programs, exhibits, and interpretation with live animals, including a hawk, an owl, turtles, snakes, and frogs.

The quarter-mile loop begins through the back doors of the nature center on a mulched trail lined with railroad ties. Off to the left are two large birdhouses where a rescued red-tailed hawk and barred owl live. An interpretive sign to the left of the trail provides a brief introduction and map. Before you descend the stairs straight ahead, a raised deck on the right offers a chance to observe birds in the tree canopy. Halfway down the stairs, the end of the loop intersects on the right; pass it to continue down the steps. At the bottom, the boardwalk extends 0.2 mile into the swamp.

Stop along the boardwalk to observe the cypress knees.

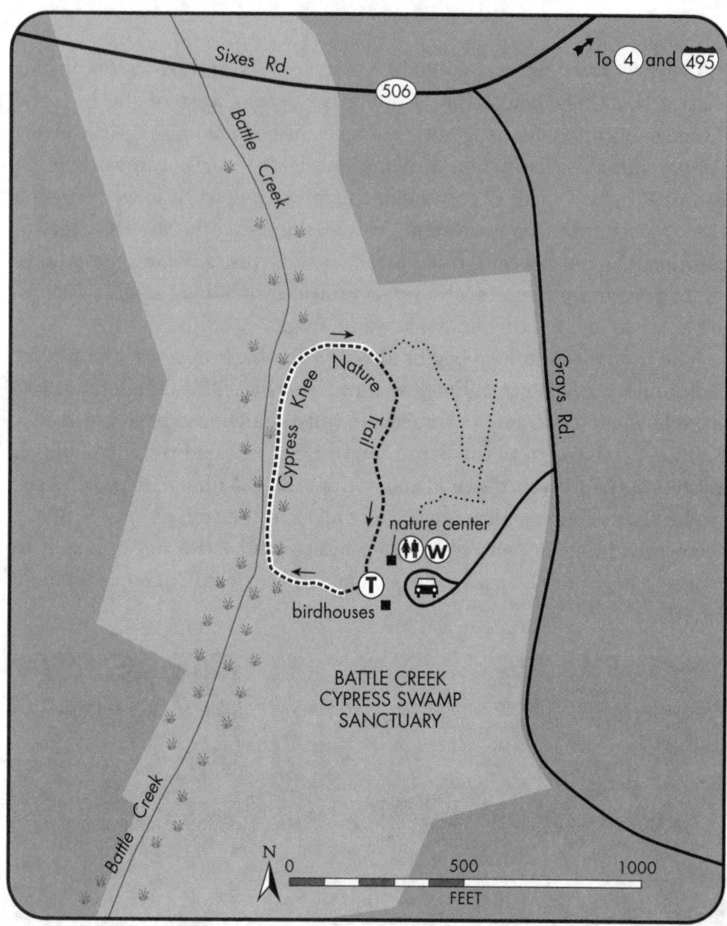

The entire hike winds through a dense forest and swamp. On the hillside above the swamp, the forest is rich with American holly, paw paw trees, and ferns. The plant life changes subtly once you reach the boardwalk and swamp. It remains dense in places where there is no standing water. Shortly after you start on the boardwalk, the first interpretive sign, which defines a bald cypress, appears on the left with two benches.

After the first interpretive sign, the boardwalk curves right and continues right to make a loop. There are two more interpretive signs and benches as you hike through the swamp and pass Battle Creek. Just

TREES WITH KNEES

A bald cypress is an evergreen tree that, unlike most, sheds its leaves (needles) every fall. The trunks stand straight and tall, up to 100 feet, and can be as wide as five feet in diameter; however, none that big exist at Battle Creek because they were harvested for their extraordinary lumber. The most unusual aspect of the bald cypress, particularly ones living in swamps, is their "knees"; their root system grows vertically from the horizontal roots just underneath the ground. These knees, generally one to three feet above the ground, provide storage for carbohydrates, oxygen for the tree's roots, and most importantly stability for the tree's structure in soil saturated with water. Bald cypress can live in drier soils, but the specimens that do may not grow knees.

before the boardwalk ends, another boardwalk and trail intersects from the left, which leads to the park's driveway and parking lot. However, continue straight on the boardwalk to reach the compact soil trail. It ascends gently above and out of the swamp where the plants subtly change back to those of a deciduous ecosystem. Where the trail intersects the stairs, turn left and climb back to the nature center to visit the exhibits and live animals.

CASCADE FALLS LOOP

BEFORE YOU GO
Map: Available at the entrance station for a small fee and on the park's website
Contact: Patapsco Valley State Park (charges a fee)
Nearest city: Elkridge, MD

ABOUT THE HIKE
Moderate/difficult, year-round
Length: 2.2 miles, loop
Hiking time: 1½–2 hours
High point/elevation gain: 420 feet/350 feet
Access: Compact soil and rock, not passable for jogging strollers

GETTING THERE

From I-495 (Capital Beltway), take I-95 north toward Baltimore. Drive 20 miles, and take exit 47A for I-195 east toward Baltimore-Washington

International Airport. Drive 1 mile, and take exit 3 for Washington Boulevard (US 1) toward Elkridge. Turn right onto Washington Boulevard toward Patapsco Valley State Park. Take an immediate right onto South Street and then an immediate left onto River Road at the park sign. Drive 1 mile, turn left onto Gun Road, and then turn right onto River Road. Drive until River Road dead-ends at the Cascade Falls parking lot.

ON THE TRAIL

Patapsco Valley State Park is just outside the Baltimore beltway of Interstate 695. Maryland's oldest park, it was established in 1907 by a newly created State Board of Forestry that received a gift of 43 acres of land from a wealthy Catonsville businessman. The park, with eight distinct recreational areas, covers more than 16,000 acres of wooded land along 32 miles of the Patapsco River. Families can participate in many activities in the park: hiking 170 miles of trails, mountain biking on the multiuse trails, horseback riding, swimming, canoeing and kayaking, camping, fishing, and picnicking.

Before leaving the Orange Grove recreational area of Patapsco, you and your children should walk on the swinging bridge. It replicates a suspension bridge that connected mill workers' homes and the flourmill on the Baltimore County side of the river. From 1856 to 1905, it was the largest mill in the Mid-Atlantic region and produced flour that was in high demand in the United States and in Europe. A fire destroyed the mill in 1905. Hurricane Agnes destroyed what was remaining of the burnt shell in 1972. All that's left these days is a retaining wall. In this southern section of the park, which is rich with outdoor activities, you can enjoy Bloedes Dam via the River or Grist Mill trails (both paved), as well as picnic areas, playgrounds, tubing (bring your own), and swimming.

The 2.2-mile Cascade Falls Trail is the primary route described here; however, you can choose to hike a shorter 1-mile loop to the falls instead. The Cascade Falls Trail can be accessed either at the beginning or end of a one-way looped parking lot. From the back of the parking lot, access the trail via the River Trail, a paved trail that extends to Bloedes Dam. Turn left onto the trail at the large "Cascade Falls Trail" sign, and hike at the edge of the woods along the parking lot. Or access the trail via stairs adjacent to the bathrooms; it curves to the right and intersects the one from the back of the parking lot. Turn left and walk uphill along the split-rail fence to the intersection with the loop. Since this loop is

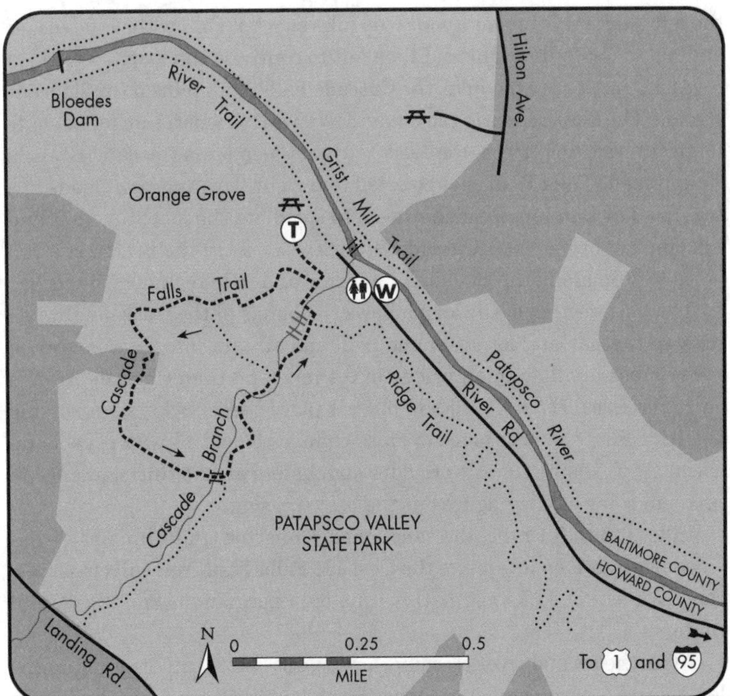

described counterclockwise, turn right at this large intersection, and walk toward the shell of an old building.

The first 0.2 mile ascends steeply up a ridge. A people's choice trail intersects from the left; however, the Department of Natural Resources, the park's management agency, has posted a "trail closed" sign here and at the other end on top of the ridge. As you hike this loop, you bypass a number of people's choice trails that either leave the loop or bisect it to create a shortcut like this one. Hike up the steep ridge past a large beech tree with many exposed roots. The trail curves to the left and reaches a flat spot at the top.

Turn right and hike on a flat trail for a few hundred yards before it descends toward and through a gulch and back up the opposite side. Continue to ascend this ridgeline finger, which began above the parking lot, and ignore a people's choice trail that intersects from the right when the trail levels off. Another people's choice trail appears 0.1 mile farther where the trail curves left. At 0.6 miles, a connector trail intersects on the left—take this to make your loop hike shorter. Follow the blue blazes and an arrow to the right and then left to continue the loop.

At 1.2 miles into the hike, the Cascade Falls Trail joins a small feeder stream. The trail curves to the left and follows it downstream for 0.4 mile to an intersection. Here, the feeder stream also joins Cascade Branch. The Cascade Falls Trail goes both left and right. Turning right leads to a trailhead at Landing Road; however, to complete the loop, turn left and hike on the bridge over Cascade Branch. Just after the bridge is a fun place to stop along the stream for a picnic and to hop among the rocks.

This last section of the loop follows the banks of the Cascade Branch back to the parking lot. After the trail and stream intersections at 1.6 miles, cross another small bridge in 0.1 mile and then Cascade Branch on rocks. Because trail builders did not place these rocks, this crossing is tricky. Plus the best place to cross changes based on water level and speed. At the same time, it provides youngsters an exciting challenge to problem solve as they figure out the best crossing.

In less than 0.1 mile, the sanctioned connector trail (unnamed) that shortens your loop intersects the Cascade Falls Trail. You will cross Cascade Branch on rocks again, this time on a permanent and purposeful route.

After the second river crossing, a people's choice trail emerges on the left to access large boulders along the streambank for some fun climbing; continue straight, following the blue blazes. Within the next 0.1

Rock hopping across Cascade Branch is a fun challenge for youngsters.

mile, pass a small waterfall. Soon after, the orange-blazed Ridge Trail intersects the Cascade Falls Trail from the right. Continue on the Cascade Falls Trail to the left and down rock steps to the second, larger waterfall, Cascade Falls. This section is limited to hikers, as opposed to most of the loop, which is multiuse and a popular mountain biking trail.

The second falls is a great place for kids to have some adventures. A large pool of water in the streambed below the falls is laden with boulders for scrambling. The Cascade Falls Trail crosses on the rocks, marked by blue blazes, in front of the waterfall.

Before you complete the loop in 0.1 mile, a steep people's choice trail on the right leads to another cascade and more boulders. Upon reaching the loop's beginning, hike straight with the split-rail fence on the right. To access the restrooms, turn right on the hiking-only connector trail after the fence ends and return to the parking lot.

CUNNINGHAM FALLS

BEFORE YOU GO
Map: Available at the entrance station for a small fee and on the park's website
Contact: Cunningham Falls State Park (charges a fee)
Nearest city: Thurmont, MD

ABOUT THE HIKE
Moderate/difficult, year-round
Length: 1.3 miles, loop
Hiking time: 1½–2 hours
High point/elevation gain: 1362 feet/250 feet
Access: Compact soil, rock, and crushed stone; not passable for jogging strollers

GETTING THERE

From I-495 (Capital Beltway), exit for I-270. Drive 28 miles; keep left for US 15 north. Drive 16 miles to the exit for MD 77. Turn right onto MD 77, heading west, and drive 3 miles. Turn left onto Catoctin Hollow Road, and turn right onto William Houck Drive into the park. The trailhead parking lot is on the left after the entrance station.

ON THE TRAIL

Cunningham Falls State Park is nestled on the eastern ridge of Catoctin Mountain. Catoctin Mountain is part of the first ridgeline that rises

Scaling giant boulders on the Cliff Trail

above the Piedmont Plateau and stretches into Virginia and Pennsylvania. Two parks cover this mountain: Cunningham Falls, a state park, and Catoctin Mountain Park, a national park. Both parks offer 47 miles of great trails that provide access to beautiful physical features like the falls in Cunningham and the rocky vistas in Catoctin. Cunningham offers a beach and lifeguards during the summer at Hunting Creek Lake, along with boat rentals, a bathhouse, picnic tables, and a campground. The lake is stocked with fish and Big Hunting Creek offers fishing as well.

The Cliff and Lower trails in Cunningham Falls State Park make a wonderful playground for kids because of the boulders that litter this loop hike. These trails offer families either a challenging loop hike, described here, or an easy out-and-back hike on the Lower Trail. Whichever you choose, your final destination is the falls.

The hike begins from the parking lot on the left side of William Houck Drive. Take the Cliff Trail, which forks to the left behind the kiosk, following the yellow blazes painted on trees or yellow triangles nailed to trees. The trail immediately rises steeply for 50 feet before the slope becomes gentler. The first half mile of the Cliff Trail rises 250 feet before it begins its descent toward the falls. The trail zigzags uphill around large trees and house-sized boulders, which requires hikers to pay attention to the single and double yellow blazes on trees and rocks. These large boulders, made of metabasalt, were formed more than 200

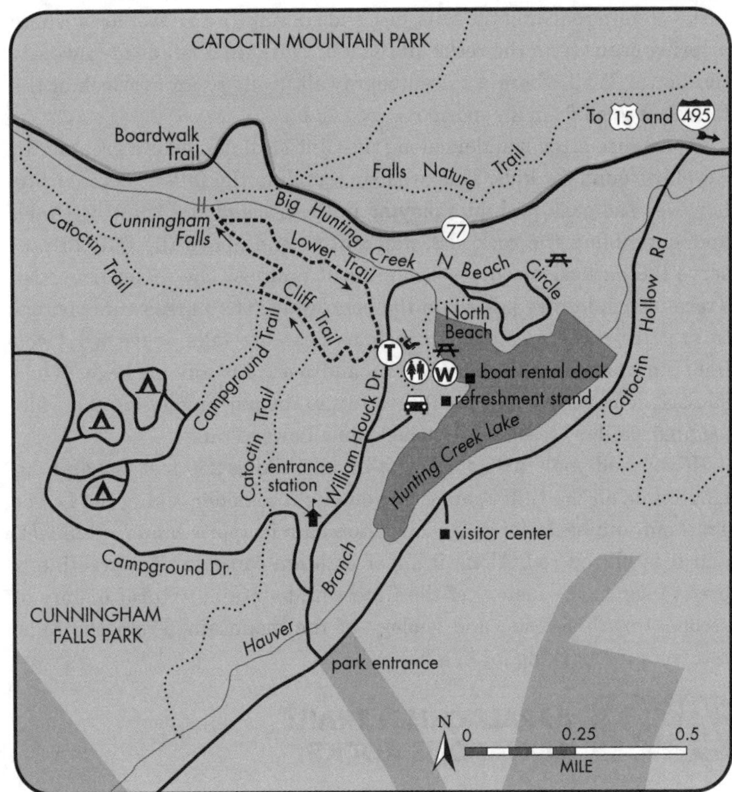

million years ago from volcanoes that inhabited the Appalachian range. It is hard to believe that the Appalachian Mountains, the oldest in the world, once resembled the Himalayas.

After you pass a couple of enormous boulders while hiking uphill on the Cliff Trail, the blue-blazed Catoctin Trail intersects from the left. At this intersection, both yellow and blue blazes mark the Cliff Trail to its crest. There, the orange-blazed Campground Trail intersects from the left. The Catoctin Trail continues straight uphill, and the Cliff veers right downhill; stay on the Cliff Trail.

The short 0.3-mile descent requires you to pay careful attention to foot placement as you maneuver across the rock outcroppings. This section allows children easy access to climb and feel like the king or queen of a rock. Pay attention to the yellow blazes; the double ones indicate turns. Before reaching the falls, descend six steps into a wet area where a spring seeps from the rocks on the left. The Cliff Trail dead-ends into the Lower Trail where a raised boardwalk leads to an overlook of the falls that gush from an enormous rock slab.

The house-sized boulders along the Cliff Trail make for a great natural playground for kids. This area surrounding the falls looks inviting; however, the park prohibits playing in the pools of Big Hunting Creek and scrambling the rock slab adjacent to and above the falls to preserve the natural resources and prevent injuries. The seven Leave No Trace principles are posted on the boardwalk. The park wants visitors to practice three particular principles near the falls: leave what you find, stay on the trail (boardwalk), and pack out any garbage. When you are done observing the falls, return to the parking lot via the wide, jogging-stroller-accessible, crushed stone Lower Trail.

If you and your little ones can't handle hiking 250 feet elevation in a half mile on the Cliff Trail, then you might consider hiking the Lower Trail out and back. Its gentle elevation gain is approximately 125 feet, and it is blazed red. Along it, older children can read its three interpretive signs: the history of the Catoctin Mountain, natural history of second-growth forests, and geology of the mountain. From the falls, return to the parking lot in a half mile.

BEFORE YOU GO
Map: Available through the Potomac Appalachian Trail Club
Contact: Appalachian Trail: Annapolis Rocks
Nearest city: Myersville, MD

ABOUT THE HIKE
Difficult, year-round
Length: 5.4 miles, out and back
Hiking time: 3½–4 hours
High point/elevation gain: 1778 feet/640 feet
Access: Compact soil and rock, not passable for jogging strollers

GETTING THERE

From I-495 (Capital Beltway), exit for I-270. Drive 28 miles, and take exit 32 for I-70 west toward Hagerstown. Drive 11 miles, and take exit 42 for MD 17 toward Myersville. Turn right onto MD 17 (Myersville Road). Drive 0.7 mile, and turn right to stay on MD 17 (Wolfsville Road). Drive 0.4 mile, and turn left onto MD 40 (Baltimore National Pike). Drive 3 miles. The parking lot for the Appalachian Trail trailhead is on the left.

ON THE TRAIL

This out-and-back hike on the Appalachian Trail (AT) is one of a few that provide families with spectacular views from atop a ridgeline. Your hiking destination is a large rock outcropping that hangs on the western ridge—a perfect place to bask in the warm afternoon sun. The stacked metamorphic boulders boast climbing routes with various degrees of challenge and multiple flat spots to sit on and enjoy a picnic while taking in the excellent views of the valley below, including Greenbrier Lake.

The trailhead is at the western edge of the parking lot on the highway. Hike the former highway for 100 yards. Before the guardrail, turn left at the blue blaze on the dirt trail. The trail leads to the edge of Interstate 70 and the pedestrian bridge over the highway, which leads hikers south toward Harpers Ferry on the AT. Walk down a few steps, and turn right (north) on the AT, which is blazed in white. Hike along I-70 for a couple hundred yards and under the MD 40 overpass. The trail turns away from the interstate, and the hum of cars and trucks soon gives way to the sounds of the forest.

At the top of a short but steep hill sits a kiosk welcoming hikers to the AT. This kiosk answers common questions about the AT, encourages hikers to reduce their impact on the environment, and educates them about what to do if they encounter bears and poisonous snakes, neither of which is common.

The trail turns left and levels off as it traverses a skinny spit of land between the highway and private land. Much of the AT sits on a sliver of federally protected land that runs from Georgia to Maine. In 1968, President Lyndon B. Johnson signed the National Trails System Act into law to create national scenic trails and protect the land around them. The AT and the Pacific Crest Trail (PCT) were the first two national scenic trails. Today, there are eleven national scenic trails in the US national trails system, which includes 60,000 miles of trails.

The trail enters a wide span of forest where it starts to gain elevation again. After you walk under power lines, a blue-blazed trail to the Pine Knob Shelter appears on the left. Shelters are provided for backpackers

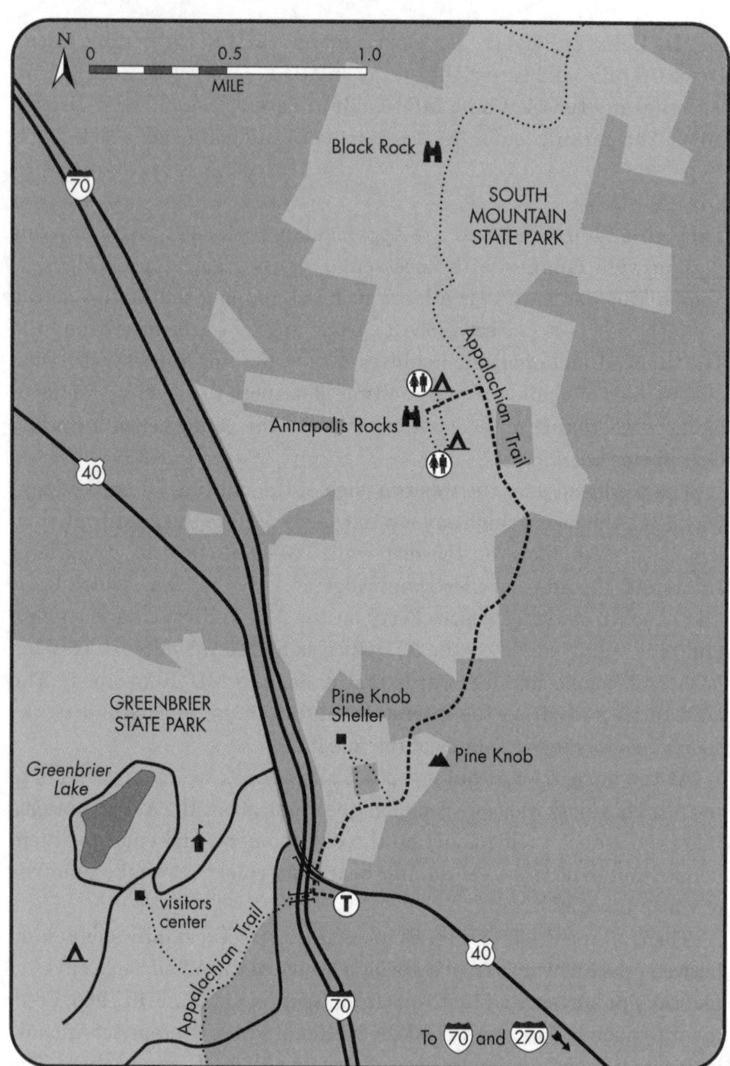

and thru-hikers about every 10 miles along the entire 2170 miles of the AT. There is another entrance to the shelter ahead for those walking south on the AT.

After the trail to the shelter, the main trail makes a few switchbacks uphill to settle into a straight path up to the crest of Pine Knob, gaining

At the trailhead for the Appalachian Trail on Route 40

more than 200 feet in elevation, the steepest stretch of the hike. The tread is full of loose rocks and multiple check dams to slow down erosion. Reaching the crest, the trail levels off for a few hundred yards and then descends 100 feet, skirting the back side of the crest to Annapolis Rocks. During winter, the ridge crest is visible to the left. To the right, rock outcroppings dot the ridge's eastern ridgeline, providing a view of the Catoctin ridge and the valley below. There are short people's choice trails to many of the outcroppings, which provide respite or an imaginative natural playgrounds for kids.

Along the AT here, red and chestnut oaks populate the stunted canopy and survive well on the dry and often windswept ridge. Black cherry dominates the understory; however, many reach the height of the oaks. Mountain laurel, which displays large, pink blooms in May, fills the understory in scattered locations along the trail and impedes a deep view into the forest.

Hike a mile of level trail on the ridge until you reach the blue-blazed trail and sign to Annapolis Rocks. Turn left and hike a quarter mile to the exposed rocks on the western ridge. After hiking 2.7 miles to get here, you and your family will enjoy the western views and chance to relax.

Before Annapolis Rocks became a formal campground, the area was known as the worst along the AT in terms of environmental impact from users. Backpackers, families, and Boy Scout groups flocked here on weekends, sometimes in the hundreds, pitching tents wherever there was a flat spot. The ground became devoid of vegetation (except for large trees), makeshift fire pits littered the area, and toilet paper flowers blew in the wind. The once-beautiful area was denuded, ugly, and smelly. The Maryland Department of Natural Resources, in partnership with the Potomac Appalachian Trail Club and the Appalachian Trail Conservancy, cleaned up the area, created designated campsites with trails, and built two composting privies. Today, the area has mostly returned to its natural state, except for the fencing that lines both sides of the trail close to the rocks. This area was so heavily impacted that it has taken years for natural succession to occur.

Annapolis Rocks has eleven primitive campsites and three group sites for backpackers, providing camping for seventy-five people. Camping is allowed here year-round without a permit. The campground has a spring. From May to October, a "ridge runner" inhabits the campground as its caretaker, educating campers on Leave No Trace and helping backpackers.

Even though you can hear the rush of cars on I-70 below and the occasional noise pollution from a drag racing track, Annapolis Rocks is a gem for camping, rock climbing, or breathing in the fresh air and absorbing afternoon sun.

When you are ready, reverse direction and return to the AT on the blue-blazed trail, then walk south 2.7 miles downhill. If you and your kids feel adventurous and have lots of energy, continue north on the AT from the blue-blazed Annapolis Rocks trail for a mile to Black Rock, another beautiful outcropping of boulders that is even more exposed. The out-and-back extends the total mileage to 7.4 miles with no additional elevation gain.

Opposite: Happy hikers having fun on the rocks at Bears Den

VIRGINIA

ARLINGTON, FAIRFAX, AND PRINCE WILLIAM COUNTIES

RIVERBEND PARK

BEFORE YOU GO
Map: Available at the visitor center
Contact: Riverbend Park
Nearest city: Great Falls, VA

ABOUT THE HIKE
Moderate, year-round
Length: 2.5 miles, loop
Hiking time: 2–2½ hours
High point/elevation change: 270 feet/290 feet
Access: Asphalt, compact soil, and gravel; not passable for jogging strollers

GETTING THERE

From I-495 (Capital Beltway), take exit 44 for VA 193 (Georgetown Pike). Turn right onto Georgetown Pike. Drive 4.5 miles, and turn right onto River Bend Road. Drive 2.2 miles, and turn right onto Jeffery Road. Drive 0.8 mile, turn right onto Potomac Hills Street, and drive to the end of the street. Park near visitor center on the left.

ON THE TRAIL

Riverbend Park is a cousin to Great Falls Park, also in Virginia, minus the crowds. It is an appealing alternative, particularly on a beautiful spring or fall day. Just north of its cousin on the Potomac River, Riverbend offers the same river scenery and great hikes through a variety of ecosystems native to the Potomac Gorge. Riverbend has six trails, some of which connect to create loops and others of which are out and back, such as the Potomac Heritage Trail (PHT). The PHT connects Riverbend and Great Falls, making an excellent long day hike with older children along the Potomac River.

The beautiful sunny deck of the Riverbend Visitor Center is a perfect place to relax in one of the many Adirondack chairs and watch the Potomac River flow by. Pack a lunch to eat at one of the many picnic tables on the grounds or on the deck. The visitor center offers public restrooms and sells cold drinks, ice cream, and fishing supplies. Inside, you can read displays about the area's natural, cultural, and geologic history and watch critters such as a copperhead and a black rat snake, a gray tree frog, and a five-lined skink in glass aquariums. On weekends, Riverbend Park offers kayak and canoe rentals for those who

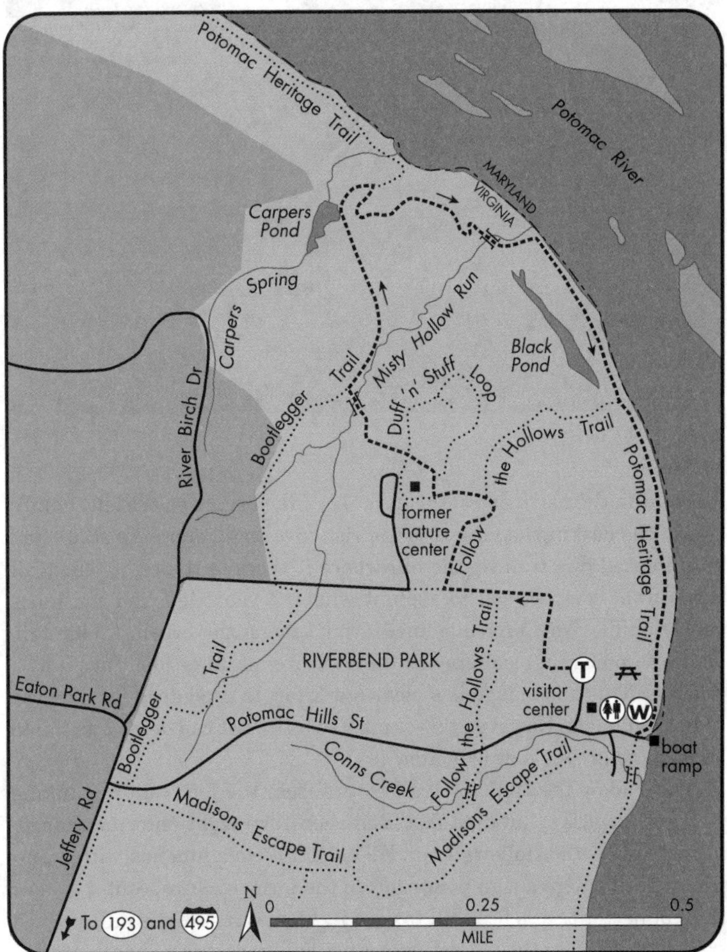

want to explore the water. The park's boat ramp on the Potomac River is always accessible to paddlers who own a boat. Whichever way you want to explore—by hiking, biking, or paddling—Riverbend Park offers multiple opportunities for you to create your own adventures along the Potomac River.

Hiking the Bootlegger Trail and the PHT via the Follow the Hollows and some connector trails offers a wonderful, moderate hike for families. This loop explores upland forests and forested floodplains along the

A five-lined skink

Potomac in the north end of the park. The hike begins on the left (uphill) side of the parking lot closest to the visitor center. Follow the stairs and an unblazed dirt trail up the hill where it veers to the right. The trail turns from compact soil to asphalt where it veers left and continues gently uphill. Watch for five-lined skink among the brush. A blue tail, which becomes charcoal gray as the creature matures, identifies it as a juvenile. This appendage is a clear mark for its predators, such as the red-tailed hawk. However, this skink has a trick: it can detach its tail to escape and grow a new one later.

The Follow the Hollows Trail enters from the left; continue hiking straight for a few hundred feet, and then turn right onto the orange-blazed Follow the Hollows Trail. Hike 0.2 mile to a junction with a connector trail where a sign points left to the former nature center. Follow this connector trail left uphill toward it. At the crest of the hill, a paved trail curves left to the old nature center. Follow this paved path around to the right of the center to the Duff 'n' Stuff Trail. Riverbend Park used to house its nature center in this building until it moved all the animals and displays to the visitor center; Fairfax County now rents this building for private functions.

A short distance along Duff 'n' Stuff, you may notice a former raptor house adjacent to the trail. The county used to rescue injured raptors and house them here. Now Riverbend Park has only a few taxidermic creatures (barred and great horned owls, a wood duck, Canadian goose, and turkey vulture) at the visitor center. Within 200 feet after the birdhouse, turn left off the paved path onto a connector trail marked with a green arrow signpost. Follow this unblazed trail downhill toward a bridge. After the bridge, this connector trail intersects the Bootlegger Trail. Turn right and follow the red blazes. The Bootlegger and connector trails used to be known as the Paw Paw Passage Trail because of the paw paw trees that line them and others in the upland forest. A native understory tree, the paw paw has large, lime-green, smooth-edged oval leaves. This tree produces a fall fruit commonly eaten by Native Americans. Many children liken its looks to that of a pear.

Hike a third of a mile downhill to a small pond at the base of two adjoining hills. Take a break here for a drink and a snack on one of the three docks that extend into the pond. Sit quietly and catch a glimpse of or listen to the twang of green frogs or the croak of bullfrogs that inhabit this pond. In spring, egg sacks and tadpoles of the wood and gray tree frogs can be found in the water. The kiosk adjacent to the pond displays information about common animals that make this forest their home.

After a rest, continue the journey on the Bootlegger Trail for a very short distance to a signpost and trail map where it ends. Continuing straight on the PHT would take you to the river's edge and then north along the Potomac; instead, make a sharp right uphill on the turquoise-blazed PHT. On the crest of this hill, an old kiosk and a people's choice trail appear on the right; continue straight on the PHT as it switchbacks downhill.

At the bottom of the hill, continue down the stairs and over the small feeder stream with a split-rail fence on the left. The PHT used to cut through the floodplain on the opposite side of the fence. However, the county rerouted the trail over the bluff because this floodplain is home to some threatened and native plant species. These plant species uniquely grow together in this floodplain due to occasional flooding by the Potomac and are threatened when humans step on them and carry invasive plant seeds into the area. Therefore, the park has permanently closed this area to people.

The last mile of this loop follows along the Potomac's edge on the turquoise-blazed PHT. Along this section, you can access the river's edge in several places. In addition, two benches along the trail are great for bird-watching. The park naturalists have placed tree identification cards adjacent to various trees that are both common in and unique to the forested floodplains. The Follow the Hollows Trail intersects the PHT; continue on the PHT until you reach the visitor center.

RIVER AND MATILDAVILLE LOOP

BEFORE YOU GO
Map: Available at the entrance station and on the park's website
Contact: Great Falls Park (charges a fee)
Nearest city: Great Falls, VA

ABOUT THE HIKE
Moderate/difficult, year-round
Length: 2.75 miles, loop
Hiking time: 2 hours
High point/elevation gain: 186 feet/110 feet
Access: Compact soil and rock, not passable for jogging strollers

GETTING THERE

From I-495 (Capital Beltway), take exit 44 for VA 193 (Georgetown Pike). Drive 4 miles, and turn right onto Old Dominion Drive (VA 738). Drive 0.5 mile to the park entrance, and park behind the visitor center.

ON THE TRAIL

Great Falls Park and its sibling across the Potomac River, the Chesapeake and Ohio Canal National Historical Park, are the best locations to view Great Falls and each provides a unique perspective of the falls. Great Falls Park has three observational decks. The first is closest to the visitor center, while the third is farthest from it and allows the best overall view.

The land around the falls has been a major attraction for thousands of years, from serving as a trading location for the Powhatan and Iroquois tribes, to acting as a site for milling and electricity generation, to housing an amusement park during the first half of the 20th century. In 1966, the National Park Service purchased the land from Pepco and Fairfax County to establish a national park. In 1972, Hurricane Agnes destroyed the carousel, one of the last remnants of the amusement park.

If your family has lots of energy, you can extend this hike another 1.5 miles (for a total of 4.25 miles) by continuing farther south and looping back; see the extension directions below. This longer route takes about another hour and a half and adds about 260 feet of elevation gain to the journey.

On beautiful warm weekends, cars are stacked for a long distance at this popular destination's fee entrance station. Once you enter the park, drive to the parking lot beyond the visitor center. The visitor center has a few caged, live animals; a theater; natural and cultural history displays of Great Falls; and a bookstore. The snack bar is open from spring to fall.

To begin your adventurous hike, walk between the two pillars of the H-shaped visitor center. Turn left and cross a small bridge over the Patowmack Canal onto the Patowmack Trail. The first observation deck for the falls is just after the bridge to the left of the main path. The other two observation points are south along the Patowmak Trail. To access the River Trail, pass the third observation area on the left, and walk 100 yards. Turn left on the River Trail, and hike toward the river.

The River Trail follows the Potomac River as the river enters and flows through the Mather Gorge. The steep metamorphic rock walls on both sides of the river squeeze the Potomac from 1000 feet wide above the falls to 100 feet wide in the gorge, forcing millions of gallons of water through the mile-long channel. The first 0.1 mile on the River Trail is dirt covered, then the trail begins to weave up, over, and around rocks that poke through the ground. Within the first half mile of the River Trail, kids will discover great rocks to climb and scramble on and places to sit atop the rocks and watch the rushing river below. They can also look and listen for frogs beside a vernal pool and discover how the force of water can erode rock to create a pothole.

Just after the trail skirts the edge of the gorge, about 0.4 mile from the trailhead, it hooks to the right and intersects the Patowmack Trail again on the right. However, continue left on the River Trail down and up the stairs and over a bridge. After climbing the stairs, head to the edge of the cliff, where you can watch kayakers paddle a series of waves in the river below, particularly on weekends. Atop the stairs, a double green blaze on a large tree directs hikers to veer right. For the next quarter mile, the trail zigzags among the rocks, providing another opportunity to peer over the edge to the river below. The trail can be wet and muddy in this section, and puncheons help keep your feet dry.

The River Trail makes a sharp turn to the right at a split-rail fence. A trail goes straight, but it dead-ends where the Patowmack Canal enters the Potomac; park rangers have placed a caution sign here to discourage people from venturing onto this peninsula, encourage revitalization of plant life, and reduce erosion. Follow the River Trail right into an open area and across the Patowmack Canal. Turn left at this third

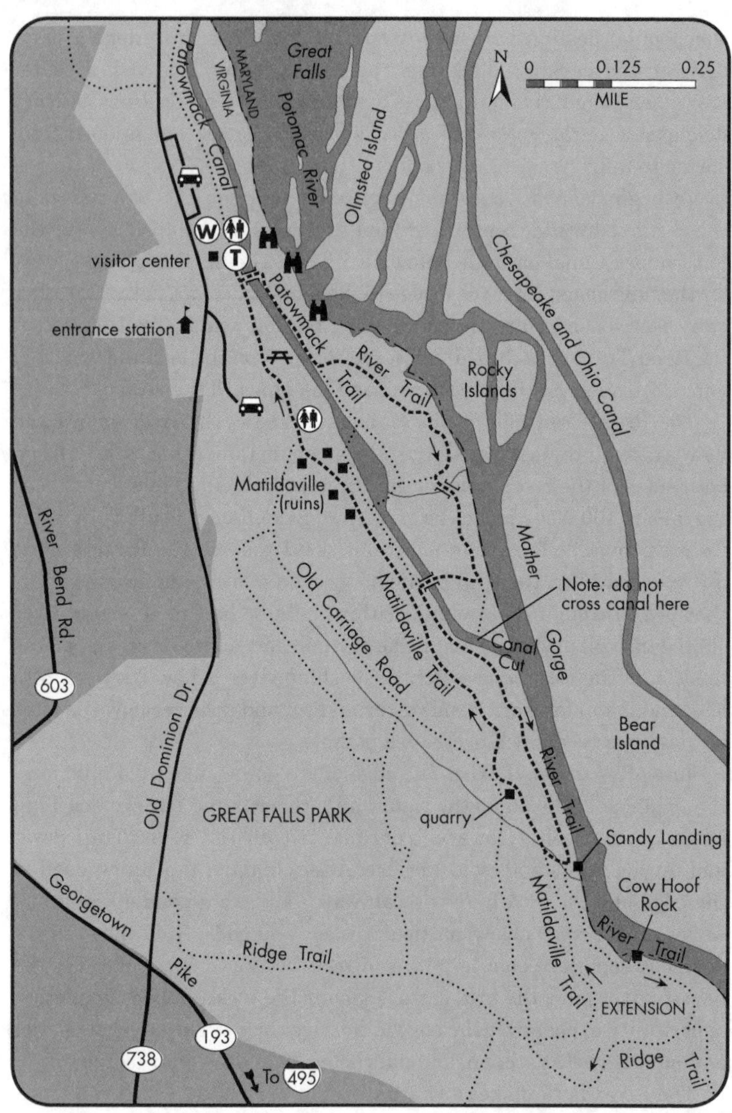

intersection with the Patowmack Trail to continue following the River Trail southeast. Stay on the trail above the canal; a lower trail provides a close view of the steep canal walls as it enters the Potomac. The lower trail joins the upper one a few hundred feet down the trail. The trail

S curves for the next quarter mile, passing spots close to the river, great rock formations, and vernal pools.

The River Trail hits a steep bedrock wall and makes a quick zigzag to the right and then left. It skirts the cliff edge with the river below on the left and the metamorphic wall rising steeply on the right. Kids have to use both hands and feet to traverse the rocky terrain for about 100 yards. Then cross a long bridge over a vernal pool situated between two walls of rock. The trail used to climb the wall of rock closest to the river, but rangers installed the bridge, creating a safer passage and reducing the environmental impact.

Within 0.1 mile, the River Trail intersects the paved road that leads to Sandy Landing, an important access point for the Fairfax County Fire Department to the Mather Gorge and Great Falls because each year, seven people on average drown in this 14-mile stretch of the Potomac River between Great Falls and Key Bridge. At the base of the landing, the river has deposited a lot of sand and freshwater clam shells. At this point, turn right onto the paved road, which quickly becomes dirt again. Within 0.2 mile, the Matildaville Trail intersects from the left, and you reach the quarry, a grass-covered open space great for eating a picnic lunch, playing a game of tag, or throwing a Frisbee. Stone was mined from this quarry to build the walls and locks of the Patowmack Canal.

PATOWMACK CANAL: BYPASSING GREAT FALLS

The Patowmack Company, a joint venture by Maryland and Virginia legislators, began building the canal in 1785 and finished it in 1802. George Washington conceived the idea; he wanted to link transportation and commerce between the east and west. However, the Potomac River falls 600 feet in elevation from Cumberland to the Chesapeake Bay, making it difficult to navigate. Canals were built along the Potomac to help boats navigate difficult terrain like Great Falls.

Indentured servants and slaves built Patowmack Canal over seventeen years. The endeavor was difficult due to the engineering needed to build five locks to drop 80 feet in less than a mile, along with drastic changes in water level due to rains and droughts, labor disputes, and financial problems. When the canal was finished, it served as a trade corridor for whiskey, flour, firearms, iron, hardware, clothing, and tobacco for twenty-six years before the Patowmack Company went broke and the Chesapeake and Ohio Company purchased it.

Leaving the quarry, turn right on the Matildaville Trail, and follow it gently uphill as it curves to the left and follows the top of the ridgeline. When the trees lack foliage, you will have a good view of the river, the River Trail below on the right, and another ridgeline of trees far off to the left. With foliage, the forest is dense with paw paw trees in the understory.

Hike a half mile from the quarry to the intersection with the Patowmack Trail. Stay left and continue to follow the Matildaville Trail for 0.2 mile to the restrooms and the intersection with the Old Carriage Road. You can view the ruins of the town of Matildaville in this last section of the Matildaville Trail.

MATILDAVILLE

The founder of the Patowmack Company, Henry Lee, established and built Matildaville in the late seventeenth century. He was the father of Robert E. Lee, the commanding general of the Confederate Army during the Civil War. Matildaville, a thriving town for three decades, supported the construction and maintenance of the canal, but it was abandoned when the Patowmack Company fell on hard times and was taken over by the Chesapeake and Ohio Company. Chimneys, front stoops, and foundations are all that is left of this short-lived boom town.

After visiting the site of Matildaville, turn right on the Old Carriage Road, and follow it a quarter mile back to the visitor center. This last quarter-mile section is grassy with shade trees and filled with picnic tables and grills. On beautiful sunny days, this area is filled with picnicking families.

Extension

Families with older children who would like a longer, more challenging hike can extend this trip by 1.5 miles and an additional 260 feet of elevation. The River and Matildaville trails both extend beyond Sandy Landing and connect via the Ridge Trail farther south. This extension requires kids to climb a short but steep ridge face, but it provides one of the most spectacular views of the Mather Gorge looking north.

To access this extension from the River Trail, cross the paved road that leads to Sandy Landing, and rejoin the River Trail through a split-rail cattle fence. Within 100 feet, cross a small cascading feeder stream on a bridge. For the next 0.2 mile, the trail tread is dirt covered, wide, and level. Within 0.2 mile, the Matildaville Trail joins the River Trail on the right; continue straight on the River Trail. Just before the trail gets rocky, an old fireplace is visible to the left. Kids can climb on boulders along the Potomac here. From the old chimney to Cow Hoof Rock, the trail has been realigned, so pay attention to the green blazes on the trees. Shortly after the old chimney, the trail rises steeply to Cow Hoof Rock and then to an intersection with the Ridge Trail. Large, flat Cow Hoof Rock sticks precariously over the edge, looking down at Purplehorse Beach across the river 400 feet below and north into the Mather Gorge.

Looking down at the Potomac River's Mather Gorge

The River Trail dead-ends into the Ridge Trail. Turn right and follow the ridgetop as it undulates for a half mile. A people's choice trail appears on the left just before the Ridge Trail intersects the Old Carriage Road; continue straight. At the next intersection, turn right on the Old Carriage Road, and then take another immediate right onto the Matildaville Trail to make a 180-degree turn. The Matildaville Trail descends the ridge back toward the Potomac. While descending 20 steps along a gulch, the trail makes a big curve to the left, eventually running parallel to the river again. This extension makes a large oblong loop with the beginning of the River and end of the Matildaville trails running parallel within feet of each other.

At the bottom of the ridge, the River Trail joins the Matildaville Trail on the right. Continue straight on the Matildaville past the cascading feeder stream on the right. Within 100 yards, the Matildaville Trail intersects the road to Sandy Landing. Turn left and head toward the quarry to play.

DIFFICULT RUN AND RIDGE TRAILS

BEFORE YOU GO
Map: Available on the park's website
Contact: Great Falls Park (charges a fee)
Nearest city: Great Falls, VA

ABOUT THE HIKE
Moderate/difficult, year-round
Length: 3.5 miles, loop
Hiking time: 2–2½ hours
High point/elevation gain: 328 feet/272 feet
Access: Compact soil, not passable for jogging strollers

GETTING THERE

From I-495 (Capital Beltway), take exit 44 for VA 193 (Georgetown Pike). Turn right onto Georgetown Pike. Drive 3.5 miles, and turn left into the parking lot after the bridge over Difficult Run.

ON THE TRAIL

The Difficult Run and Ridge Trail loop is located in the southern section of Great Falls Park. You could park at the Main Visitor Center and hike this loop, but that would be an 8-mile loop via the River, Ridge, Difficult Run, and Matildaville or Old Carriage Road trails. This 3.5-mile loop allows families with younger children to hike the southern section of the park.

This shorter hike used to be passable for jogging strollers; however, in 2012 heavy rains eroded the tread on a huge section of the Difficult Run Trail—in one place washing all the soil from the trail, leaving the bedrock exposed. The trail is now difficult to traverse: Hikers have to either climb a people's choice trail up the steep ridge 25 feet or climb down and up the exposed rock for 15 feet. Either way, it is now an obstacle. The National Park Service plans to rebuild and reinforce the trail during the fall of 2014. After that time, the hike will be jogging-stroller passable. Contact Great Falls Park for current trail conditions.

The hike begins at the southern end of the parking lot adjacent to Difficult Run. Follow the green blazes of the Difficult Run Trail along the stream for 100 yards, and then turn left, hiking away from the run and parallel to the road. At the left turn, a people's choice trail continues straight and follows the run; however, it is constantly flooded, muddy, and difficult to follow. Follow the green-blazed sanctioned trail that runs parallel to the road for a quarter mile until you reach the bridge. Here, the people's choice trail intersects from the right. Hike under the bridge, and follow the trail 100 feet to where it meets a dirt road and a trail sign. Emergency vehicles use this wider road, still Difficult Run Trail, to access the Potomac River.

This wide section of the Difficult Run Trail continues with the run on the right and the steep ridge walls to the left. Difficult Run is one of the prettier streams in the region to hike along because of the large boulders that line the banks and bed, creating small cascades in its final 1.5-mile descent to the Potomac River. These boulders are a great natural playground for kids; one such area can be easily accessed within a quarter mile of the trail sign. A good portion of this hike on the Difficult Run Trail looks down upon the cascading stream.

The trail was washed away a half mile from the trail sign; it can be traversed but with caution. After the washout, the trail gains gentle elevation, while the run descends toward the Potomac. About 0.4 mile from the washout, Difficult Run Trail intersects the Ridge Trail at a trail sign. Here, you can choose to turn right and descend the ridge to a waterfall and an outcropping of rocks along the run if you like. From this intersection, hike straight on the Difficult Run Trail until it dead-ends at the Potomac River, a quarter mile down the trail.

Viewing the waterfall on Difficult Run

At the mouth of Difficult Run, the trail has been heavily eroded away. You can access the point, but you must scramble on hands and feet among rocks, tree roots, and felled trees. If they have good gross motor skills, kids will love the challenge this obstacle provides. At the point, the Potomac has left the Mather Gorge and widened. It is fun to watch kayakers play in the waves of the Maryland Chutes here. Though the river looks placid at the mouth of Difficult Run, it has a strong undertow and swift invisible currents.

To finish the loop, scramble back and hike uphill to the intersection with the Ridge Trail. At the intersection, turn right onto the Ridge Trail and hike uphill to the top of the ridge overlooking the Potomac. The Ridge Trail comes to a T intersection. Turning right will lead you above the point where Difficult Run and the Potomac meet, providing a nice view through the trees. To continue the loop, turn left and continue walking uphill until you reach a small open area with a horse corral and

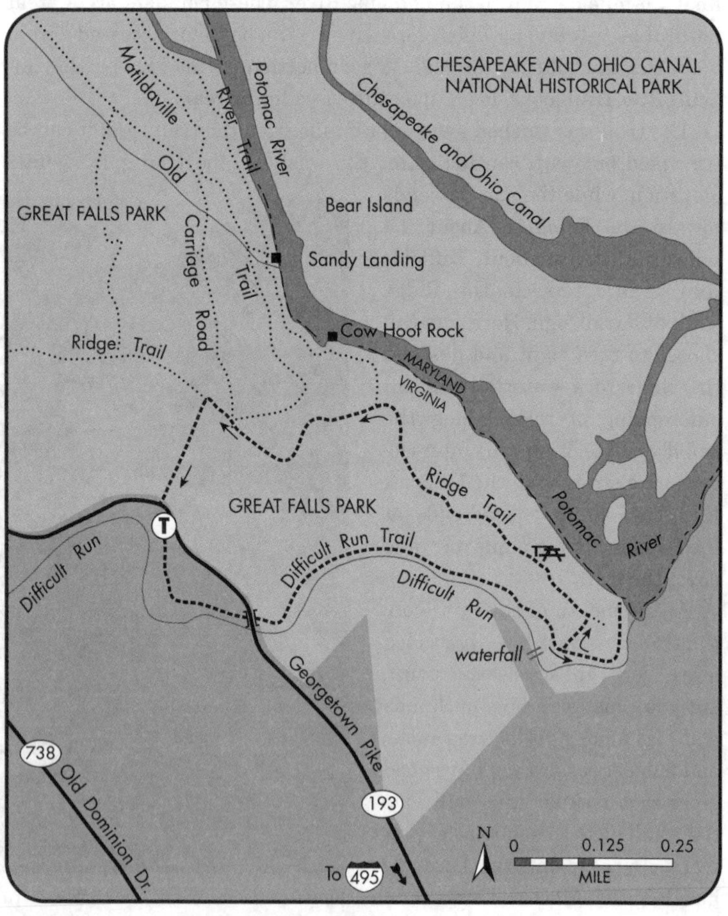

a picnic table. (The Difficult Run, Ridge, and Old Carriage Road trails are all horse trails in Great Falls Park.) From this rest stop, continue hiking on the Ridge Trail. The wide trail follows the rolling contours of the ridgetop.

In a quarter mile, the River Trail intersects the Ridge Trail on the right. Pass it and continue hiking a quarter mile to the three-way intersection with the Old Carriage Road and the Matildaville Trail. Stay on the Ridge Trail by walking down nine steps, crossing the Old Carriage Road, and heading up the berm. In 0.1 mile, a people's choice trail appears on the left at half of a split-rail fence and a couple of large stumps sitting on the right side of the Ridge Trail. Turn left on the people's choice trail, and walk 0.3 mile to Georgetown Pike and the trailhead parking lot. Be very careful crossing Georgetown Pike; there is no crosswalk on this heavily traveled road. To discover more of Difficult Run and its trail, you can hike north along the run from the entrance to the parking lot.

SCOTTS RUN NATURE PRESERVE

BEFORE YOU GO
Map: Not available online or at the park
Contact: Scotts Run Nature Preserve
Nearest city: McLean, VA

ABOUT THE HIKE
Moderate, year-round
Length: 3.2 miles, loop
Hiking time: 2–2½ hours
High point/elevation gain: 341 feet/240 feet
Access: Compact soil; passable for jogging strollers; water shoes recommended in warm weather

GETTING THERE

From I-495 (Capital Beltway), take exit 44 for VA 193 (Georgetown Pike). Turn right onto Georgetown Pike. Drive 0.6 mile, and turn right into the second Scotts Run parking lot across from Swinks Mill Road.

ON THE TRAIL

Scotts Run Nature Preserve, a 336-acre preserve that buttresses the Potomac River, contains some of DC's oldest trees. It was established

Hikers scramble on rock to view the waterfall at the end of Scotts Run.

in 1970 when the residents of the neighboring communities fought developers Miller and Smith Associates, who bought the land from the Burling family for $2.4 million to build 309 luxury homes. Neighboring residents discovered the purchase from a posted public notice and took action to prevent the developer from removing trees and building homes. After a long battle, a referendum was passed to increase residents' taxes in order to purchase the land for the public. Today, Scotts Run Nature Preserve hosts 8 miles of trails on a rolling landscape and in a virtual cathedral of trees. Hiking on the bluff above the river provides an adventure for a young child, while hiking down the bluff to the Potomac offers a cardiovascular challenge for all.

Scotts Run offers a multitude of trail combinations, and this wide, well-maintained route accommodates jogging strollers. One note of caution: The trails in this park are not blazed; therefore, they don't provide the visual reminder that reassures hikers that they are on the correct path. However, mounted trail maps help guide the way at various intersections.

To hike in this cathedral of trees, such as hemlock, beech, tulip poplar, oak, hickory, and maple, begin by walking up a set of tiered stairs in the middle of the parking lot. During spring, hikers may spot wildflowers such as mayapples, trout lilies, and bloodroot. At the top, the trail veers to the right; follow it to the first intersection. Turn left, hop over the small brook just after the intersection, and climb the small hill. The trail curves to the left before the second intersection. At the intersection, a very large downed tree that lived for more than a century lies off to the side adjacent to a trail sign. Its trunk makes a great spot to rest. When you're ready, turn right at the second intersection and follow the trail uphill. Hike 0.5 mile to the third intersection, observing the tall structures of the poplar, the mighty oaks, and the ever-present American holly.

Reaching a large four-way intersection, make a left turn to continue the journey among the steeples. Shortly thereafter, the fourth intersection appears; continue hiking left at this Y intersection. The wide trail undulates and ends up in front of a spot where a cabin owned by the Burling family once stood. Seeking quiet and solitude, Edward Burling, a prominent DC lawyer, frequented his property into his nineties. The fireplace and front stoop still stand. The corners of the hearth are favorite places for spiders to hang out and wait for their next meal. Perched on a bluff above the Potomac River, the old cabin site is one of the highest spots in Scotts Run.

To descend toward the river, the trail bears right from the cabin site. A series of water bars and check dams litter the descent to prevent the trail from eroding. Just before it bends to the right above a set of stairs, you reach a spot where one of the oldest beech trees in the park unfortunately met its demise. Half of the enormous trunk, which was struck by lightning, lies on the ground and makes for a fun play structure for kids. Beech trees are known as graffiti trees because their smooth, thin bark makes it easy for people to leave their permanent mark—please do not do so. To visit the Potomac and the waterfall at the base of Scotts Run, descend the stairs, and turn right to hike downhill on the wide

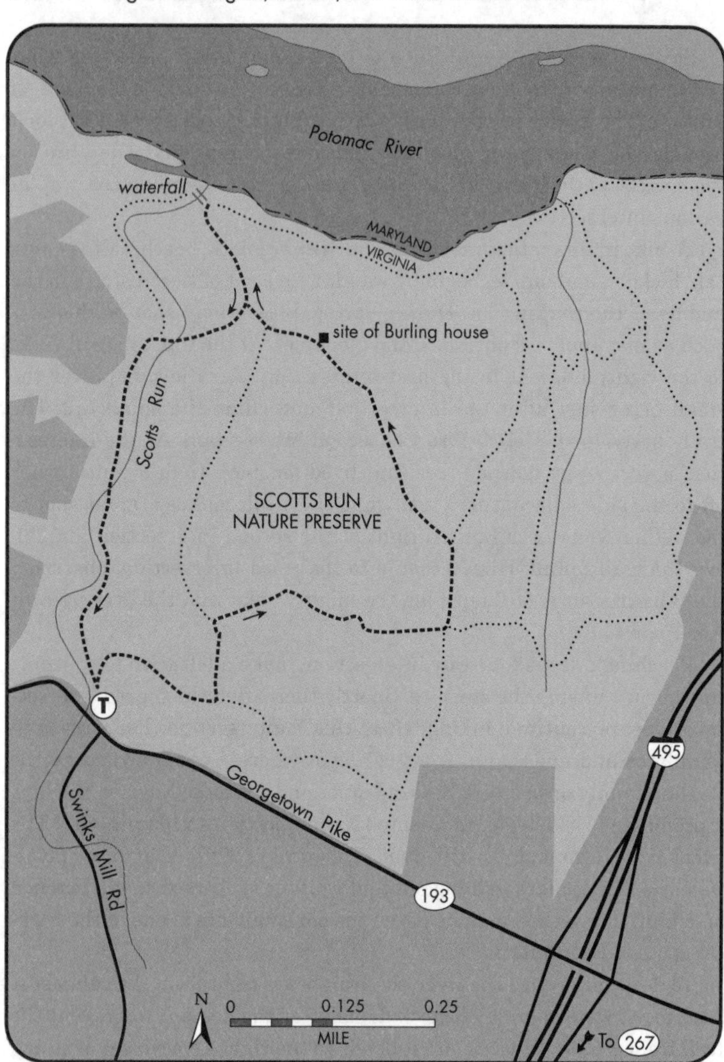

gravel path. The waterfall is to the left at the bottom of the bluff. Hang out along the edge of the Potomac River to spot great blue herons, great and snowy egrets, hawks, and bald eagles.

To close the 3.2-mile loop, walk back uphill on the gravel path past the stairs. Over the crest of the hill, a series of cement pilings in Scotts Run make it easy to keep your feet dry while you cross it. If you are inclined to cool your hot feet in the stream, wear water shoes. Be careful because the algae on the paved bottom makes it slippery. The wide trail veers to the left as it follows the boulder-strewn run. In no time, the kids get to have fun again crossing a second set of pilings. Every once in a while, you might smell a slight stench of sewer—no, there is no sewage in the stream, but there is a sewer line buried nearby. Fairfax County (and many counties in DC) built its municipal sewer lines along stream valleys. The hike ends in another quarter mile back at the parking lot.

TURKEY RUN LOOP

BEFORE YOU GO
Map: Available on the parkway's website
Contact: Turkey Run Park
Nearest city: McLean, VA

ABOUT THE HIKE
Moderate, year-round
Length: 1 mile, loop
Hiking time: 1 hour
High point/elevation gain: 220 feet/170 feet
Access: Compact soil, not passable for jogging strollers

GETTING THERE

From I-495 (Capital Beltway), take exit 43 for George Washington Memorial Parkway. Drive 1.4 miles, and take the exit for I-495 and Turkey Run Park. After 0.4 mile, turn left onto Turkey Run Road. Take the first left into the C-1 parking lot.

ON THE TRAIL

Turkey Run Park is a section of land within the George Washington Memorial Parkway, near Interstate 495. The 7174-square-acre parkway stretches from Great Falls to Mount Vernon. The park offers two loop trails that travel up and down the bluff and three large picnic areas that overlook the Potomac River. The Potomac Heritage Trail (PHT) runs through the park and makes up part of each loop. The PHT is a network of trails, not all connected yet, that runs on both sides of the Potomac from Point Lookout in Maryland and the Northern Neck of Virginia to Seward, Pennsylvania.

The shorter of the two loop hikes, the 1-mile Turkey Run Trail descends steep switchbacks and stairs to the river to return back up the

Looking down Turkey Run

bluff adjacent to Turkey Run. The trail traverses through mature forest and crosses Turkey Run twice. The run cuts a deep ravine through the bluffs, just like a lot of the streams along the Potomac in Virginia, providing an intimate experience in the forest. Standing on the bluff gives you an opposite experience—expansive views of Maryland and the river.

Begin at the north side of the parking lot by descending seven steps and turning left to follow yellow blazes. In a couple hundred yards, the trail forks to begin the Turkey Run Trail loop. Stay to the right and follow the trail as it descends steeply 0.2 mile to the river via steps and five switchbacks. At the bottom, a trail sign greets hikers with destination points and mileage on the PHT. Turn left and follow the PHT for 0.1 mile to Turkey Run. This trail is blazed both yellow and blue. The PHT follows the fence to the left and up the ravine 100 feet to cross the run on rocks, with steps on both streambanks. On the opposite bank, the PHT continues to the right; however, turn left and follow the Turkey Run Trail.

The trail stays 10 to 15 feet above the run with minimal access to it except for the two crossings. Wide trees tower over the trail, providing deep shade and protective growth for native plants like viburnum, paw paw trees, spicebush, jack-in-the-pulpit, and bloodroot, to name a few. When breaks in the canopy occur, they create strong patches of sunlight where invasive plants often take hold and strangle out native plants.

In 0.2 mile, the trail crosses the run again on rocks, and on the opposite side, it forks. The trail on the right is a people's choice trail under the parkway. Follow the Turkey Run Trail to the left and uphill. For the remaining 0.5 mile, the trail ascends the bluff gradually, following the fluctuations of the topography and meandering left and right among the trees. The trail crosses a bridge over an artificial ditch caused by water flowing out of a storm drainpipe from the parkway. Next to the bridge kids can observe the network of a tree's major roots.

GUSHING STORMWATER

Pollution from the George Washington Memorial Parkway flows into a storm drain along the road and through a drainpipe to be released into nature. Trees and vegetation usually serve as a valuable filter for polluted water, preventing it from entering streams and rivers. However, the volume of water entering the storm drain from the parkway instead erodes the soil and provides a chute to channel the polluted water directly into the Potomac. In this case, the forest isn't an effective buffer zone to capture and filter gasoline, fertilizers, oil, and trash from entering the Potomac, the DC region's source for drinking water.

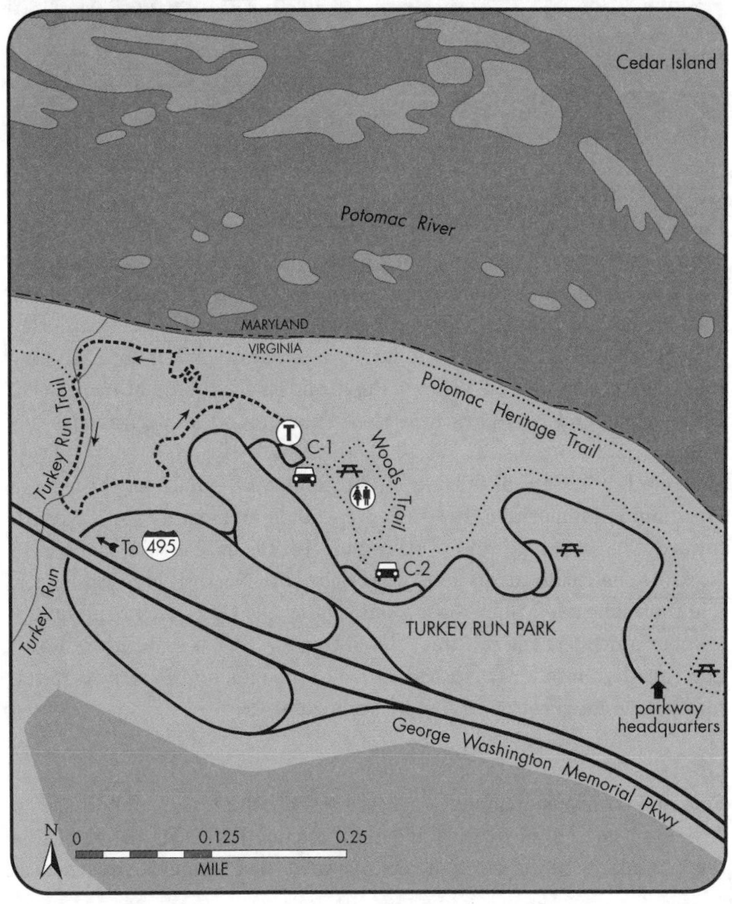

The Turkey Run Trail turns right to return to the parking lot. The picnic area east of the parking lot provides a shady respite after hiking the bluff to and from the Potomac River.

POTOMAC OVERLOOK REGIONAL PARK

BEFORE YOU GO

Map: Available inside the nature center

Contact: Potomac Overlook Regional Park

Nearest city: Arlington, VA

ABOUT THE HIKE

Moderate, year-round

Length: 2.7 miles, loop and spur

Hiking time: 2–2½ hours

High point/elevation gain: 289 feet/180 feet

Access: Compact soil, not passable for jogging strollers

GETTING THERE

From I-495 (Capital Beltway) in Maryland, take exit 40 for the Cabin John Parkway (becomes the Clara Barton Parkway) toward Glen Echo. Drive almost 5 miles, and turn right onto the Chain Bridge. In 0.5 mile, turn right onto North Richmond Street. Then take a left immediately onto North Old Glebe Road and finally another quick left onto Military Road. Drive 1.5 miles on Military Road, and turn left onto Marcey Road. Drive to the end, and park next to the playground and restrooms just before a gate.

From I-495 (Capital Beltway) in Virginia, take exit 43 for the George Washington Memorial Parkway. Drive 4 miles, and exit for VA 123 south toward Chain Bridge and Washington. In 1.3 miles, turn right onto North Glebe Road. In 0.5 mile, turn right onto North Richmond Street, and then take a left immediately onto North Old Glebe Road and finally another quick left onto Military Road. Drive 1.5 miles on Military Road, and turn left onto Marcey Road. Drive to the end, and park next to the playground and restrooms just before a gate.

ON THE TRAIL

Potomac Overlook Regional Park is tucked behind a neighborhood in Arlington on a bluff overlooking the Potomac River. To visualize this bluff, think about fingers that reach toward the Potomac; between each

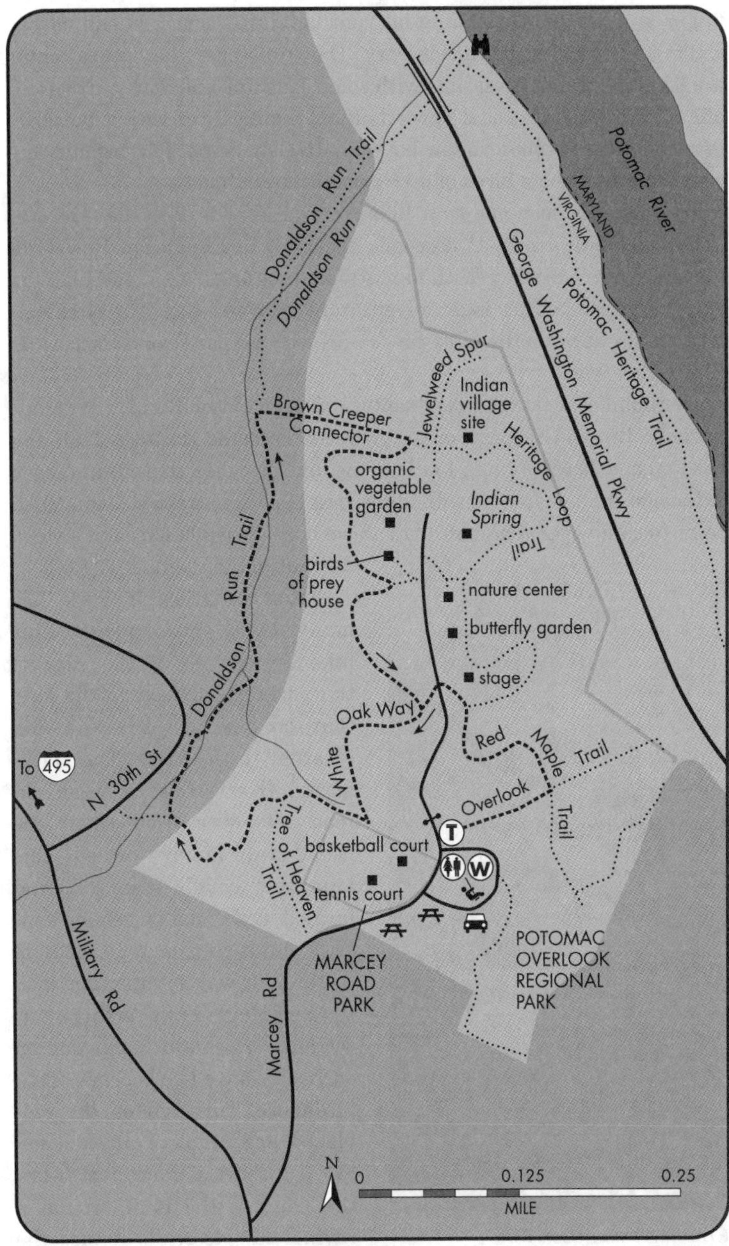

Potomac River
MARYLAND
VIRGINIA
Potomac Heritage Trail
George Washington Memorial Pkwy
Donaldson Run Trail
Donaldson Run
Jewelweed Spur
Indian village site
Brown Creeper Connector
Heritage Loop Trail
organic vegetable garden
Indian Spring
birds of prey house
nature center
butterfly garden
stage
Donaldson Run Trail
Oak Way
Red Maple Trail
White
Overlook Trail
To 495
N 30th St
Tree of Heaven Trail
basketball court
tennis court
Military Rd
Marcey Rd
MARCEY ROAD PARK
POTOMAC OVERLOOK REGIONAL PARK
N
0
0.125
0.25
MILE

finger is a ravine. Depending on your children's age, you can choose a combination of trails in this park. The trails near the nature center are jogging-stroller accessible with some easy ups and downs. The park offers several educational opportunities; families can visit a butterfly garden and see a photovoltaic board, native shade garden, organic vegetable garden, and a birds of prey rehabilitation house.

The 2.7-mile loop-and-spur hike starts and ends with the Overlook and Red Maple trails. It descends the bluff to Donaldson Run Trail via the White Oak Way. With four stream crossings (six if you hike the extension), Donaldson is an adventurous trail for kids. The clockwise loop climbs back up the bluff via the Brown Creeper Connector back to White Oak Way.

For families seeking more adventure, the Donaldson Run Trail extends past the Brown Creeper Connector to the Potomac Heritage Trail and the Potomac River. Adding 1 mile to the hike distance, this out-and-back extension challenges kids with many rock hops across the stream, fallen trees to climb over, a narrow trail above high streambanks, and a steep descent to the river.

Crossing Donaldson Run

Potomac Overlook Park has many trail entry points. This hike commences at the edge of the parking lot, next to the gate that crosses the driveway and adjacent to the kiosk. The black-blazed Overlook Trail is an old road left over from when the Donaldson family owned this land; they bought it in 1842 and farmed it for many generations. Walk down steps and go 0.2 mile to the four-way intersection with the Red Maple Trail. At this intersection, two raised boxes, one on each side, have two benches and a birdhouse. Turn left on the red-blazed Red Maple Trail, and follow it a short distance just below the edge of the bluff around a ravine that descends toward the

Potomac. This trail rises to the top of the bluff and forks; stay left at the intersection with the driveway. Continue for a couple hundred feet on the opposite side of the driveway before intersecting with White Oak Way.

Turn left on the white-blazed White Oak Way to hike clockwise on this loop. This trail follows the higher contour line of the bluff and dips twice. The first dip is within a quarter mile. Most of the time, the gulch here is dry except when it is raining and the rainwater runs off the driveway, tennis courts, and park to find the path of least resistance to Donaldson Run. At this gulch, turn right and cross over a small wooden bridge. The trail ascends back up the bluff. American beech populates the oak understory in this section of the park.

DO TREES GET TUMORS?

A number of the American beech trees in this park have galls or burls, which look like bark-covered tumors that extrude from the tree's trunk or branches. They can also appear on leaves and stems. Insects, fungi, bacteria, and environmental damage cause galls and burls. The cells of the cambia multiply at exponential rates creating a growth in that layer of the tree. Some insects burrow or find an entry point into the tree and lay eggs. The tree responds with rapid cell production to contain the infestation. The effect creates a safe habitat and food source for the eggs and larvae when they hatch. Most galls are not fatal to the tree, but they can reduce its life span.

All along the White Oak Way, benches are positioned for hikers to look out over the bluff and view the tree canopy. The Tree of Heaven Trail intersects White Oak from the left; continue straight as White Oak curves to the left along the bluff. From the Tree of Heaven Trail, White Oak Way used to perpendicularly descend the bluff to Donaldson Run. However, the park rerouted it to reduce runoff and make the descent (and ascent) of the bluff family friendly. It now bisects the contour lines of the bluff, providing a less strenuous incline, and has a few steps at its steepest point. White Oak Way curves to the right to its intersection with the yellow-blazed Donaldson Run Trail.

North 30th Street is accessible ahead at two points: a left at this intersection with Donaldson Run Trail and again on the left farther down the trail. To continue on the loop, turn right and follow the trail to its first stream crossing on a set of cement pilings. This type of crossing is less natural than rocks, but it is a typical trail construction technique of the Northern Virginia Regional Park Authority. You cross Donaldson Run four times in 0.6 mile before you reach the Brown Creeper Connector.

After the pilings, turn right to stay on the trail, and head a few steps down. The trail stays to the left of the stream for a few steps before you need to cross it again, this time on rocks. Before the crossing, there is a sandy area for free play in the stream. For the next 0.2 mile, the trail stays to the right of the stream before it crosses for a third time. At this crossing, a large boulder on the streambank serves as a perfect place to hang out for a snack or drink. Within a short distance, the trail crosses the stream for the fourth time and stays to the right of it to intersect the Brown Creeper Connector. Turn right here.

The Brown Creeper Connector ascends the bluff with an often dry gulch to its right. When trail builders construct a trail, the best place to ascend is alongside a stream or along contours where two ridges connect. This point of intersection provides the gentlest ascent or descent for hikers and reduces the erosive impact on the land. Hike 0.3 mile on the brown-blazed Brown Creeper Connector. Before the intersection with White Oak Way, a demonstration area on the left side of the trail educates visitors about invasive species. Furthermore, this area is being reforested due to the destruction caused by the derecho in the summer of 2012. Each sapling is wrapped with a deer cage to ensure its survival—deer eat the sapling's tender leaves and twigs, and bucks rub the trunks to remove the fuzz from their antlers.

Take a short side trip to the demonstration gardens a few hundred feet away from the end of the Brown Creeper Connector. To complete the loop on White Oak Way, turn right off Brown Creeper Connector, and follow the trail as it winds along the edge of the bluff. Along the way, benches allow you and your kids to take a respite and watch the birds fly in the tree canopy. Within 0.3 mile, a very short connector to the nature center intersects from the left. The nature center has educational displays, live animals such as snakes and turtles, a small library, and a cave for kids to explore.

White Oak Way continues for 0.2 mile before another connector trail intersects from the left. Turn left here, and cross the driveway to head back on the Red Maple Trail and then the Overlook Trail. When you reach the intersection with the Overlook Trail, turn right to head back to the parking lot next to the playground and restrooms.

Extension on the Donaldson Run Trail

This 1-mile out-and-back extension is difficult because it has many stream crossings, an old cement wall to climb, a narrow trail with steep streambanks, and an occasional tree trunk to climb over. It is an exciting adventure for kids who have the gross motor skills to handle the obstacles. At the intersection of the Donaldson Run Trail and Brown Creeper Connector, continue north along Donaldson Run. Almost immediately, cross the stream over rocks. You will cross it two more times on rocks before you reach an old cement wall, which was built in the late 1800s to dam the stream and create a swimming area. Follow the trail on the right bank and over the cement wall; steps on the other side assist you. Choose dry rocks to follow the trail across the stream and onto the left bank.

Just before you reach the George Washington Memorial Parkway's overpass, cross the run for the final time. The narrow trail with a steep drop-off descends a few hundred feet on rocky tread before it intersects the Potomac Heritage Trail, which stretches from Theodore Roosevelt Island into Loudoun County. To access the river, make a slight left and follow the white arrows painted on the rocks down a few hundred steep feet to where Donaldson Run enters the Potomac River. When you and your children have had your fill of the river, hike back a half mile and over the same stream crossings to return to the Brown Creeper Connector and Potomac Overlook Park.

UPTON HILL REGIONAL PARK

BEFORE YOU GO
Map: Available on the park's website
Contact: Upton Hill Regional Park
Nearest city: Arlington, VA

ABOUT THE HIKE
Easy, year-round
Length: 0.8 mile, loop
Hiking time: ½–1 hour
High point/elevation gain: 417 feet/39 feet
Access: Asphalt, compact soil, cinder, and mulch; jogging-stroller friendly

GETTING THERE

From I-495 (Capital Beltway), take exit 45B for I-66 east toward Washington. Drive 2.8 miles on VA 267, and exit left onto I-66. Drive 1.7 miles, and take exit 69 for US 29, VA 237, and Washington Boulevard (Lee Highway). In 0.2 mile, stay straight on Washington Boulevard. Drive 0.3 mile, and turn right onto North Sycamore Street (VA 237). After 1 mile, turn left onto Wilson Boulevard. Drive 0.5 mile to Patrick Henry Drive, and turn right into the park driveway immediately after Patrick Henry Drive (at the stoplight).

ON THE TRAIL

Upton Hill Regional Park is one of the most popular parks in Northern Virginia because it offers trails, a playground, bocce ball and horseshoe courts, batting cages, miniature golf, picnic facilities, and a water park. Families can make a day of it at Upton Hill.

The land Upton Hill sits on has historical significance related to the Civil War. It was one of the largest hills on the western front to protect Washington, DC, during the war. The Union Army occupied it until July 1861 when it lost the first Battle of Manassas and retreated to Washington. The Confederate Army followed the Union in its retreat to establish a fortified line on Upton Hill. Confederates used an old Quaker defense tactic of building cannon lines made of black painted tree trunks. The Confederate Army did not hold the hill for long. In

Climbing a Quaker-style Civil War cannon

September 1861, it retreated to Manassas, and the Union Army held the hill for the remainder of the war, during which it built Fort Ramsey and a large observation and communication tower near the Upton family home. Upton Hill was also made famous during the Civil War because the song "Battle Hymn of the Republic," written by Julia Ward Howe, is based on events that occurred during the Union's occupation of Upton Hill in November 1861.

Upton Hill is in a densely populated area of Arlington; therefore, the Northern Virginia Regional Park Authority made good use of the wooded hill to create three trails: red, orange, and yellow (all blazed in their corresponding colors). They connect within short distances at various points and to trailheads on neighboring streets. However, these multiple connections can be confusing at times. Traversing the interior of the park from the park entrance to North Livingston Street, this hike is shady and wide with a mixture of four different trail surfaces: pavement, soil, cinder, and mulch. Encourage your kids to stay to the center of the wide trail to avoid the poison ivy along it.

Before you leave Upton Hill Park, take advantage of the many other high-quality activities that families can engage in. The waterpark will refresh you after a hike on a hot, sweaty day, or you and your family might take on the challenge of an eagle putt on the longest miniature golf hole in the world.

The hike begins at the parking lot between the batting cages and miniature golf and waterpark areas. The trailhead is at the end of the lot beyond the batting cages and next to the picnic shelter. From the trailhead, hike downhill on the paved service road for 0.1 mile to the intersection with the Yellow Trail. Turn right on the dirt Yellow Trail, and hike another 0.1 mile to the intersection with the Red Trail. On the Yellow Trail between the service road and the Red Trail, ignore a people's choice trail on the left.

At the intersection with the Red Trail, a large grassy area with a small stage appears to the right of the trail. Turn left on the Red Trail, and descend a series of check dams for 150 feet. Intersect the Yellow Trail again, and turn right onto it to curve left and downhill before intersecting the Orange Trail in 250 feet. The Orange Trail forks both left and right. Turn right then reach another fork in the Orange Trail within 50 feet. This time turn left to follow the Orange Trail as it curves to the left. Soon the Orange Trail splits in three different directions. The trails straight ahead and to the right lead to North Livingston Street.

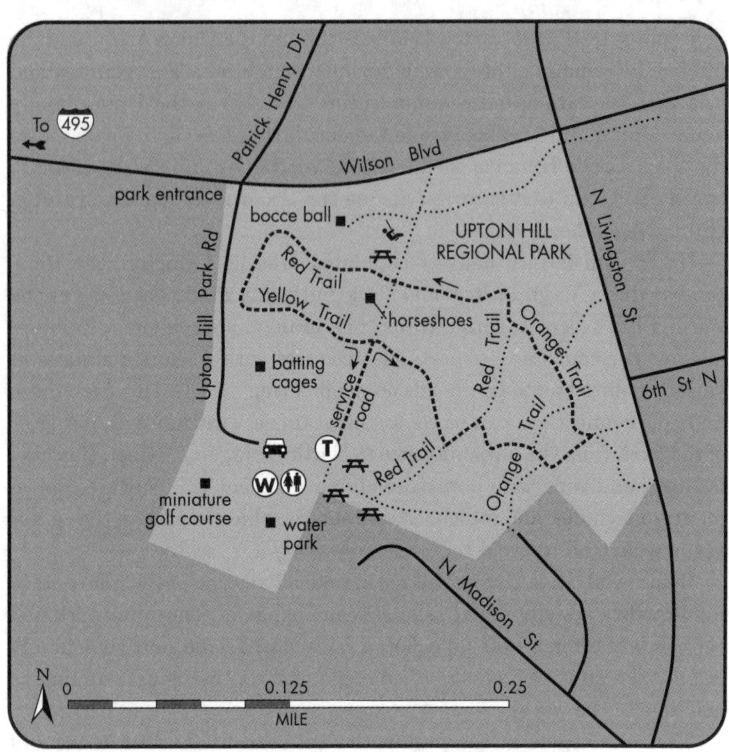

Turn left and follow the Orange Trail past an orange-blazed trail on the left and then another one 100 feet farther on the right. Continue straight on the Orange Trail for 300 feet more until it intersects the Red Trail. Turn right on the Red Trail, and follow it 0.15 mile to the service road.

At the intersection with the service road, your kids can take a break to play on the park's playground, which is on the right side of the Red Trail after the service road. The Red Trail continues on a narrower path through the woods. The trail heads toward the intersection with Patrick Henry Drive and the park's entrance. Before reaching the entrance driveway, the Red Trail curves left, passing a people's choice trail on the right. For 300 feet, the Red Trail runs adjacent to the driveway but in the woods. The Red Trail dead-ends at the Yellow Trail—take a left here to follow the Yellow Trail for 0.15 mile until it reaches the service road. Turn right on the paved service road, and head uphill to the parking lot.

WOLF TRAP TRAIL

BEFORE YOU GO
Map: Available at the visitor center and on the park's website
Contact: Wolf Trap National Park for the Performing Arts
Nearest city: Vienna, VA

ABOUT THE HIKE
Moderate, year-round
Length: 3 miles, loop
Hiking time: 2–2½ hours
High point/elevation gain: 364 feet/102 feet
Access: Compact soil and boardwalk, not passable for jogging strollers

GETTING THERE

From I-495 (Capital Beltway), take exit 45 for VA 267 (Dulles Toll Road) west. Drive 3 miles, and take the Wolf Trap exit. Drive 0.5 mile, and turn right into Wolf Trap. Follow the driveway to the parking area to the right of the main entrance on the circle. Hikers may park here when there is not a performance; otherwise, park in a lot during a performance.

ON THE TRAIL

When families in DC hear the phrase *Wolf Trap,* they often think of the fantastic outdoor performing arts center where they can bring a picnic to eat while listening to great concerts. However, Wolf Trap National Park is also a great place to hike through high-quality forests and along streams and a pond. In 2011, the National Park Service (NPS) partnered with the Potomac Appalachian Trail Club to design and build the 3-mile Wolf Trap Trail that traverses the park's ridges and streams. NPS also partnered with Kids in Parks, a program funded by the Blue Ridge Parkway Foundation, to implement a TRACK Trail in the park. This hike follows some of and extends beyond the blue-blazed trail described here. Families can visit the NPS Wolf Trap website for printable nature brochures to bring on the hike.

While you are at this park, enjoy the short trail that bisects the meadow in the driveway circle. The NPS and volunteers have planted hundreds of native plants to provide an interpretive area for visitors and a meadow ecosystem for birds, bees, butterflies, dragonflies, and other insects.

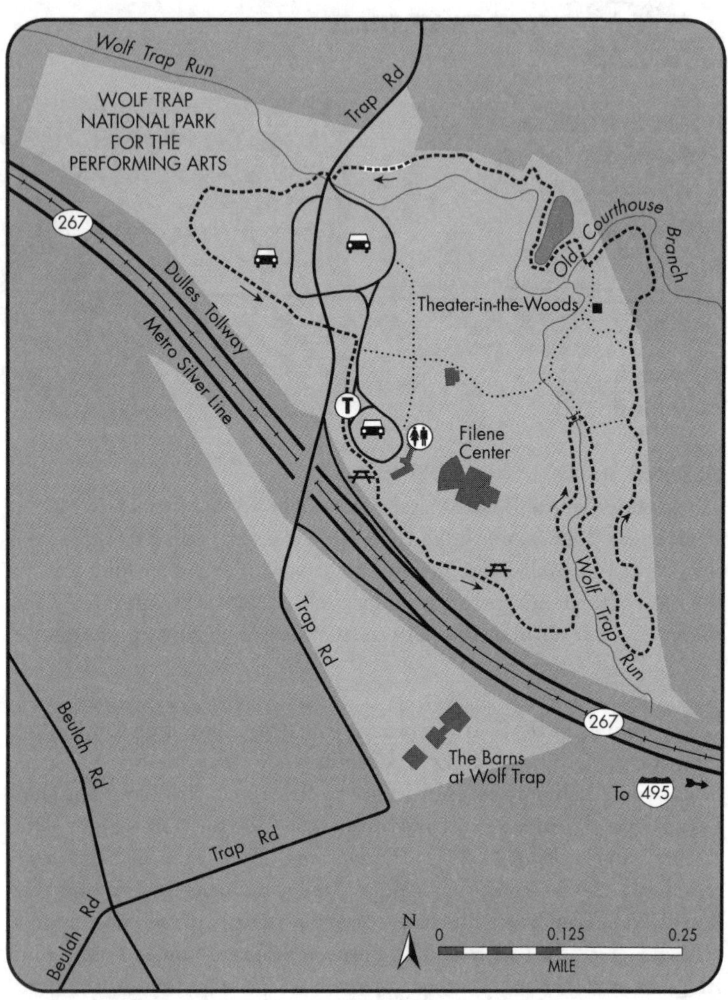

The hike follows a blue-blazed trail that zigzags through heavily wooded land to the north and east sides of the property. NPS has also placed small trail posts with blue arrows at intersections or major turns. The almost complete circuit starts at the Filene Center's entrance gate and ends at the maintenance building on the opposite side of Trap Road. The hike meanders alongside and up and down the ridges that Wolf Trap Run and Old Courthouse Branch have carved into the land beginning millions of years ago. The park is named after the run. Halfway through, you can choose to shorten your hike by approximately 1 mile.

A boardwalk crosses a wetland along the Wolf Trap Trail.

Wolf Trap Trail begins to the right of the Filene Center's entrance where there is a cluster of picnic tables under the trees and against the highway jersey wall. Look for a trail post, and hike past the tables and through pine trees, keeping the jersey wall on the right. The jersey wall remains on the right for a quarter mile. The trail continues through pines and over a bent barbed-wire fence and goes downhill. This area lost trees during the construction of the highway and jersey wall. Fast-growing pine trees were planted to reduce the erosion damage into Wolf Trap Run, but numerous wet snowfalls have toppled many of them. Introducing this once shady area to sunlight has caused invasive plants, trees, bushes, vines, and ground cover to take over.

At a double blaze, turn left and walk through an area that is often wet from stormwater drainage. Shortly thereafter, the trail curves right at a double blaze and post and ascends a short hill. At the top, Composers Cottage picnic area is on the left and on the right is a fenced area. White-tailed deer have heavily browsed the understory in this area; therefore, the park installed a fenced deer management area to study the regrowth rate of native species. In stark contrast, the healthy forest on the ridge just northeast of Wolf Trap Run boasts a native plant ecosystem of large oaks, mountain laurel, and blueberry bushes.

After the picnic area, the trail curves to the left and switchbacks down the ridge toward Wolf Trap Run. At the final switchback, a people's choice trail enters from the left, allowing access to the center's back parking lot. Between the parking lot and trail, there is a small wetland filled with skunk cabbage. Continue following the trail along the run where kids have their first opportunity to access the stream. The trail zigzags along the stream before intersecting a bridge; follow the trail post arrow over the bridge. At the end of the bridge, turn right to continue following the blue blazes. The green blazes on the left lead to a shortcut to the Theater-in-the-Woods. To reduce the hike by 0.7 mile, turn right after the bridge, hike 100 feet and turn left at the green blaze. Walk uphill to where it reconnects with the blue-blazed trail in 100 yards. From here, turn left and hike uphill to pass the Theater-in-the-Woods.

To hike the full 3 miles, follow the blue-blazed trail at the end of the bridge, keeping Wolf Trap Run on your right again. Two locations here along the stream provide great natural play spaces for kids. Within 0.1 mile, the trail makes a sharp left turn and switchbacks once above the stream. Within 100 yards, the trail descends back down to the stream and makes a left turn at a double blaze to stay along it for another 0.2 mile. Close to the jersey wall again, the trail turns left and ascends the ridge to follow private property lines for the next 0.3 mile. On this ridge you can observe a healthy, deciduous ecosystem.

At 1.3 miles, the blue-blazed trail intersects the green trail (the shortcut described earlier). Follow the blue arrow to the right, past a people's choice trail accessing private property, over a bridge, and uphill through cedar trees. In 0.1 mile, at the Theater-in-the-Woods, turn right to follow the arrow on the trail post. Pass the theater and a people's choice trail on the right. The trail tread becomes rocky and descends on a few switchbacks to Old Courthouse Branch. The trail turns left to follow the stream for 0.1 mile to a bridge over the branch where there is a great access point to throw rocks into the water or climb on its boulders. This stream feeds into Wolf Trap Run just beyond the bridge.

The Wolf Trap Trail turns right over the bridge; a left here leads back to the Theater-in-the-Woods. At the end of the bridge, the trail turns left where Turtle Pond appears on the right. The trail sits atop a berm between Wolf Trap Run on the left and Turtle Pond on the right. It follows the pond for two-thirds of its circumference. Tell your kids to keep their eyes peeled for great blue herons and turtles.

At 2 miles into the hike and at the end of the pond, Wolf Trap Trail turns left at a double blue blaze. For the next 0.2 mile, Wolf Trap Run continues to the left of the trail and you can access a rockbar in the stream and a large boulder on its streambank. At a trail post, the trail makes a sharp left turn. Don't follow the people's choice trail straight ahead. Ahead after the left turn, a boardwalk allows you to walk through a wetland, which ends just short of Trap Road. Before crossing Trap

Road, turn left and walk alongside it until you reach the driveway. The trail continues across Trap Road.

On the other side of Trap Road, look for the trail post with a blue arrow pointing hikers straight back into the woods. The hike finishes with another 0.2 mile along Wolf Trap Run before it ends at the parking lot next to the maintenance facility. The trail does continue on the other side of the maintenance building adjacent to the dumpster, but you should walk across the parking lot toward Trap Road and a tunnel that goes under it. After the tunnel, walk to the driveway, and turn right on the sidewalk to return to the parking lot.

STONE BRIDGE LOOP

BEFORE YOU GO
Map: Available at the trailhead, visitor center on Route 234, and on the park's website
Contact: Manassas National Battlefield Park
Nearest city: Manassas, VA

ABOUT THE HIKE
Easy/moderate, year-round
Length: 1.4 miles, loop
Hiking time: 1–1½ hours
High point/elevation gain: 344 feet/102 feet
Access: Asphalt, compact soil, and boardwalk; passable for jogging strollers

GETTING THERE

From I-495 (Capital Beltway), exit for I-66 west. Drive 13 miles, and take exit 52 for US 29 (Lee Highway) toward Centerville. Turn right onto US 29, and drive 3 miles. The parking lot is on the right.

ON THE TRAIL

In 1940, the National Park Service created the 5000-acre Manassas National Battlefield Park to preserve the land and history of the first and second battles of Manassas, which occurred during the Civil War. The park offers 20 miles of interpretive hiking trails and historic places to learn about both battles. Some of the trails pass historic houses, such as the Stone House—a Union field hospital—and Henry Hill House, which were significant places during the battles. The park's visitor

Walk over wetlands toward Stone Bridge on a wide boardwalk.

center has exhibits and an educational video to explain in detail the events that occurred during both the 1861 and 1862 battles at Manassas.

Stone Bridge was a pivotal location during both battles. In 1861, Union General George McClellan sent a diversionary unit of soldiers across Stone Bridge to distract the Confederates from their main point of attack at Sudley Spring Ford on Bull Run. In 1862, the Confederates pushed Union troops east to Chinn Ridge and finally to Henry's Hill after three days of battle that started at Groveton Woods. It was here at Henry's Hill that the Union Army raised the white flag and retreated across Stone Bridge toward Washington.

The 1.4-mile Stone Bridge Loop Trail gives you and your kids a historical perspective on both battles and information about the natural history of the area, including the plants and animals that create the meadow, forest, and stream ecosystems in the park. The Kids in Parks program, sponsored by the Blue Ridge Parkway Foundation, offers four brochures to educate kids: trees, birds, nature tales, and activities such as a game of hide-and-seek and a cell phone interpretation guide. At each point of interest, a sign indicates which number to press after you call the telephone number. Green is the adult explanation, and orange is the children's.

The hike begins on a paved trail over Stone Bridge and continues on compact soil along Bull Run and the meadows of the battlefield—which can be hot and sunny on a summer day—and finally on a boardwalk through wetlands. Along the first section of the loop, there are multiple people's choice trails and access points to Bull Run. The trail is marked at intersections but is not blazed. The trail gains most of its elevation along Bull Run and then descends from the meadow to the wetlands parallel to US 29.

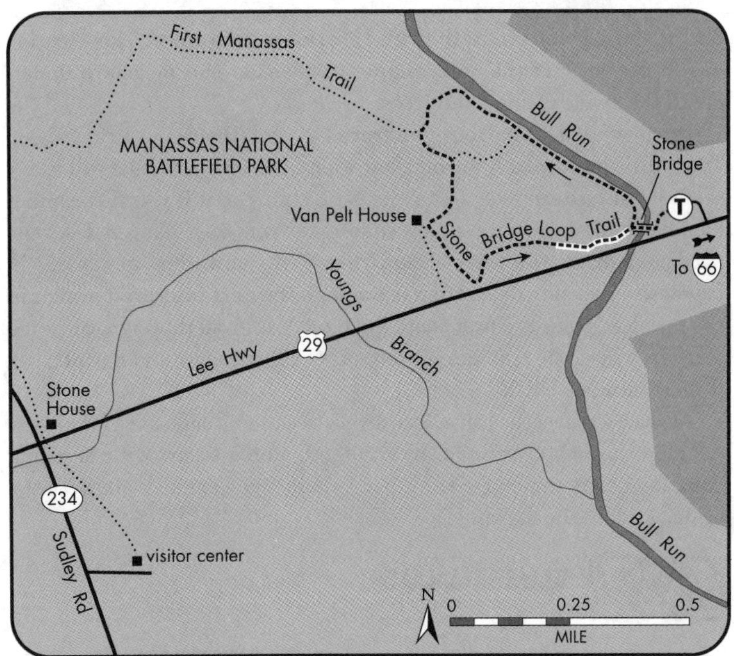

The hike begins at two interpretive signs at the end of the parking lot, where you can find a trail map and brochures. Follow the paved trail 0.1 mile past two interpretive signs that explain what occurred at Stone Bridge during both battles and continue over Stone Bridge. The loop begins at the end of the bridge. Turn right and hike along Bull Run. The run remains on the right until the loop's second intersection with the First Manassas Trail.

The first 0.3 mile is level until just past the intersection with the First Manassas Trail. Continue straight uphill above Bull Run. At the top of the hill, pass an interpretive sign about Farm Ford during the First Battle of Manassas. Farm Ford is where General William Sherman led his Union troops across Bull Run. The trail curves left and continues gently uphill over a small bridge where it again curves left and then right. The Stone Bridge Loop Trail intersects the First Manassas Trail for the second time at the edge of the forest. Turn left and follow the loop along the edge of the woods for 0.1 mile. The loop turns right to continue along the forest's edge, while the First Manassas Trail turns left and returns to the woods. Follow the loop to the right, and hike another

0.1 mile to a point where the Van Pelt House once stood. This location has a nice view of the surrounding battlefields and meadows underneath the shade of a few tall trees.

From the Van Pelt House interpretive sign, the Stone Bridge Loop Trail turns left through the meadow where you and your kids will likely see a lot of butterflies flying about on a sunny day. Butterflies cannot metabolize their own heat like we humans can. Just like turtles, they need sunlight to heat their bodies. That is why butterflies are sparse in meadows on cloudy days. Hike 0.1 mile to the next interpretive sign in the meadow about the first shots fired in 1861. From this sign, continue straight where the trail curves left out of the meadow and downhill as it then parallels US 29.

At the bottom of the hill, a boardwalk begins and continues for almost 0.2 mile through a wetland. In spring, this area teems with breeding amphibians. At the end, Stone Bridge is in sight again; walk over the bridge back to the parking lot.

BLUEBELL LOOP

BEFORE YOU GO
Map: Available at the park entrance or on its website
Contact: Bull Run Regional Park (charges a fee)
Nearest city: Manassas, VA

ABOUT THE HIKE
Easy, year-round (best in April)
Length: 2 miles, loop
Hiking time: 1–1½ hours
High point/elevation gain: 150 feet/20 feet
Access: Compact soil and raised-wooden walkways, jogging-stroller friendly

GETTING THERE

From I-495 (Capital Beltway), exit for I-66 west. Drive 13 miles to exit 52 for US 29 (Lee Highway), and turn right onto US 29. Drive 2 miles, and turn left onto Bull Run Post Office Road. Drive 1 mile, and turn right onto Bull Run Drive. Drive 1 mile to the park entrance, and park in the pool parking lot.

ON THE TRAIL

The Bluebell Trail looped with the Bull Run Occoquan Trail is by far

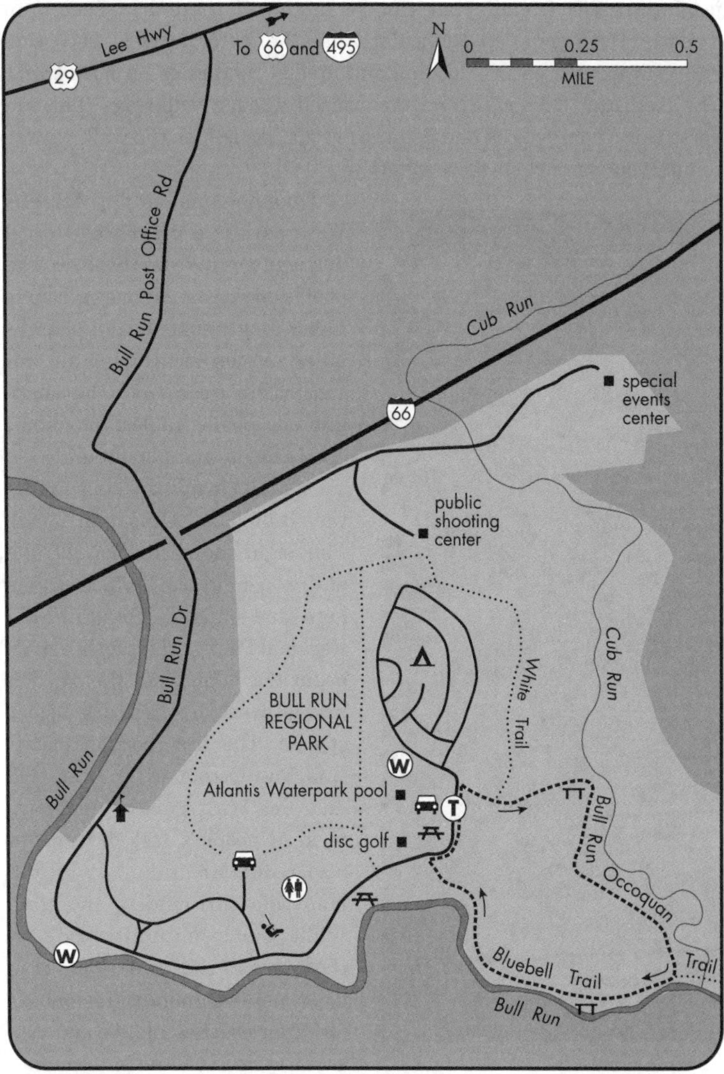

the best way to see huge patches of bluebells in the floodplains along Cub and Bull runs. The bluebells usually bloom the third week of April—earlier if it is a warm spring, and closer to the last week of April and beginning of May in a cold spring. This easy, wide 2-mile loop is jogging-stroller friendly but can be muddy if there has been rain recently. Downpours in particular raise the water level of both Cub and Bull runs, creating flooding and muddy conditions on both trails. The Bull Run Occoquan Trail has raised wooden walkways that traverse this swampy area and its many vernal pools. Use the walkways to reduce your impact on the vegetation.

Virginia bluebells

On a hot summer day, Atlantis Waterpark is a great way to cool down after a hike on this loop. The pool is open from Memorial Day to Labor Day weekend and charges an admission fee. During all seasons, visitors can enjoy the campground, picnic tables, pavilions, sports fields, and playgrounds.

A large trailhead sign marks the Bull Run Occoquan Trail. The sign shows a map of the entire 17-mile trail, which begins here and ends in Fountainhead Regional Park to the southeast. To begin the hike, cross the wooden bridge over an often dry feeder stream. The first portion of the Bull Run Occoquan Trail is wide and flat with raised walkways to keep people's feet dry and to also reduce their impact on the plant life surrounding the trail. While people naturally walk on the edges of the trail where it is drier and less muddy, this behavior often crushes plants and creates a cycle of increasing standing water, reducing vegetation along the trail's edges, widening the trail, and increasing erosion on it and into streams. The Northern Virginia Regional Park Authority (NVRPA) has built raised walkways or puncheons on this trail to protect the environment.

Reach Cub Run within 0.4 mile. There is a rockbar below the steep streambank for playing and a bench atop it for taking a rest. The Bull Run Occoquan Trail turns right here and follows Cub Run for the next 0.8 mile to where it empties into Bull Run. The trail zigzags to follow the flow of the stream and provides some easy access points for kids to play in it. In addition, another bench in this section makes for a great snack stop. Cross a wooden bridge 0.3 mile into this section and enter a meadow to hike under power lines. After you return to the woods, follow a small raised wooden walkway over an often wet area and then cross another small wooden bridge before the Bull Run Occoquan Trail intersects the Bluebell Trail.

A trail sign marks this intersection. The Bull Run Occoquan Trail turns left and across the mouth of Cub Run. The Bluebell Trail turns right and follows Bull Run all the way back to Bull Run Drive. Bluebells are found along the entire loop; however, they are most concentrated along the Bluebell Trail.

BLUEBELLS

Virginia bluebells are spring ephemeral plants, meaning that they last only a short time. Their habitat is in riparian zones (along rivers and streams) and they are most abundant in floodplains where the soil is wet. Their pink bud turns blue upon opening to signify to insects that it is ready to be pollinated. The flower's alkalinity changes the pigment to increase its chances of pollination. Once the flower is pollinated and a seed is created in the ovary, the flower drops to the ground to grow a new plant next year.

Unlike the Bull Run Occoquan Trail, which has blue blazes, the Bluebell Trail is blazed with single posts sporting an NVRPA emblem. Just like sections of the Bull Run Occoquan, this trail has wet, muddy spots. There are a number of places to access Bull Run along the trail: one is at a bench 0.3 mile from the trail intersection with the Bull Run Occoquan Trail. Within a couple hundred yards after the bench, walk under power lines in a meadow. On warm sunny days, look for butterflies. After the power lines, hike the last half mile on the Bluebell Trail. About 0.1 mile before the hike ends, Bull Run turns away from the trail.

Once you reach Bull Run Drive, turn right and walk 0.2 mile along the road back to the parking lot at the pool.

BULL RUN TRAIL

BEFORE YOU GO
Map: On trailhead kiosk
Contact: Hemlock Overlook Regional Park
Nearest city: Clifton, VA

ABOUT THE HIKE
Moderate, year-round
Length: 2.4 miles, loop
Hiking time: 1½–2 hours
High point/elevation gain: 338 feet/190 feet
Access: Compact soil, not passable for jogging strollers

GETTING THERE

From I-495 (Capital Beltway), take exit 54A–B for Braddock Road (VA 620) west. Keep right for Braddock Road west. Drive 1.6 miles, and turn left onto Burke Lake Road (VA 645). Drive 4.8 miles, and continue on Clifton Road. Drive 4 miles, and turn left onto Yates Ford Road. Drive 2 miles until the road dead-ends at the park.

ON THE TRAIL

Hemlock Overlook Regional Park is one of five regional parks along Bull Run from Interstate 66 to the Potomac River. The other four are Bull Run Regional Park (Hike 52), Bull Run Marina (not described in this book), Fountainhead (which primarily offers mountain biking, fishing, and boating), and Sandy Run (which does not have trails). The Northern Virginia Regional Park Authority (NVRPA) preserved 4000 acres of land along Bull Run, which provides an excellent buffer zone of forested land to help protect the Potomac watershed. The Bull Run Occoquan Trail runs 17 miles from Bull Run Regional Park to Fountainhead Regional Park. Adventure Links, an outdoor education organization, uses Hemlock Overlook in partnership with NVRPA. The public has the right to hike the trails at Hemlock but cannot use the ropes course or any of the buildings or pavilions.

This 2.4-mile loop descends a gulch between two steep slopes to Bull Run, follows Bull Run, and ascends a ridgeline at Bull Run's intersection with Popes Head Creek. Along Bull Run, the trail undulates to follow the topography as Bull Run carved a steep, sloped valley millions of years ago. There are many places to access the stream from the trail via the bank or at rockbars in the stream. The dirt trail has some rocky

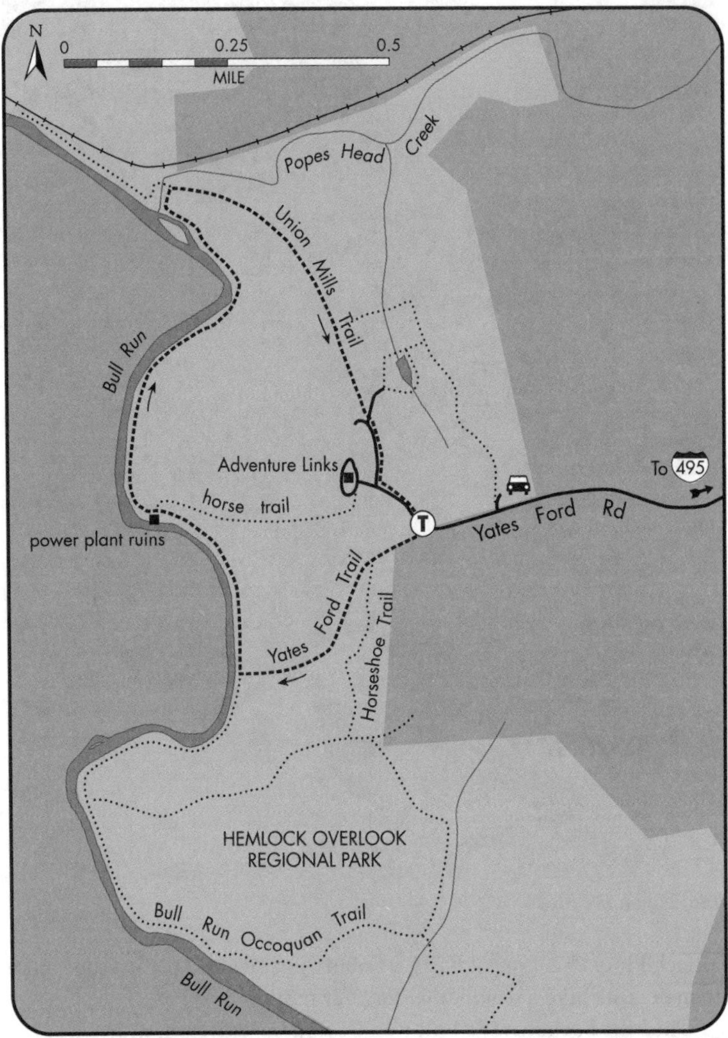

areas. Even though the trails are named, these names are not marked. However, the Yates Ford and Union Mills trails are blazed in yellow, and the Bull Run Occoquan Trail is blazed in blue.

Paradise Winery, which neighbors Hemlock Overlook Park on Yates Ford Road, is an excellent place to stop off for a glass of wine and a picnic

Playing on Bull Run

after hiking. This area of Fairfax County is quiet and picturesque; plan to make this hike a destination for your family.

The hike begins at the Bull Run Occoquan Trail sign, which is at the end of Yates Ford Road. From the start, the Yates Ford Trail descends gradually downhill. The Horseshoe Trail (blazed with yellow horseshoes) intersects on the left 0.1 mile from the start; continue straight on the Yates Ford Trail as it steepens where the trail meets a feeder stream on the left that has carved a gulch between two slopes. Hike another 0.3 mile to its intersection with the Bull Run Occoquan Trail and turn right. The word *occoquan,* from the Powhatan tribe's language, means "at the end of the water."

The Bull Run Occoquan Trail follows Bull Run for 1.3 miles. At 0.3 mile after turning right onto the trail, cross a feeder stream on some rocks. Soon there is a short clearing where some power lines cross the trail and the stream. Hike 0.1 mile to some power plant ruins and a horse trail that intersects the Bull Run Occoquan Trail from the right. Continue straight down an embankment, and stay to the right where a people's choice trail goes left to access the stream.

For the next 0.8 mile, follow the trail as it continues next to Bull Run. About 0.4 mile into this section, the trail tread becomes rocky and may be wet when the stream has flooded. Shortly after this rocky section, the trail and run gently curve left and you can see an island in the run. The trail curves to the right, and two double blazes appear on a tree at 1.75 miles. The Bull Run Occoquan Trail turns left and over Popes Head Creek on concrete pillars (a great place to hang out and play); however, to complete the loop, turn right and follow the Union Mills Trail up the ridgeline.

Most of the first 0.4 mile on the Union Mills Trail rises steeply on soil, steps, and rocks—a majority of the rocks that make up the ridges along the hike are schist, a category of metamorphic rock. The trail gentles just before you reach the Adventure Links property.

CREATING SCHIST

Schist is created when shale, mudstone, and some igneous rock are exposed to heat and pressure within the earth. The type of schist formed depends on the mix of crystals and minerals in the rock, such as mica and basalt. Schist is characterized by foliation, a layering of crystals that are visible to the human eye.

At 2.1 miles into the hike, the trail is indistinguishable and unmarked as it crosses a grassy area used by Adventure Links. The trail reenters the woods after 0.1 mile, and within 100 yards it forks at a sign stating "parking" and "lodge." Follow the left fork toward the parking area. Head behind the Adventure Links maintenance area with the ropes course on your left. Cross a road (it leads to a pond down the hill to the left) and follow the trail until it ends at the Adventure Links driveway. Turn left and left again back toward Yates Ford Road in 0.1 mile.

HUNTLEY MEADOWS

BEFORE YOU GO
Map: Available at the visitor center and on the park's website
Contact: Huntley Meadows Park
Nearest city: Alexandria, VA

ABOUT THE HIKE
Easy, year-round
Length: 1.6 miles, loop
Hiking time: 1–1½ hours
High point/elevation gain: 82 feet/75 feet
Access: Cinder, asphalt, and boardwalk; jogging-stroller friendly

GETTING THERE

From I-495 (Capital Beltway), take exit 177A for US 1 south toward Fort Belvoir. Drive 4.2 miles, and turn right onto Lockheed Boulevard. After 0.6 mile, turn left into the park.

ON THE TRAIL

Situated in Alexandria south of the beltway, Huntley Meadows provides a 1500-acre green space for hiking and nature watching—especially bird-watching. More than 200 species of birds either migrate through the park or make it their home. Species commonly found in the park include great blue herons, great and snowy egrets, kingfishers, and red-winged blackbirds, to name a few. The boardwalk and observation tower in the wetland provide many opportunities to observe these birds and other animals, such as turtles, beavers, dragonflies, butterflies, and frogs.

The 1.6-mile loop is flat and wide on either cinder, asphalt, or boardwalk, making it easy for parents to manipulate strollers on all three trails: Cedar, Heron, and Deer. The loop is particularly great for families with younger kids. The hike may be shortened by 0.15 mile, but that option leaves out the observation tower. The trail is marked with signs at the intersections and has fifteen knee-high trail posts with maps indicating with a red dot where you are on the three trails that complete the loop. Throughout the hike, the park has placed benches and interpretive signs to educate hikers about the wetlands and the plants and animals that inhabit it.

Watch for wildlife while hiking the large inland wetland at Huntley Meadows.

The park visitor center has restrooms, exhibits about the wetlands and the history of the park, and staff to answer your questions. It also sells a small selection of nature-related children's books.

The hike begins on the Cedar Trail at the front entrance of the visitor center. For 0.3 mile, the Cedar Trail meanders through the forest until it reaches a fork. Turn right onto the Heron Trail. In the next 0.1 mile, the first interpretive sign about the importance of wetlands appears and the boardwalk begins.

WETLANDS: AN ENVIRONMENTAL POWERHOUSE

A wetland is an area of land, tidal or nontidal, in which the soil is covered by or saturated with water for most of the year. Huntley Meadows' wetland is a nontidal marsh or wet meadow created by a depression in the land from an ancient tributary of the Potomac River. Certain plants like cattails and creatures like carpenter frogs are characteristic of this wetland.

Wetlands prevent flooding, store water during droughts, collect runoff, improve water quality by filtering pollutants and nutrients, and provide habitat for plants and animals and highly productive breeding grounds for crustaceans, fish, amphibians, and reptiles. Furthermore, wetlands are economically viable because they draw tourists and also because humans consume a lot of the biological life they produce.

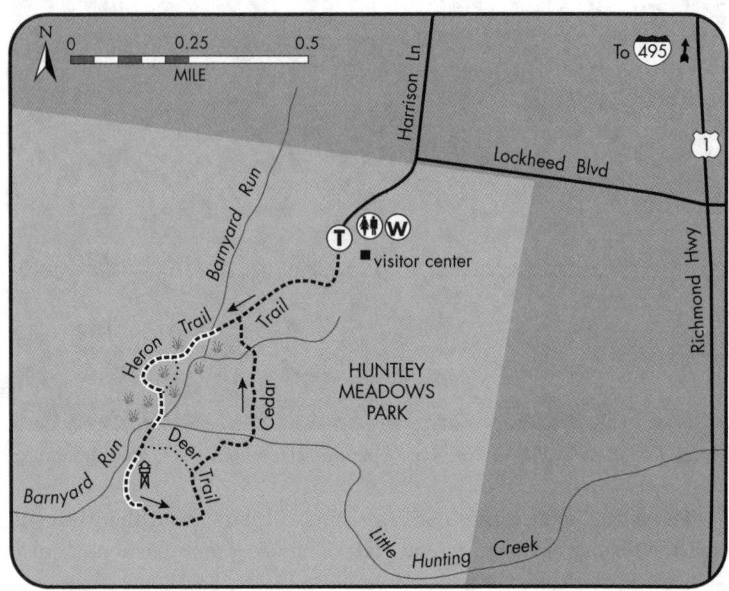

Shortly after you step onto the boardwalk, you and your kids will see a large beaver lodge that has taken over a tree trunk, a bench, and half of the boardwalk. Play "I Spy" with your kids to see if they can find a turtle, beaver, frog, great blue heron, egret, cattail, snake, and fish. Keep your eyes peeled; there is a lot to observe. When I scouted the park with my family, we saw a large snapping turtle adjacent to the boardwalk. Remember to keep a safe distance from animals as we humans are visiting their homes.

In 0.1 mile, the boardwalk splits, but since it reconnects, it doesn't matter whether you go left or right. To the right, there is a raised-deck with interpretive signs and a few benches overlooking the wetland. Once the forks rejoin, the boardwalk continues through the wetland for another 0.1 mile where it becomes cinder and reenters the forest. The cinder lasts for 100 yards before another boardwalk begins and the Deer Trail intersects from the left. Continue straight on the Heron Trail. In 100 feet, look for a two-tiered observation tower, where photographers and birders with binoculars often observe and wait for the perfect photo.

About 0.1 mile after the observation tower, the boardwalk and the Heron Trail end. Continue straight on the Deer Trail. Pass an informal trail on the right (posted with a sign) as it leads to a neighborhood surrounding the park. Walk another 0.1 mile, and pass a people's choice trail, marked with a "trail closed" sign, that intersects from the left and right. Cross a wooden walkway, and follow the trail as it curves left. In 0.1 mile, the Deer Trail intersects the Cedar Trail.

Turn right onto the Cedar Trail for 0.3 mile as it meanders through the woods back to its intersection with the Heron Trail. At this intersection, a large sign directs hikers to turn right back to the visitor center, which is 0.3 mile away.

HAUL ROAD TRAIL AT DYKE MARSH

BEFORE YOU GO
Map: Available on the preserve's website
Contact: Dyke Marsh Wildlife Preserve
Nearest city: Alexandria, VA

ABOUT THE HIKE
Easy, year-round
Length: 1.5 miles, out and back
Hiking time: 1–1½ hours
High point/elevation gain: 36 feet/30 feet
Access: Cinder and boardwalk, jogging-stroller friendly

GETTING THERE

From Maryland, take I-495 (Capital Beltway) to exit 177A and B for US 1. Make a slight right toward Mount Vernon off the exit ramp. Curve right onto Church Street. Turn right onto South Washington Street, which turns into Mount Vernon Memorial Highway (also known as George Washington Memorial Parkway). Drive 1.2 miles, then turn left into Belle Haven Park and Marina. The parking lot is on the left.

From Virginia, take I-495 (Capital Beltway) to exit 177A and B for US 1 south toward Fort Belvoir. Keep right for US 1 south. Drive 400 feet, and turn left onto Old Richmond Highway. Drive 200 feet, and make a slight right onto Fort Hunt Road. Drive 0.7 mile, and turn left onto Belle Haven Road. After 0.4 mile, turn right onto Mount Vernon Memorial Parkway (also known as George Washington Memorial Parkway). Drive 0.1 mile, and turn left into Belle Haven Park and Marina. The parking lot is on the left.

ON THE TRAIL

Dyke Marsh Wildlife Preserve is part of the George Washington Memorial Parkway, which is owned and maintained by the National Park Service. This 485-acre tidal marsh contains marsh, floodplains, and swamp forest. It is affected by a three-foot tide originating from the Chesapeake Bay. The floodplain and swamp forest are four feet above high tide but are sometimes flooded due to heavy winds during high tide and large amounts of rainfall. Dyke Marsh can be explored on foot via the Haul Road Trail or in a canoe or kayak (motorized boats are prohibited in the marsh).

The unmarked Haul Road Trail is 1.5 miles out and back on a wide, cinder road that changes to raised boardwalk at the end of the marsh. The trail is mostly shady with exposure to the sun on the boardwalk. Interpretive signs along the trail describe the marsh and what

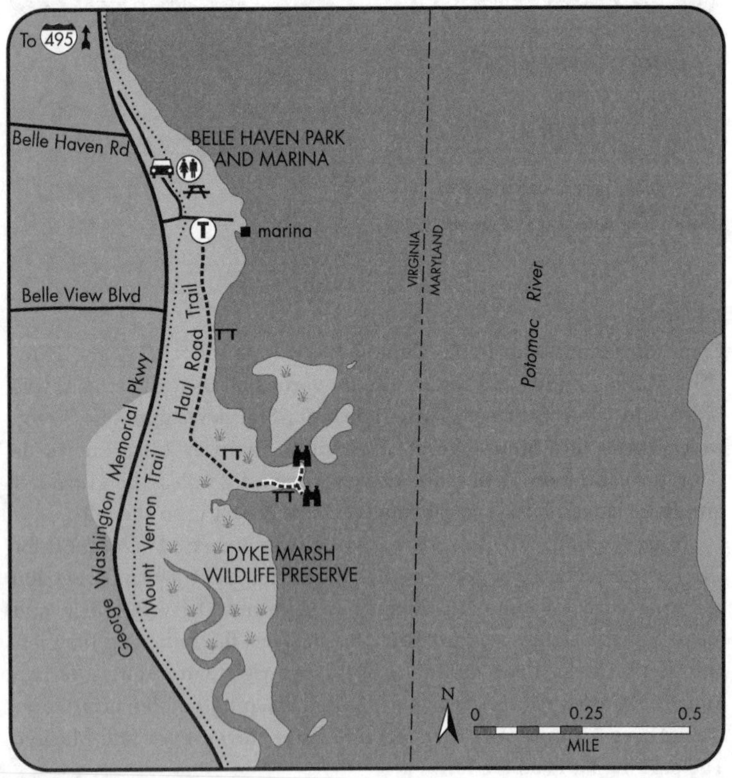

hikers see. During most of the hike, you can see the Potomac River through openings in the swamp forest and access the river at a number of locations. Belle Haven has many picnic tables, river access, and open grass for hanging out and playing before you leave the park.

Watch for birds and kayakers in Dyke Marsh.

The hike begins on the right side of the driveway leading to the marina. A large sign, kiosk, interpretive sign, and gate indicate Dyke Marsh and the trail. The first 0.5 mile traverses straight through the edge of the swamp forest with the Potomac on the left side of the trail. A quarter mile into the hike, a large opening in the forest provides a beautiful view of the boats in the marina and National Harbor across the Potomac. There is a bench here and an interpretive sign about the kinds of birds, such as bald eagles, that inhabit this marsh. Continue down the trail for another half mile where the trail curves left and out of the swamp forest into the floodplain.

In less than 0.1 mile, cross a bridge over a tidal gut where there is a bench and another interpretive sign about the important functions of each part of Dyke Marsh. A tidal gut is a channel that moves water, both salt and fresh, around a marsh. The vegetation in a marsh collects sediment flowing downstream, oxygenates the water, provides habitat and food for animals, and serves as a giant filter that absorbs nitrogen.

ALGAL BLOOMS

When there is too much nitrogen (the fertilizers we put on our lawns and crops are one source) in our waterways, then algal blooms occur. Algal blooms prevent underwater sea grasses from receiving sunlight for photosynthesis. Furthermore, when the algae dies and decomposes, it depletes the waterway of dissolved oxygen, a vital nutrient for fish. Algal blooms create dead zones in waterways.

After the bridge, the trail zigzags left and right a few times; at 0.1 mile, a people's choice trail on the right leads to an inlet in the marsh. At low tide, there are some large scraps of cement pilings along the inlet's shoreline. Shortly thereafter, the boardwalk begins with a big open deck, a few benches, and some interpretive signs. The view here looks south on the Potomac River. The boardwalk turns left and then it ends in 100 yards with a view looking into the guts of the marsh. From here, turn around and retrace your footsteps 0.75 mile back to the marina driveway.

56 BEAVER POND AND GREAT BLUE HERON TRAILS

BEFORE YOU GO
Map: Available at the trailhead kiosk
Contact: Accotink Bay Wildlife Refuge
Nearest city: Fort Belvoir, VA

ABOUT THE HIKE
Easy, year-round
Length: 1.5 miles, loop and spur
Hiking time: 1–1½ hours
High point/elevation gain: 59 feet/62 feet
Access: Compact soil, passable for jogging strollers

GETTING THERE

From I-495 (Capital Beltway), take the exit for I-95 south. Drive 5 miles, and take exit 166A for VA 286 (Fairfax County Parkway) toward Fort Belvoir and Newington. After 3.3 miles, turn left onto Richmond Highway (US 1). Drive 0.3 mile, and turn right onto Pohick Road. The parking lot is on the right before the Fort Belvoir security gate.

ON THE TRAIL

Accotink Bay Wildlife Refuge was created in 1979 by Fort Belvoir to protect the land surrounding Accotink Bay on the Potomac River. The 1360-acre refuge has 12 miles of trails and is home to Accotink Creek, marshes, ponds, and forests. It is well known for excellent birding for migratory birds and shorebirds; both bald eagles and peregrine falcons may also be observed. Beyond birds, hikers may see beavers, snakes, turtles, and frogs in the refuge. The refuge has an environmental education center on the Fort Belvoir base that offers videos and

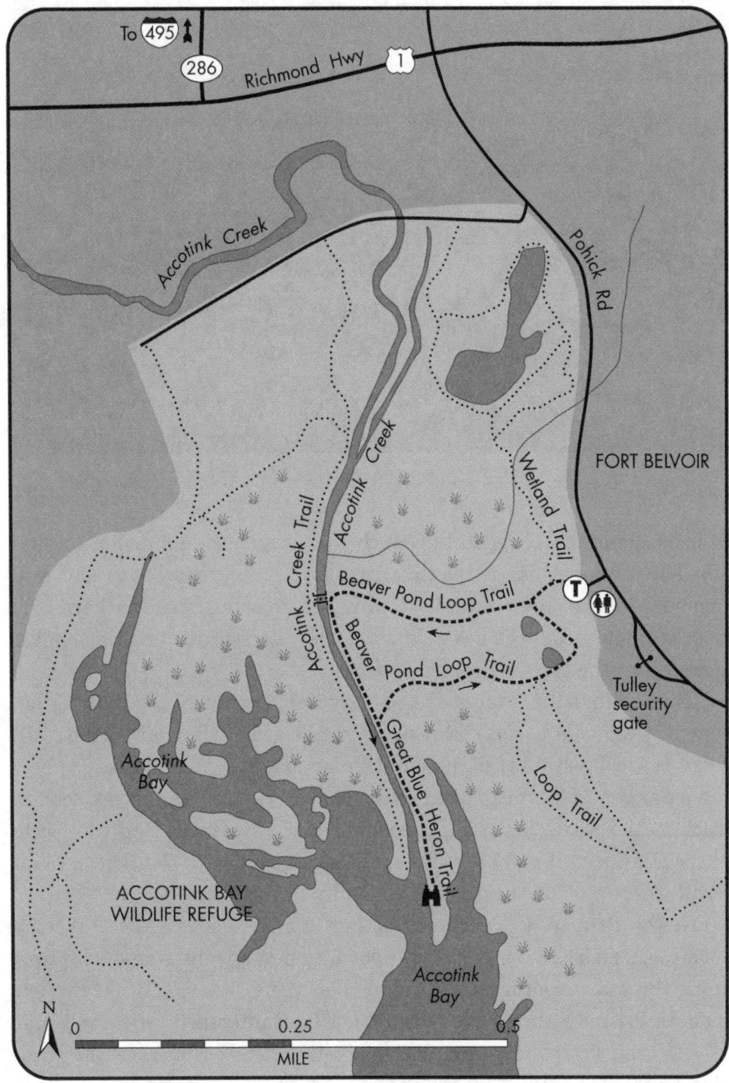

displays about the refuge and its wildlife. Note that you must have government-issued identification to pass through the security gate, but the trails are open to everyone.

The Beaver Pond Loop and Great Blue Heron trails travel up and down berms of land that slope to marshes on either side. These berms

Look out through the bird blind at the marsh—what birds do you spot?

house upland forest vegetation, such as beech trees and mountain laurel. The 1.5-mile hike is blazed with small green metal tags and well signed at each intersection; it provides quarter-mile markers and benches. The trail does not gain much elevation at any one time, but it does follow the terrain over the berms.

The trailhead is located at the back right corner of the parking lot, which is adjacent to the Tulley security gate at Fort Belvoir. At the trailhead, a kiosk with a trail map and a sign explains that because of possible danger from unexploded ordinances in the refuge, hikers need to stick to the trails. The trail turns left at the trailhead and intersects the Wetland Trail in 50 feet. Continue straight toward the Beaver Pond Trail where the loop begins in 100 yards.

At the Beaver Pond Loop Trail sign, continue straight to hike the loop counterclockwise. A marsh appears on the right side of the trail until the quarter-mile marker, and then there is a marsh on the left side. In 0.1 mile, the Beaver Pond Loop Trail intersects with the Great Blue Heron Trail and a bridge over Accotink Creek with access to Accotink Creek Trail. Built by one of the units at Fort Belvoir, this suspension bridge is fun for kids to walk on. Like the Great Blue Heron Trail, the Accotink Creek Trail travels on a narrow spit of land between the creek and a marsh to a boardwalk for bird-watching.

Return to the Beaver Pond Trail and head south. The trail tread becomes sandy after the bridge and along the creek. Follow the creek for 0.15 mile to its intersection with the Beaver Pond Loop Trail. (The 0.5-mile marker is just before this intersection.) Hike the Great Blue Heron Trail straight for 0.3 mile to a boardwalk and a bird blind at the end overlooking a huge marsh at the mouth of Accotink Bay. Bird blinds provide camouflage for people to observe birds up close without disturbing them.

Return on the Great Blue Heron Trail to the Beaver Pond Loop Trail. Turn right on the Beaver Pond Loop Trail, and cross a stream. After the bridge, the trail gently climbs a berm. The Beaver Pond Loop Trail travels for a quarter mile to its first intersection with the Loop Trail on the right; pass this intersection and the next one. The trail bisects a small pond with frogs and turtles. After the pond, the trail curves left, ascends a berm, and heads back down on a few steps. In 0.1 mile, a pond appears on the left just before the intersection with the connector trail to the parking lot. Turn right, and hike less than 0.1 mile back to the parking lot.

WOODMARSH TRAIL

BEFORE YOU GO
Map: Available at the trailhead kiosk and on the refuge's website
Contact: Elizabeth Hartwell Mason Neck National Wildlife Refuge
Nearest city: Lorton, VA

ABOUT THE HIKE
Easy/moderate, year-round
Length: 2.4 miles, loop and spur
Hiking time: 1½–2 hours
High point/elevation gain: 82 feet/43 feet
Access: Compact soil and boardwalk, passable for jogging strollers

GETTING THERE

From I-495 (Capital Beltway), take the exit for I-95. Take exit 166A for VA 286 (Fairfax County Parkway) toward Fort Belvoir and Newington. Drive 3.3 miles, and turn right onto Richmond Highway. After 3 miles, turn left onto Gunston Road (VA 242 and 600). Drive 4 miles, and turn right onto High Point Road. Drive 1.2 miles, and turn left, before the fee station for Mason Neck State Park, into the parking lot.

ON THE TRAIL

The 2227-acre Elizabeth Hartwell Mason Neck Wildlife Refuge was preserved in 1969 to protect bald eagle habitat on the Potomac River. Both the refuge and Mason Neck State Park together cover more than 4000 acres of land on the Mason Neck peninsula, which is bordered by Gunston Cove to the north and Belmont Bay to the south. Mason Neck State Park, Pohick Bay Regional Park, and Gunston Hall (the former

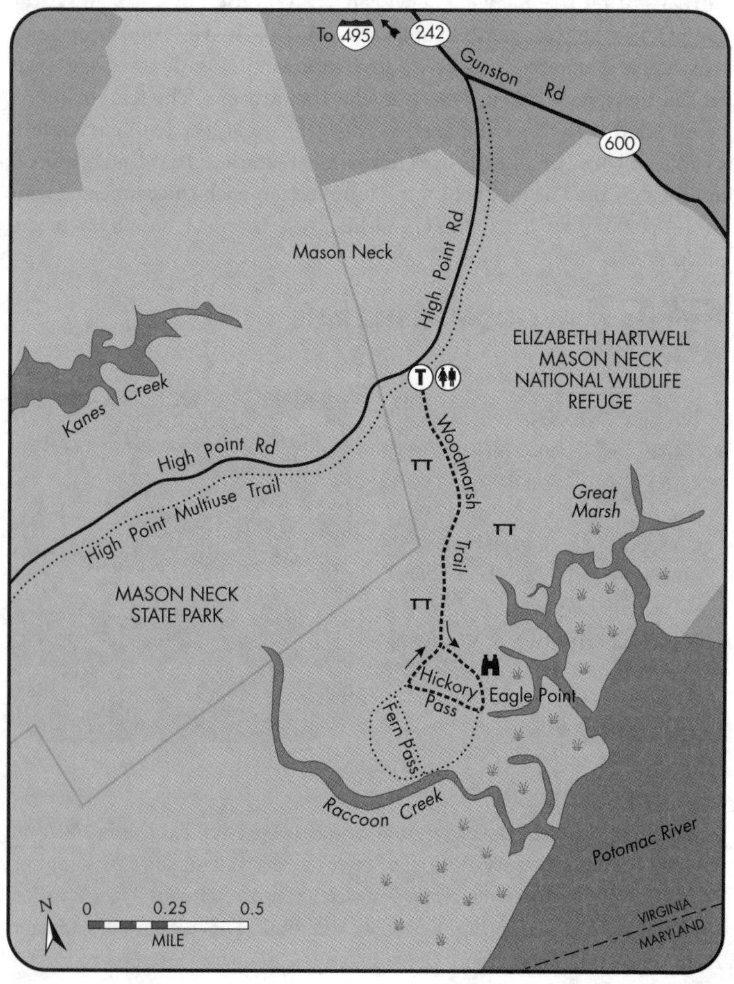

The pavilion overlooking the Great Marsh is a great spot to observe bald eagles.

5500-acre corn and tobacco farm owned by George Mason) are also located on this same peninsula.

Great Marsh, a freshwater tidal marsh within the refuge, is 207 acres and supports one of the largest great blue heron colonies in Virginia. Elizabeth Hartwell was a local resident who stopped the development of a housing community and airport on the peninsula. She observed the value the land had for the endangered bald eagle and wanted to preserve its habitat.

The Woodmarsh Trail is a 0.9-mile out-and-back hike with a variety of loop opportunities from 0.6 mile to 1 mile, including Eagle Point or Hickory and Fern passes. Hikers follow a shady trail through forests with pine, oak, and hickory trees blazed in yellow and with signs at each intersection. The highlight is a large pavilion overlooking Great Marsh where you can look for bald eagles; don't forget to bring binoculars. The trail follows the shallow undulations of the land, and boardwalks traverse low, wet areas.

The trailhead is in the back parking lot next to a kiosk with a trail map. Shortly after the trailhead, the trail curves left and crosses over its first bridge at 0.1 mile. The first bench appears at about 0.2 mile, and then a puncheon helps you cross a low, wet place on the trail at 0.3 mile. At 0.4 mile, the trail curves left where there is a second bench and bridge, after which the trail curves right. Just before 0.7 mile, a third bench appears.

At 0.7 mile and 0.8 mile, cross the third and fourth bridges on the spur, and then at 0.9 mile a trail sign at the intersection points you left toward Eagle Point in 0.2 mile. A large pavilion at Eagle Point sits just off the loop atop the Great Marsh. The view of the marsh from here is spectacular; you and your kids may spot bald eagles and great blue herons.

BALD EAGLE: ENDANGERED NO MORE

In the mid-1900s, the bald eagle population dramatically declined due to hunting, trapping, and widespread use of DDT, a pesticide used in US agriculture. In 1978, with only 500 left in the Lower 48, the bald eagle was put on the endangered species list. With its protection and the ban of DDT, the bald eagle has made a dramatic recovery, boasting tens of thousands in the United States. In 2007, bald eagles were taken off the endangered species list, but they still receive protection, particularly through the establishment of wildlife refuges like Mason Neck.

After leaving the pavilion, turn left to continue the loop. In 0.1 mile, the trail makes a hard turn to the right, and then it goes left over a bridge, up a short hill, and left again. The trail zigzags left and right before coming to the intersection with Hickory Pass; turn right and hike 0.1 mile. At the second intersection, Hickory Pass continues left; however, turn right to follow the arrow for the parking lot. In 0.2 mile, the trail curves right before completing the loop. Turn left to return to the parking lot on the spur in 0.9 mile.

BAYVIEW TRAIL

BEFORE YOU GO
Map: Available at the entrance station and trailhead kiosk
Contact: Mason Neck State Park (charges a fee)
Nearest city: Lorton, VA

ABOUT THE HIKE
Easy, year-round
Length: 1 mile, loop
Hiking time: ½–1 hour
High point/elevation gain: 101 feet/95 feet
Access: Compact soil and boardwalk, not passable for jogging strollers

GETTING THERE

From I-495 (Capital Beltway), take the exit for I-95. Take exit 166A for VA 286 (Fairfax County Parkway) toward Fort Belvoir and Newington. Drive 3.3 miles, and turn right onto Richmond Highway. After 3 miles, turn left onto Gunston Road. Drive 4 miles, and turn right onto High

The views along Belmont Bay on the Potomac River

Point Road. Drive 3 miles to the entrance station; continue to the parking area at the end of High Point Road, next to the visitor center.

ON THE TRAIL

Mason Neck State Park covers 1825 acres of land on a Virginia peninsula into the Potomac River with Belmont Bay to the south and Gunston Cove to the north. Much of the peninsula is protect by either the state park or Elizabeth Hartwell Mason Neck National Wildlife Refuge. The state park offers many recreational opportunities for families: hiking, a paved bike trail, birding, a playground, picnic areas, swimming, fishing, a visitor center, a boat launch, and canoe and kayak rentals for exploring Belmont Bay. Most of the trails are shorter than 1.5 miles, but they provide excellent opportunities to hike through upland forests, meadows, and wetlands and alongside open water. There are plenty of picnic tables adjacent to the trailhead for barbecuing or picnicking.

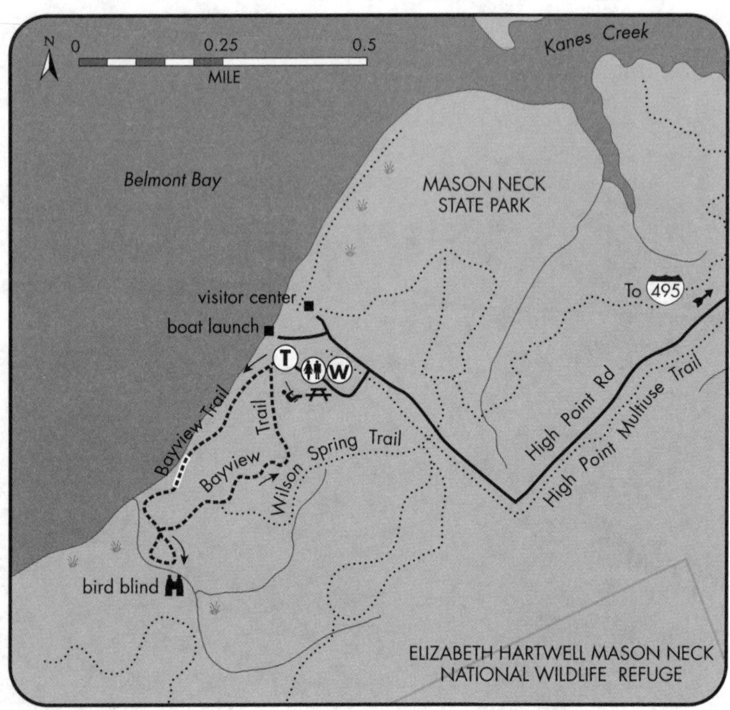

The 1-mile Bayview Trail starts above Belmont Bay and then weaves down to the water before turning through a marsh and back up into the forest. The wide trail is well marked with red blazes and signs at the intersections. It has two sets of stairs, which makes it difficult for families with jogging strollers to navigate.

The hike begins at a kiosk at the end of the circular driveway near the playground. It goes counterclockwise around the loop. From the kiosk, hike straight toward the water, and turn left to walk alongside Belmont Bay. Hike 0.2 mile above the bay until the trail curves right, descends some steps, and crosses a bridge. At this point, you are next to the bay on a boardwalk where an interpretive sign explains the erosion of the shoreline. The break walls were built to prevent further erosion of the riverbanks. Healthy streambanks gently slope toward the water line, and they are covered by vegetation to hold the soil in place and prevent erosion. These banks are cut and steep with a lot of soil exposed to the water. Marshes along the Potomac River, or any waterway, provide a buffer zone against erosion and filter pollutants from the water.

The boardwalk ends in a little less than 0.1 mile where the trail curves left and becomes sandy. Through the trees on the left, you can see a wetland. The trail curves right where another boardwalk crosses a small inlet. Hikers can access the sandy riverbank on Belmont Bay before and after the boardwalk. The trail turns left at 0.4 mile and traverses a wetland on a boardwalk. During summer, the marsh is abuzz with many different types of insects. The boardwalk over the marsh is 100 yards long, and at the end, you ascend some stairs. At the top, the trail levels off, and the Bayview Trail makes a small secondary loop to visit a large wetland in the upland forest.

At the intersection, continue hiking straight on the Bayview Trail toward the bird blind. The trail curves to the right, and a bird blind appears to the left. The blind sits slightly above the large wetland where hikers may spot a bald eagle. The trail follows the wetland for 100 yards before circling back into the forest to the same intersection. This secondary loop is a little more than 0.1 mile. At the intersection, continue straight for 0.2 mile on the Bayview Trail through a mixture of pine, oak, American holly, and beech trees until you reach the Wilson Spring Trail on the right. Pass this trail, and continue straight on the Bayview Trail for the next 0.2 mile over a boardwalk and through the forest. The trail ends at the same kiosk where it began.

LITTLE STONEY MOUNTAIN TRAIL

BEFORE YOU GO
Map: Available at the visitor center
Contact: Claude Moore Park
Nearest city: Sterling, VA

ABOUT THE HIKE
Easy/moderate, year-round
Length: 1.5 miles, loop
Hiking time: 1–1½ hours
High point/elevation gain: 427 feet/103 feet
Access: Compact soil and boardwalk, passable for jogging strollers

GETTING THERE

From I-495 (Capital Beltway), take exit 45A for VA 267. Drive 1.7 miles, and take exit 16 for VA 7 (Leesburg Pike) west toward Leesburg. Drive 10 miles, and turn left onto Potomac View Road (VA 637). After 1 mile, turn left onto Cascades Parkway (VA 1794). Drive 0.2 mile, and turn left onto Old Vestals Gap Road. Park at the visitor center.

Waterfowl paddle the ponds at Claude Moore Park.

ON THE TRAIL

Claude Moore Park has 357 acres of woodlands, meadows, wetlands, and ponds in eastern Loudoun County. The park offers 11 miles of hiking trails, two ponds for fishing, picnic areas, a sports complex, Lanesville Heritage Area, Loudoun Heritage Farm Museum, and educational programming at the Frogshackle Nature Center and in the Discovery Room at the visitor center.

Steeped in history, Old Vestals Gap Road was once walked by the Manahoac tribe thousands of years ago as evidenced by the hunting tools discovered there during archaeological digs. In the late 1700s, settlers moving to the Shenandoahs walked the road from Alexandria. George Washington traveled the road from Mount Vernon during the French and Indian War. In 1814 when the British were burning Washington, DC, the Declaration of Independence and Constitution were carried by wagon to a safe place on Old Vestals Gap Road. When you hike this road, imagine the stories of the people whose feet once traveled it.

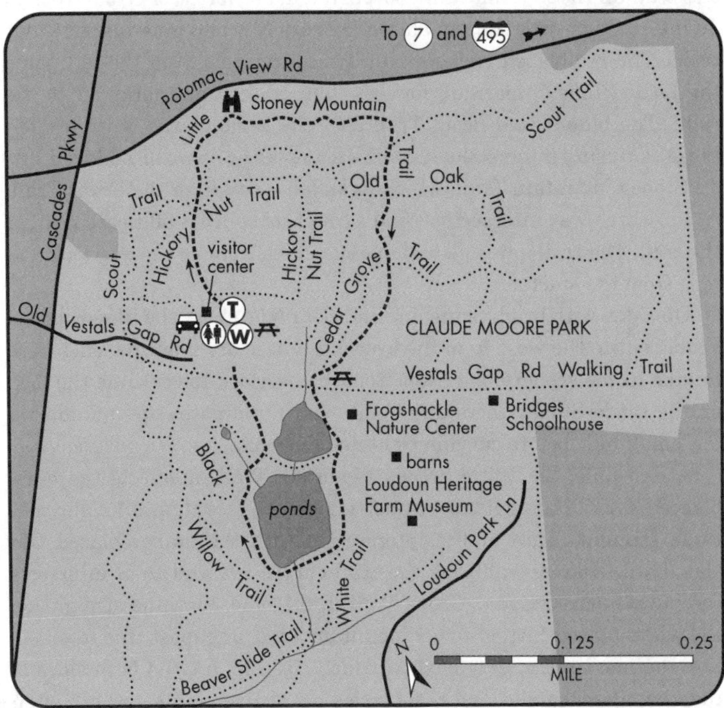

Before you leave the park, check out the historic buildings that are clustered together along Old Vestals Gap Road: Frogshackle Nature Center, an old log cabin built in the 1700s; Bridges Schoolhouse, built in 1870; Lanesville Ordinary, a tavern; the barns; and the Loudoun Heritage Farm Museum, which is open Tuesday through Saturday, 10:00 AM to 5:00 PM, and Sunday, 12:00 PM to 5:00 PM, and closed on Mondays.

This 1.5-mile hike traverses a little more than a mile of the white-blazed Little Stoney Mountain Trail. The park has a spaghetti network of trails, all color coded and well marked at each intersection. The clockwise hike gains most of its elevation on the Little Stoney Mountain Trail behind the visitor center on the way up to the overlook. The first half of the trail is well shaded in a maturing forest of deciduous and conifer trees and then much less so around the two ponds.

The hike begins at the northeast corner of the visitor center on a boardwalk adjacent to a small trail sign with a white blaze labeled Little Stoney Mountain. Shortly after beginning the hike, pass an interpretive trail on the left, and walk through a dense forest of cedar trees to an intersection with the red-blazed Hickory Nut and blue-blazed Scout trails. The red-blazed Hickory Nut Trail intersects from the left, joins the Little Stoney Mountain for less than 50 feet, and forks off to the right. The blue-blazed Scout Trail does the same as the red. Through these confusing intersections, continue to stay on the white-blazed Little Stoney Mountain Trail, which forks left away from the Scout Trail. At this three-way intersection, find a couple of benches off to the right of the trail. The trail gains elevation and curves right to the overlook, 0.3 mile from the start.

On a day with bright sunshine and clear blue skies, the Blue Ridge is visible out to the west from the overlook. There are a few benches here to take in the scenery. Turn left from the overlook to continue the loop on the Little Stoney Mountain Trail, which undulates up and down a few small hills before curving right and downhill.

At 0.6 mile, the Little Stoney Mountain Trail intersects the blue-blazed Scout Trail again; continue straight. In less than 0.1 mile, continue straight again at the intersection with the orange-blazed Old Oak Trail. Hike downhill as the trail curves left and then intersects the purple-blazed Cedar Grove Trail in 0.1 mile; continue straight on the white-blazed Little Stoney Mountain Trail. Just past this intersection there are blackberry bushes, which ripen in July, on both sides of the trail. Blackberries and raspberries are native plants and are often found on sunny forest edges or in meadows. The plants grow from the seeds inside their fruit; the seeds, which are indigestible by birds and mammals, are deposited in the animal's droppings. Both plants develop fruit when pollinators like honeybees fertilize their flowers.

HONEYBEE DECLINE

Over the last thirty years, the honeybee population in the United States has declined by almost half with not one specific cause, but many. Pesticides, pests, pathogens, colony collapse disorder, and a lack of a food sources have all contributed to the decline in honeybees. In recent years, farmers growing crops such as almonds, blueberries, strawberries, and alfalfa have become alarmed by the decline because they depend on honeybees to pollinate their crops.

The Little Stoney Mountain Trail crosses a bridge and enters a grassy area with a picnic pavilion. Cross the grass diagonally to the right toward Old Vestals Gap Road, where a wooden post sports a white blaze. There is no trail tread through the grass before or after Old Vestals Gap Road. Hike over the grass toward the pond, and evidence of a trail tread appears at the pond's edge. Follow the trail tread with the pond on the right and a small meadow on the left. After about 50 feet, the trail curves left away from the pond through the meadow. Then the trail curves right at the edge of the meadow and grass. Follow the edge of the meadow for 20 feet back into some trees where the trail forks. Follow the arrow left to stay on the Little Stoney Mountain Trail.

For 0.1 mile, the trail continues through immature trees and heavy vegetation between the second pond and a parking lot, neither of which hikers can see. A connector trail intersects the Little Stoney Mountain Trail from the right; turn right to hike halfway around the second pond.

This pond has a few small islands where hikers can view native and migrating birds. There are benches along the pond and multiple places for fishing access. The park stocks both ponds with catfish, largemouth bass, and blue gill; children younger than sixteen can fish without a license. The pink-blazed Beaver Slide Trail intersects the connector trail on the left; however, continue to follow the connector trail as it curves right around the pond.

In 0.1 mile, the connector trail veers left away from the pond where it intersects the green-blazed Black Willow Trail on the left. In 20 feet, turn right and over a small bridge to head back to the first pond. Pass an access trail on the right to the second pond, and continue straight on a boardwalk as it curves to the left toward the first pond. At the pond's edge, turn left and walk through the grassy area toward Old Vestals Gap Road and the driveway to the visitor center on the opposite side of the road.

RUST NATURE SANCTUARY

BEFORE YOU GO
Map: Available at the welcome center and on the society's website
Contact: Rust Nature Sanctuary
Nearest city: Leesburg, VA

ABOUT THE HIKE
Easy, year-round
Length: 0.9 mile, loop
Hiking time: ½–1 hour
High point/elevation gain: 538 feet/65 feet
Access: Compact soil, passable for jogging strollers

GETTING THERE

From I-495 (Capital Beltway), take exit 45 for VA 267 toward Leesburg. Drive 25 miles, and take exit 1A for US 15 south (VA 7 west). Drive 1 mile, and keep left for VA 7 west. After 1.6 miles, exit for VA 7 business toward Leesburg. Drive 0.2 mile, and turn right onto West Market Street. Follow this for 0.1 mile, then turn right onto Catoctin Circle. Drive 0.3 mile, and turn right onto Children's Center Road. Drive 0.5 mile to the parking lot beside Rust Manor.

ON THE TRAIL

Rust Nature Sanctuary, a 68-acre preserve, offers meadows, forests, and a pond close to downtown Leesburg. Henry Harrison built the manor on the property in 1910 for his wife Anna Lee, cousin of Robert E. Lee. Upon Anna Lee's death in 1928, the manor and property were donated to the St. Emma Agricultural and Industrial Institute, a school for young black men. The Rust family purchased the estate from St. Emma shortly thereafter. In 2000, the family gave the estate to the Audubon Naturalist Society. The property provides animals, migratory birds in particular, with a place of refuge from a rapidly developing community;

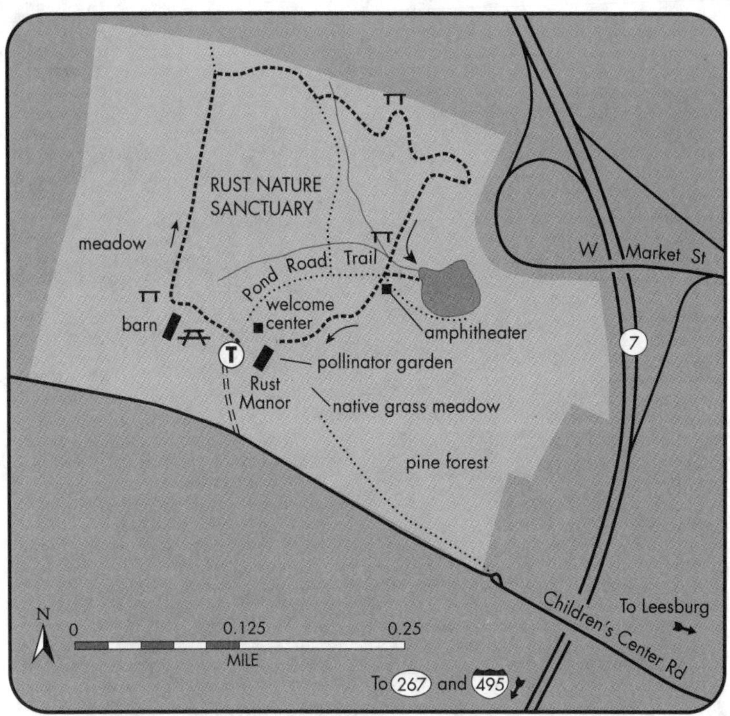

some birds need large areas of forest to reproduce and prefer to nest in the interior of a forest with little to no human impact. The sanctuary has a pollinator garden, nature programs, interpretive trails, a picnic area, and a small natural playground. The Audubon Naturalist Society rents the manor and grounds to the public for social gatherings; however, the trails are still open to the public for hiking during those occasions. If the manor is not rented out, enjoy a picnic on its quiet, expansive grounds with large canopy trees before you leave.

The 0.9-mile loop passes through all three ecosystems here: meadow, forest, and pond. The trails are not named, except for the Pond Road Trail, nor are they blazed or signed. However, the small property and trail system are easy to navigate. This hike follows the outermost trails on the property. It is mostly shaded except for the meadow at the beginning of the loop. The trail undulates with the landscape; hiking it is like riding a baby roller coaster through the meadow; it then makes a gentle descent toward the pond and finally rises back toward the manor.

Listen for frogs at the Rust Sanctuary pond.

The hike begins on the west side of the manor adjacent to the parking lots and picnic area. There is no identifiable path until you reach the meadow. Walk toward the natural playground and the north side of the barn. Just past the barn, there is a kiosk, birdhouse, and bench; turn right onto the trail. The meadow is on your left and the woods on your right for the next 0.15 mile. There are some bluebird houses in the meadow and a few signs identifying trees, such as a pignut and mockernut hickory that stand side by side.

PIGNUT VS. MOCKERNUT

Hickory trees, members of the walnut family, produce a meaty nut that is covered by a hard, sometimes thick outer shell. Pignut and mockernut are common native hickories found in the Mid-Atlantic. How can you tell them apart? What differences do you observe between the two trees standing at the forest edge next to the trail? Their bark is similar with deep, vertical creased ridges; however, the ridges on the mockernut's bark furl at the edges.

The easiest way to tell them apart is to compare their leaves. The hickory tree has compound leaves instead of simple leaves. A compound leaf has multiple leaflets on a single stem. A pignut hickory has five to seven leaflets per stem, while a mockernut has seven to nine. Finally, the fruit (nut) they produce is similar but has subtle differences. The mockernut shell is thicker with a ribbed nut, while the pignut shell is thin with a smooth round nut. Hickory nuts are edible and used to be a staple food of Native Americans.

About 0.2 mile into the hike, turn right into the forest. The trail descends gently and curves right within 100 yards before it forks. Turn left and walk on a bridge over an often dry streambed. After the streambed, hike up a short and gentle gulch created by the stream. Shortly after, the trail curves right twice, first at a post marked with the number seven and then at a bench. The trail enters a patch of pines where the ground is covered with pine needles and sparse ground cover due to the trees' acidic nature. Among the pines, the trail makes two more curves to the right and then turns left and over a bridge. Within 50 feet, cross another bridge, where there is a bench, before reaching the kiosk at the amphitheater. To reach the pond, turn left at this four-way intersection, and hike 0.1 mile down a wide dirt road.

The pond is home to fish, many frogs (particularly carpenter frogs, which produce hammering sounds), turtles, butterflies, and dragonflies. A large dock at the end of the dirt road has tall cattails on its right side. The pine trees surrounding the pond provide sight and sound cover from the VA 7 ramp.

When you're ready, hike back to the kiosk and amphitheater, and turn left around the back of the amphitheater. The trail turns right behind it and continues uphill 0.1 mile to the manor. It ends at the pollinator garden in front of Rust Manor.

BANSHEE REEKS NATURE PRESERVE

BEFORE YOU GO
Map: Available at visitor center kiosk and on the park's website
Contact: Banshee Reeks Nature Preserve
Nearest city: Leesburg, VA

ABOUT THE HIKE
Moderate, year-round
Length: 3.2 miles, loop
Hiking time: 2–2½ hours
High point/elevation gain: 351 feet/154 feet
Access: Compact soil and grass, passable for jogging strollers

GETTING THERE

From I-495 (Capital Beltway), take exit 45 for VA 267 toward Leesburg. Drive 22 miles, and take exit 3 for Shreve Mill Road. Turn left onto Shreve Mill Road. Drive 1 mile, and turn left onto Evergreen Mills Road (VA 621). Drive 2.7 miles, and turn right onto The Woods Road (VA 771). Drive 1.3 miles, and turn left into the preserve. Drive 0.8 mile to the visitor center.

ON THE TRAIL

Nestled in the rolling meadows and forests just south of the town of Leesburg, quiet and unknown Banshee Reeks Nature Preserve has 725 acres and offers 20 miles of hiker-only trails. Hikers can create many different loops in the preserve because its many short and connecting trails were constructed to help visitors experience the area's varied ecosystems and wildlife. The preserve is open to visitors only on weekends and offers a primitive campground available with special permission for groups.

Banshee and *reeks* are Gaelic terms; the name comes from a story told by the first property owner, who was Irish and Scottish. *Banshee* means a female spirit, and *reeks* is a hill. The early nineteenth-century farmer went to Leesburg to conduct business and drink some spirits before returning home. Upon his return, the wind kicked up and the animals howled. A bit bewildered when he arrived home, he told his family that he had heard a banshee on the reeks.

The loop follows the rolling terrain of the hills and ridges above Goose Creek, which borders the preserve for 2 miles. The loop described here

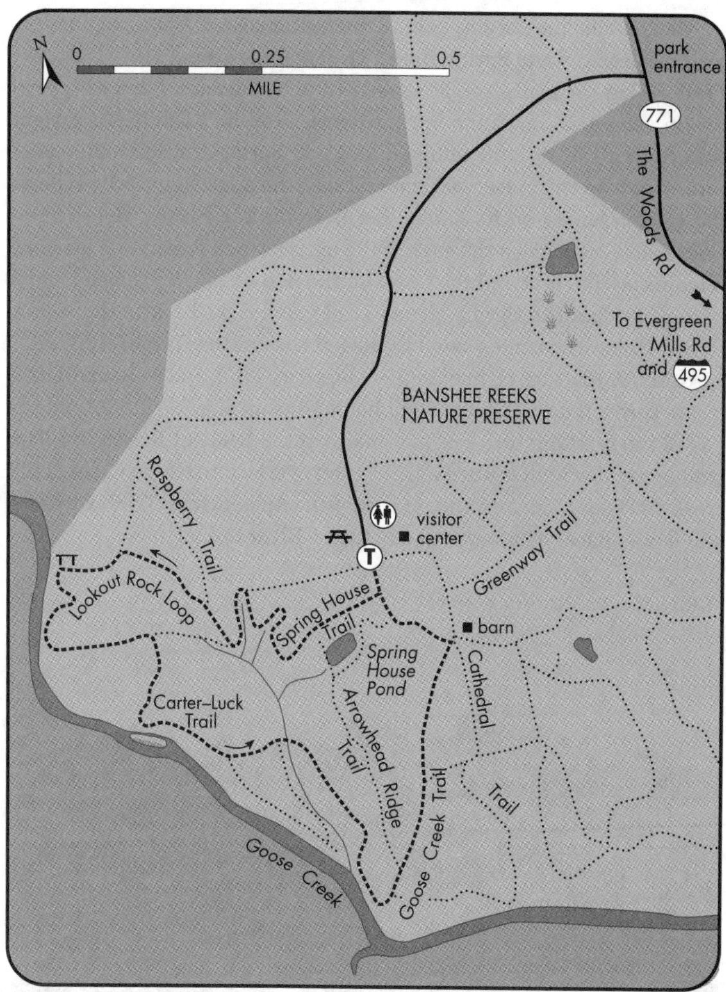

covers the preserve's southwestern section with opportunities to shorten or lengthen the hike to suit your family. The trails are not blazed, but each intersection is marked with arrows and trail names on plastic stakes. The greatest elevation gain on the hike is the return trip to the visitor center from Goose Creek at the end of the loop. The hike passes through sunny meadows and shady hardwood forests. A few tables in the shade at the trailhead make a great spot to spread out a picnic.

The 3.2-mile hike begins behind the visitor center. A trail sign marks two trailheads: one to Spring House Trail and the other to the Greenway Trail. Follow the trail straight ahead through a meadow filled with flowers (in season) to reach the Spring House Trail in 0.1 mile. Turn right onto Spring House Trail to hike alongside Spring House Pond, one of three ponds in the preserve. On a still day, the pond beautifully reflects the trees situated on its banks. For 0.2 mile the Spring House Trail weaves like a snake on the edge of the meadow and forest. The meadow remains on the right and the forest on the left. At the fourth bend, cross a small bridge. The Spring House Trail veers right back to the visitor center. Follow the bend around to the left toward the Raspberry Trail.

In 100 yards, turn right onto the Raspberry Trail, and walk uphill 200 feet to turn left onto Lookout Rock Loop. Hike up a gentle hill 0.1 mile to a trail intersection; turn left to remain on the Lookout Rock Loop. The trail heads downhill toward a bench and overlook to Goose Creek. This creek starts in Linden on the ridge that the Appalachian Trail traverses and flows almost 54 miles to the Potomac River in Sterling.

Meadows near the visitor center

From the overlook, the Lookout Rock Loop turns left and curves inland, then back to the right. From the bench, hike a quarter mile downhill and around the base of the ridge to an intersection; turn right on Carter-Luck Trail. Wind through the thick lowland forest for a quarter mile until it forks; turn left toward the Goose Creek Trail. In 250 feet, a trail intersects from the right; however, continue straight over the bridge onto Goose Creek Trail. This trail turns right after the bridge and follows the creek to the left for 0.2 mile. Arrowhead Ridge rises above the trail to the left.

Goose Creek Trail meets Goose Creek at the end of the ridge. On the right, a people's choice trail descends the bank to a rocky streamside. The creek is wide and shallow with a few riffles, a great spot to play in the stream and skip rocks. After you have played in the creek, return to Goose Creek Trail. In 100 feet, Cathedral Trail intersects on the right; however, continue straight on Goose Creek Trail, passing Arrowhead Ridge Trail on the left in another 100 feet. Goose Creek Trail continues uphill for 0.3 mile through a large meadow covered with milkweed, black-eyed Susans, and thistle, some taller than six feet. On a sunny day, you can observe hundreds of butterflies here, all kinds of swallowtails: zebra, tiger, black, and spicebush, to name a few. A third of the way uphill in the meadow, a trail connector intersects from the right toward the Cathedral Trail; continue straight to the barn. On the side of the barn facing the trail intersection, look for a bat box.

BATS: A FLYING MAMMAL

Bats are nocturnal and live in caves, small tree cavities, bat boxes, or old buildings. The only flying mammal, bats get a bad rap. Vital to our ecosystems, they play an integral role in the food web, eat up to 3000 insects each night, and are prey for owls, hawks, raccoons, and skunks. Bats use echolocation, emitting high-frequency sound, to locate insects and navigate. Out of the 1232 bat species worldwide, 17 species (3 endangered) inhabit Virginia, and 10 species inhabit Maryland.

At the barn, turn left and hike 0.1 mile toward the Spring House Trail. The trail forks and continues to the right around an enormous white oak and back toward the visitor center in 0.1 mile. Halfway up the hill to the visitor center, the Spring House Trail intersects from the left; continue straight.

62 RED ROCK WILDERNESS OVERLOOK REGIONAL PARK

BEFORE YOU GO
Map: Available on the park's website
Contact: Red Rock Wilderness Overlook Regional Park
Nearest city: Leesburg, VA

ABOUT THE HIKE
Easy/moderate, year-round
Length: 1.6 miles, loop
Hiking time: 1–1½ hours
High point/elevation gain: 308 feet/82 feet
Access: Compact soil, passable for jogging strollers

GETTING THERE

From I-495 (Capital Beltway), take exit 45 for VA 267 toward Leesburg. Drive 25 miles, and take exit 1B for US 15 north. Drive 2 miles, and turn right onto Edwards Ferry Road (VA 773). After 1.5 miles, turn left into the park.

ON THE TRAIL

Red Rock Wilderness Overlook Regional Park, a 67-acre park, sits on a bluff on the banks of the Potomac River. A trail in the northern corner allows access to the river along about half of the park. While the Potomac is not accessible from the eastern half due to steep cliffs that abut the river, this area provides a spectacular view of the Potomac and Maryland.

The trails at Red Rock are named for and blazed with colors. The longest loop, the 1.2-mile White Trail, follows the park's circumference with a jaunt along its largest stream. The other trails intersect the White Trail, which allows you to shorten or lengthen your hike.

Before your hike, visit the park's historic buildings and read the interpretive signs describing their past uses. In 1869 Charles Paxton, a wealthy businessman, bought 765 acres of land along the Potomac in what is now Loudoun County. In 1872 he built Carlheim Mansion and in subsequent years a farm on what is now Red Rock Wilderness Park. This farm and its buildings, such as the granary, well, and ice and carriage houses, were considered advanced for the late 1800s. Furthermore, the use of concrete for the buildings (a material not commonly

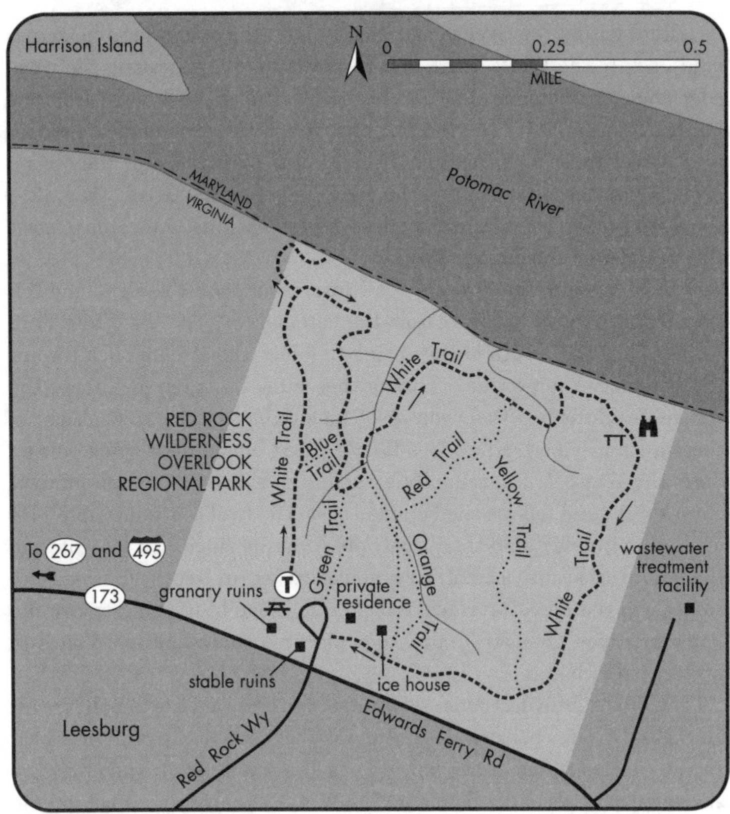

used in the late 1800s) and the buildings' larger-than-normal sizes showcased Paxton's wealth.

The White Trail loop begins at the far northeast corner of the parking lot and is marked with a trail sign. The first 0.2 mile is straight and flat. The trail leads through a century-old forest that sprang up when the land succumbed to natural succession after the Paxton family no longer farmed it. A little after 0.1 mile, the Blue Trail intersects the White Trail on the right; continue straight. The trail makes a gradual descent on the ridge toward the Potomac. At 0.3 mile from the trailhead, turn left on a trail that descends steeply on the ridge to the Potomac, the only trail in the park that provides access to the river. When the Potomac floods, this area can be muddy.

After visiting the river's edge, climb up the ridge on the same access trail back to the White Trail, and turn left to follow it along the ridge edge above the Potomac. In 0.1 mile, the trail curves right away from the Potomac. The trail follows the ridge above a small stream for a quarter mile. Cross three small wooden bridges over springs. After the second bridge, pass the Blue Trail on the right and then the Green Trail after the third bridge. The White Trail descends steeply just after this to meet the stream and the Orange Trail.

At the stream, the Orange Trail intersects from the right and follows the stream valley away from the Potomac. Stay on the White Trail as it crosses the mouth of the spring to follow the stream back toward the Potomac. A large tree spanning the valley walls ten feet above the stream lets kids test their balance. The stream remains to the right of the trail until the trail crosses it 100 yards ahead on a bridge. From here, the White Trail gradually ascends the ridge for 0.1 mile until it curves right and follows the Potomac east. The trail continues uphill for a few hundred feet and then levels off. Atop the ridge, you lose sight of the Potomac because a small stream has carved an S curve between two ridges. On the opposing ridge, a dramatic, steep bluff looms above the Potomac River. Loudoun County has placed a chain-link fence on it to protect park visitors.

The White Trail descends steeply again to cross another small stream on rocks. On the opposite side, it climbs the ridge to the bluff overlook. At the overlook, stop at the bench for a snack and drink and enjoy the spectacular views of the Potomac. The White Trail continues behind the bench, heading away from the Potomac and toward a water treatment facility. For the next 0.3 mile, the trail follows the park's property line with the facility. The level trail often has muddy patches, but its meandering line through cedar and pine trees makes it feel intimate and cozy.

The last 0.2 mile of the White Trail parallels Edwards Ferry Road. Shortly after the trail curves to parallel the road, the Yellow Trail intersects from the right. The Orange Trail intersects from the right just before the icehouse. During winter, the Paxton family would chisel chunks of ice from the Potomac and would layer them and cover them with straw to insulate them. The house's thick concrete walls also preserved the ice during summer. Next to the icehouse is another picnic table where you can snack or picnic before you leave the park. To return to the parking lot, follow the grass-covered trail in front of the private residence, being careful not to disturb the residents.

Spectacular views of the Potomac River at the White Trail overlook

63 BALLS BLUFF BATTLEFIELD REGIONAL PARK

BEFORE YOU GO
Map: Available on the park's website
Contact: Balls Bluff Battlefield Regional Park
Nearest city: Leesburg, VA

ABOUT THE HIKE
Moderate, year-round
Length: 2.6 miles, loop
Hiking time: 1½–2 hours
High point/elevation gain: 341 feet/147 feet
Access: Compact soil, passable for jogging strollers

GETTING THERE

From I-495 (Capital Beltway), take exit 45 for VA 267 toward Leesburg. Drive 25 miles, and take exit 1B for US 15 north. Drive 3 miles, and turn right onto Battlefield Parkway Northeast. After 0.2 mile, turn left onto Balls Bluff Road. Drive 0.5 mile, and in a cul-de-sac, drive straight onto the dirt park road. Park at the end of the road.

ON THE TRAIL

Like most parks along the Potomac River in Virginia, Balls Bluff Battlefield Park sits on a bluff overlooking the Potomac in Loudoun County. Besides being a scenic and fun place to hike, this park is full of Civil War history. The Civil War began on April 12, 1861, with the firing on Fort Sumter. During the summer of 1861, fighting was heavy along Bull Run in Manassas. After multiple defeats, the Union Army retreated to home territory across the Potomac into Maryland. On October 21, 1861, the Battle at Balls Bluff occurred with both the Confederate and Union armies evenly manned and armed. However, by the afternoon, the Union soldiers were outmatched strategically. The Confederate soldiers killed Colonel Edward Baker, a senator from Oregon. His death was a devastating blow to the Union, and they retreated across the Potomac to Harrison Island. During the retreat, many soldiers died in the river because they were shot or drowned. Oliver Wendell Holmes, who later became a US Supreme Court justice, fought at Balls Bluff.

A meadow stands where a majority of the battle took place that fateful day. The white-blazed Battlefield Interpretive Trail loops around the battlefield. Interpretive signs at the trailhead adjacent to the parking lot and along the trail inform hikers of the battle's events. The rest of the trails at this 223-acre park create a network of hikes through this woodland forest overlooking the Potomac. This park is one of many regional parks along the Potomac River that provide large, natural spaces for birds of prey and large mammals to forage and reproduce. Covering most of the park's circumference, the hike described here leads first through the battlefield and then south along the Potomac to circle back inland up and down the ridges to the parking lot.

The hike begins at the interpretive signs and benches adjacent to the parking lot. Follow the wide, dirt road east to reach the cemetery in 0.3 mile. The Battlefield Interpretive Trail (with white blazes) turns left in 0.1 mile; however, continue straight on the dirt road as it leaves the tree canopy and enters the meadow. The white-blazed trail changes names

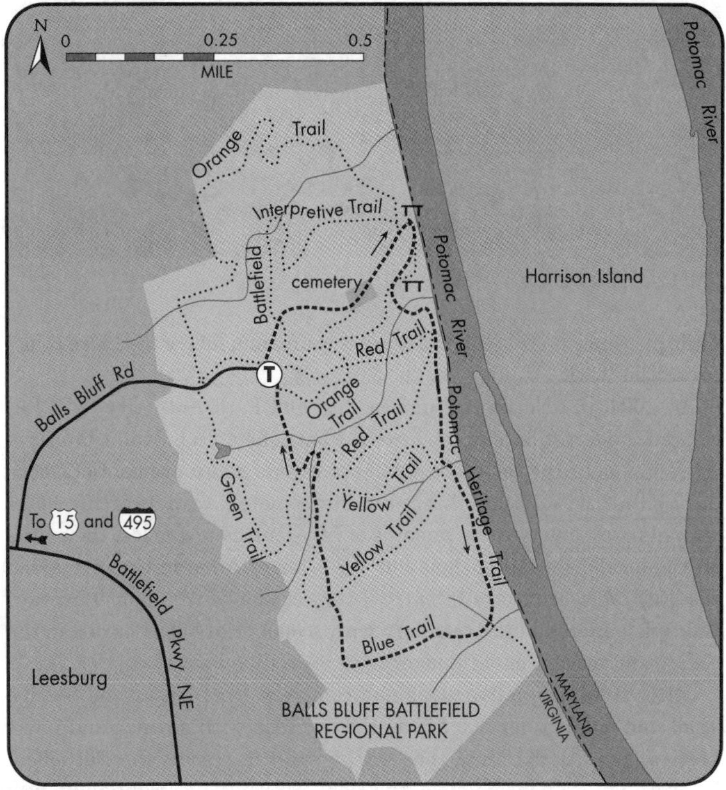

The Civil War cemetery at Balls Bluff

multiple times on this hike, making it confusing; follow the blaze colors to stay on track.

In 2004, the Northern Virginia Regional Park Authority (NVRPA) cleared the forest here to replicate the battlefield. In 0.2 mile, interpretive signs near the cemetery detail the events and movement of troops during the battle. Within this red-walled cemetery with its arched black wrought-iron gate are the remains of fifty-four men who lost their lives on the battlefield. All of them but one—James Allen in Company H of the 15th Massachusetts Infantry—were unidentified. Colonel Edward Baker is honored in the cemetery with a memorial but is buried in the San Francisco National Cemetery.

After the interpretive signs and cemetery, turn left on the Orange Trail and follow it for 500 feet to the overlook with a bench and interpretive sign. At the bluff, the Orange Trail intersects the Battlefield Interpretive Trail, now named the Holmes Trail. Turn right and follow the Holmes Trail (with white blazes) along the edge of the bluff, looking down at the Potomac. Along this bluff, the NVRPA has placed benches, which provide a respite with great views. The trail curves right and away from the river.

In 0.1 mile, a people's choice trail intersects from the right. Continue straight to the intersection with the Potomac Heritage Trail (PHT, with turquoise blazes). The best option to access the bank of the Potomac is to hike out and back 0.4 mile (this detour is not accounted for in the total mileage of the loop). Otherwise, continue straight on the white-blazed Holmes Trail 100 feet before it splits right and back to the parking lot. However, to continue hiking the 2.5-mile loop, turn left onto the PHT, and descend the ridge toward four steps and a small bridge that crosses the stream. Across the stream, follow the trail along it for 100 feet. Turn right at the turquoise double blaze, and then a quick left up the knoll to stay on the PHT. A turquoise blaze appears on a tree just after the turn, but there is no double blaze at the turn.

The PHT continues on top of the bluff for a half mile, intersecting the Red Trail in 0.2 mile on the right. The PHT descends the bluff steeply to a stream. The Yellow Trail intersects on the right before the stream crossing and again on the right halfway up the bluff on the opposite side of the stream. Continue hiking straight on the PHT, rising above the Potomac again until you reach the intersection with the Blue Trail. Descend the bluff toward two streams that bisect a ridge. The PHT crosses the left stream and ascends the bluff back toward the Potomac. However, cross the stream on the right, and ascend the ridge on the Blue Trail to hike inland.

The Blue Trail travels 0.3 mile up the ridge and levels off before reaching a forked intersection. The left fork is a people's choice trail. Follow the blue double blaze right to continue on the Blue Trail. The trail parallels a neighborhood on the left. For the next 0.3 mile, this trail undulates to follow the rolling topography and intersects the Yellow Trail twice. At the second intersection with the Yellow Trail, follow the blue double blazes left to continue on this trail. Before the Blue Trail dead-ends at the Red Trail, the Green Trail intersects from the left. Continue straight to the Red Trail, and turn left to descend the ridge and cross the stream.

Ascend the hill, and turn right at the red double blazes. The Green Trail intersects from the left here. Follow the Red Trail across the last stream and uphill to the parking lot.

FARMSTEAD LOOP

BEFORE YOU GO
Map: Available at trailhead and on the center's website
Contact: Blue Ridge Center for Environmental Stewardship
Nearest city: Purcellville, VA

ABOUT THE HIKE
Moderate, year-round
Length: 2.6 miles, loop and spur
Hiking time: 1½–2 hours
High point/elevation gain: 663 feet/194 feet
Access: Compact soil, passable for jogging strollers

GETTING THERE

From Maryland, take I-495 (Capital Beltway) to I-270. Drive 28 miles to exit 32 for I-70 west. Drive 1.2 miles to exit 52 for US 340 south. Drive 16.6 miles, and turn left onto VA 671 (Harpers Ferry Road). Drive 2 miles, and turn right into the Blue Ridge Center for Environmental Stewardship.

From Virginia, take I-495 (Capital Beltway) to VA 267 (Dulles Toll Road) west. Drive 26 miles to exit 1A for US 15 south (VA 7 west). Drive 1 mile to VA 7 west, and follow it for 4 miles to VA 9 (Charles Town Pike) toward Charles Town, West Virginia. Turn right onto Charles Town Pike. Drive 10 miles, and turn right onto Harpers Ferry Road. Drive 6 miles, and turn left into the Blue Ridge Center for Environmental Stewardship.

ON THE TRAIL

The Blue Ridge Center for Environmental Stewardship (BRCES), 2 miles from Harpers Ferry in Loudoun County, sits between Short Hill and Blue Ridge. The Robert and Dee Leggett Foundation bought the sprawling 900-acre farm in 1999. In 2004, the foundation established the nonprofit BRCES to provide environmental education, 10 miles of trails, and an organic farm. By purchasing the land, the foundation preserved the property's rich history, the historic Demory–Wortman House, and the remnants of a settlement built along Piney Run.

This 2.6-mile loop follows the Farmstead Loop with two spurs, the Mountain View Trail and Piney Run Spur. The hike passes Wortman Pond and Demory Field, a large group camping field and pavilion that

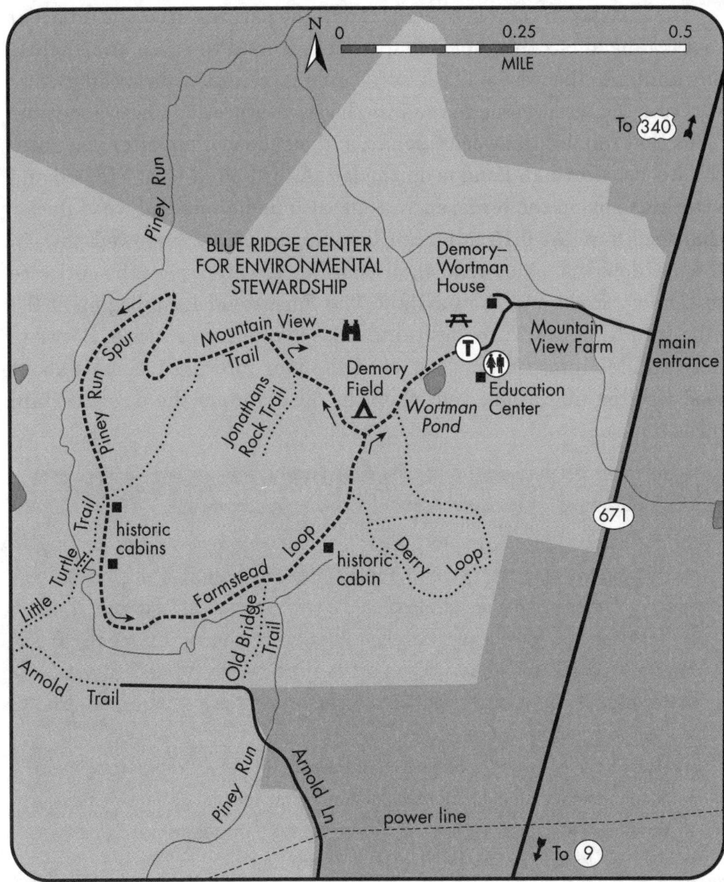

can accommodate eighty people. The loop is best hiked counterclockwise so that you can enjoy the interpretive signs about the birds in the forest and ascend a small ridge early in the hike. A 0.2-mile out-and-back spur on the Mountain View Trail provides you with an unobstructed view of Short Hill and a beautiful meadow. The red-blazed Farmstead Loop passes three historical log-hewn and cobblestone houses and a fun split-log bridge over Piney Run. Parts of Piney Run Spur and the loop may be muddy in places where the trail holds standing water after heavy rains. A picnic table at the trailhead makes for a great after-hike picnic so that you can continue to take in the beautiful scenery of the mountains.

The hike begins at a gate across from the parking area and adjacent to a trailhead box that holds maps; walk around the gate and slightly downhill into the woods. The first 0.3 mile is on a wide, dirt road. Before entering the woods, stop to read the large interpretive tower about the birds that inhabit the woods, ponds, and meadows. Just after you enter the woods, Wortman Pond is on the left. A bird blind here lets you and your kids spy on the birds, such as great blue herons and wood ducks, that feed here. At 0.15 mile, continue straight past a mowed path in the meadow and a historical sign. Shortly thereafter, pass the entrance to Demory Field and the pavilion. The Farmstead Loop begins at 0.3 mile into the hike. Turn right and hike it counterclockwise. Between here and Mountain View Trail, read the four interpretive signs about food, shelter, migration, and where in the layers of the forest certain birds live.

FOREST DENSITY AND BIRDS

The forest has four layers: forest floor, understory, midstory or canopy, and emergent—the crowns of the tallest trees in the forest, such as tulip poplars. Different species of birds utilize various aspects of a forest from the forest layers for nesting to fallen logs for drumming for mates. The density of a forest's understory indicates the health of the ecosystem. The denser it is, the more viable a forest is for nesting, foraging, and protection from predators.

The wood thrush, a species inventoried at BRCES, for example, nests in the understory of a forest, as do American robins. Different species of birds also inhabit forests with different percentages of canopy cover or closure, which is determined by the amount of shade or coverage provided by tree crowns. White-throated sparrows and blackburnian warblers, both species that have been inventoried at BRCES, nest and forage in different canopy closures. White-throated sparrows inhabit forests in early succession with less than 30 percent coverage, while blackburnian warblers like deep forest with coverage of at least 80 percent. BRCES has inventoried 130 species of birds.

After you turn right onto the Farmstead Loop, the trail gains elevation for the next quarter mile along its steepest section just before the intersection with the Mountain View Trail. While ascending the hill, you can access Demory Field again in two places on the right. At the

Hikers play on the split-log bridge over Piney Creek

top of the small ridge, turn right onto Mountain View Trail, and hike 0.2 mile out and back to the overlook, where there is a bench. At the meadow here, you can observe some of the 60 species of moths and butterflies the park has inventoried.

Back at the intersection with the Farmstead Loop and Mountain View, continue straight back onto the Farmstead Loop downhill to reach the Piney Run Spur in 0.2 mile. (Here, you can shorten the hike by a quarter mile by staying on the Farmstead Loop instead of taking the Piney Run Spur.) At the Piney Run Spur trail sign, turn right and make three switchbacks down the ridge toward Piney Run where the trail parallels the stream for a half mile. The trail is never adjacent to its streambanks, but you can hear its riffles. Piney Run Spur is narrow (but not overgrown) and wet in a few places. At the intersection with the Farmstead Loop, turn right to stay on the loop.

Immediately after you turn right to rejoin the Farmstead Loop, the Little Turtle Trail appears on the right, allowing horses to cross Piney Run. To the left of this trail intersection is the first of three historic cabins along the loop. Pass this trail and hike 100 yards to where Piney Run comes closest to the Farmstead Loop. Built by a Boy Scout as his Eagle Scout project, a split-log bridge on the Little Turtle Trail crosses Piney Run. The stream provides a great place to wade and play. On the left of the Farmstead Loop at this trail intersection is the second of three historic cabins.

When you are done playing in the stream, head back on the Farmstead Loop. In 0.1 mile, the loop curves left and then intersects the Old Bridge Trail in 0.2 mile on the right. Stay on the Farmstead Loop for another 0.3 mile, and pass the last of the historic cabins, this one built with cobblestone. Shortly thereafter in a small clearing, the loop intersects the Derry Loop where the Farmstead stays left and reenters the woods. Continue straight on the dirt road back to the parking lot past Demory Field and Wortman Pond.

BEARS DEN TRAIL CENTER

BEFORE YOU GO
Map: Available outside the lodge
Contact: Bears Den Trail Center (charges a fee)
Nearest city: Bluemont, VA

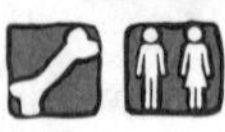

ABOUT THE HIKE
Moderate/difficult, year-round
Length: 1.5 miles, loop
Hiking time: 1–1½ hours
High point/elevation gain: 1362 feet/213 feet
Access: Compact soil and rock, not passable for jogging strollers

GETTING THERE

From I-495 (Capital Beltway), take exit 45 for VA 267 toward Leesburg. Drive 25 miles, and take exit 1A for US 15 south (VA 7 west). Drive 1 mile, and keep left for VA 7 west. After 17.5 miles, take a left onto Blueridge Mountain Road. Drive 0.5 mile, and turn right into Bears Den driveway. Park in the day-use parking lot on the right.

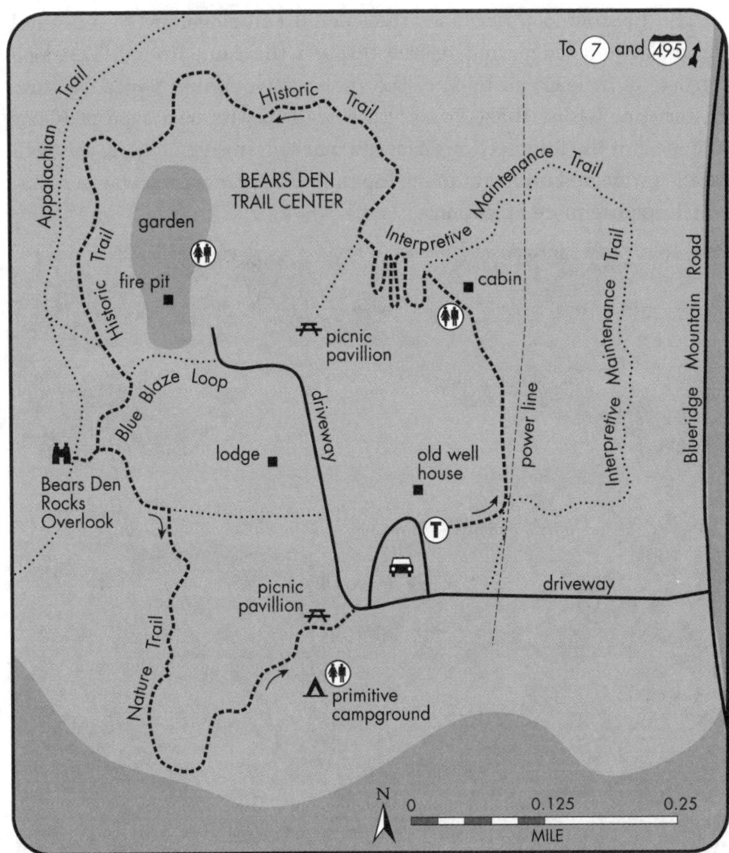

ON THE TRAIL

Bears Den is a trail center just yards from the Appalachian Trail (AT). The Appalachian Trail Conservancy (ATC) owns 66 acres of land along this famous trail, and the Potomac Appalachian Trail Club manages the property, which includes a lodge, hiker hostel, cabin, campground, and surrounding trails. Bears Den is best known for a large outcropping of rocks on the ridgeline and trail that overlooks the Shenandoah Valley toward Winchester. This outcropping creates a natural playground for climbing over and under massive boulders and through their crevices. If you are looking for a place to spread a blanket for a picnic or throw a Frisbee, there are two grassy areas on the north side of the lodge.

The 1.5-mile loop traverses the sidehill and ridgeline, goes around the cabin and lodge, and passes through the campground. The loop consists of at least portions of the Interpretive Maintenance, Nature, Historic, and Blue Blaze trails. Each trail has its own type of blaze, and most of the intersections are well marked. In some places, the trail tread is wide and even, but along the ridge, it is strewn with large rocks, which require more attention.

Bouldering on the rocks at Bears Den

COPPERHEAD SNAKES

Copperheads are cold-blooded animals, which means that they need the sun to warm their bodies to convert food into energy. Copperheads are venomous, but their venom is less powerful than that of rattlesnakes. However, more people in the United States are bitten by copperheads because, unlike rattlesnakes, which can rattle their tails, copperheads lack a warning system. Copperheads warn by biting, and so they use less venom to strike a human than they would when they prey on a small mammal. But their venom destroys red blood cells and the surrounding tissue.

According to North Carolina State University's Cooperative Extension, copperhead bites are not life-threatening; however, if you are ever bitten by a copperhead or any venomous snake, seek medical attention immediately. If you see a copperhead, give it a wide berth so that it feels less threatened and can escape. They will slither away from people when given the chance.

The hike begins at the day use parking lot next to the old well house. A sign here states "foot traffic only." The trail follows power lines downhill for 0.1 mile to its intersection with the Interpretive Maintenance Trail. The trails merge for 100 yards and then separate; the Interpretive Maintenance Trail continues straight, and the trail to the cabin turns left. Follow the cabin trail for 0.1 mile to where it passes between the back of the cabin and a privy. The trail passes a water spigot between the two and continues straight for 50 feet to an intersection with the Interpretive Maintenance Trail. Turn left and climb the sidehill on a few switchbacks, one of the hike's two short, steep sections. The white-diamond-blazed Interpretive Maintenance Trail intersects the yellow-blazed Historic Trail in 0.15 mile after crossing an old stone wall.

Turn right on the half-mile Historic Trail, which starts downhill, curves left, and then heads uphill on rocky tread. It continues uphill but at a much gentler slope as it meanders through the woods on rocks rather than on soil. The Historic Trail ends at the Blue Blaze Loop, which connects the AT with the trail that heads around the lodge. At the "Historic Trail" sign, turn left on the Blue Blaze Loop, and walk 100 feet to turn right to stay on the same trail. In 0.1 mile, you reach an access trail to the rock outcropping on the ridgeline that overlooks the Shenandoah Valley. The sunsets are amazing here as the sun rests over the next ridgeline to the west. If you are visiting during the day, plan to spend a half hour to an hour here so that your kids can climb up, down, under, and through the large boulders and slabs of rock. On sunny, warm afternoons, be cautious because copperhead snakes are known to sun themselves on or between these rocks.

After visiting the rocks, return to the Blue Blaze Loop, and turn right. In less than 0.1 mile, turn right on the Nature Trail (blazed with a white bear paw) at the posted sign. The trail curves left to face a wall of rocks with obvious signs that they have been climbed many times. From here, the Nature Trail continues to the right, gently downhill, and then steepens a bit before curving left to ascend the sidehill and through the campground. Pass the pavilion with its beautiful stone fireplace on the left to return to the driveway and parking lot.

NICHOLSON HOLLOW TRAIL

BEFORE YOU GO
Map: Available at the NPS shed on weekends (spring through fall) or on the park's website
Contact: Shenandoah National Park (charges a fee)
Nearest city: Sperryville, VA

ABOUT THE HIKE
Moderate, spring to fall
Length: 3.8 miles, out and back
Hiking time: 2½–3 hours
High point/elevation gain: 1200 feet/300 feet
Access: Compact soil and rock, not passable for jogging strollers

GETTING THERE

From I-495 (Capital Beltway), exit for I-66. Drive 22 miles, and take exit 43A for US 29 toward Gainsville. Drive 11 miles. Stay right to take US 211 west toward Luray. Drive 29 miles to Sperryville, and turn left onto US 522 (Sperryville Pike). After 0.8 mile, turn right onto VA 231 (Fort Valley Road). Drive 8 miles, and turn right onto VA 601 (Nethers Road), which becomes VA 707, then VA 600. Drive 3 miles to the parking lot on the left.

ON THE TRAIL

The tranquil Nicholson Hollow Trail follows the Hughes River in the central district of Shenandoah National Park. It offers families rock scrambling adjacent to the river or on the ridge side of the trail. Furthermore, the river's small cascades and swimming holes are great places to cool off in the heat of summer. The hike is 3.8 miles out and back, including 0.6 mile of walking on VA 600 each way to the trailhead, and it gains 300 feet of elevation in 1.9 miles. It is in the very popular Old Rag Mountain section of the park. The small parking lot closest to both the Old Rag trailhead and the Nicholson Hollow Trail is restricted to park staff. Therefore, you must park 0.6 mile east of the trailhead on

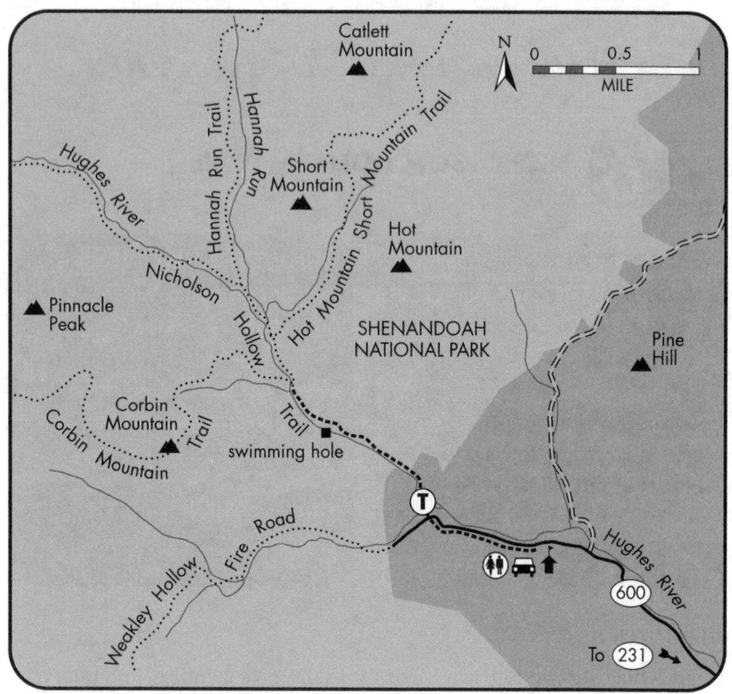

VA 600 in a large lot in a field. NPS operates a fee and information station with maps at this parking lot.

To begin the hike, turn left and walk up VA 600 for 0.6 mile to a forked trailhead with the traditional Shenandoah National Park Service cement trail post. The Old Rag trailhead is to the left, and the Nicholson Hollow Trail is to the right down a dirt driveway toward a gate. The Nicholson Hollow Trail begins just before the gate where there is a large trail sign along with a blue double blaze; the length of the trail is blazed in blue. To the right, a culvert drains water off the trail to prevent erosion. In 100 yards, about a dozen large boulders help hikers cross a fork in the Hughes River. Within another 100 yards on an island in the river, cross the second fork on another dozen large boulders. Little ones may need a hand to hold for both of these crossings because the space between some of the boulders is wide.

For the next 1.3 miles, the blue-blazed Nicholson Hollow Trail is fairly level with occasional elevation gains of 10 to 30 feet over soil-covered boulders. It is also fairly straight until it zigzags around an

This swimming hole and cascade in the Hughes River is a perfect spot to cool off on a hot hike.

obstacle, such as a rock ledge or a large tree. The Hughes River remains on your left; you sometimes walk adjacent to it, but even when you can't see it, the sound of water accompanies you. When the trail is close to the river, kids have excellent opportunities to scramble among the large boulders. The steep slopes on the right side showcase thickets of mountain laurel, rock outcroppings, and mature canopy trees. There are no trail intersections, people's choice trails, or feeder streams to cross—only two small culverts halfway along the hike that divert springwater through the trail and to the river.

At 0.9 mile, a cascade and swimming hole, the hike's best features, are accessible from the trail. A lightly traversed trail on the left leads over some large rocks to a couple of car-sized boulders on the river. The swimming hole is small but deep enough to cool off your whole body on a hot summer day. Leaving this area, continue hiking upstream to find truck- and house-sized boulders on the right, a great natural playground for kids to exercise their gross motor skills.

Past the boulders, the trail curves right and then left as it gains elevation, the most at any point in the hike. Shortly before the Nicholson Hollow Trail intersects the Corbin Mountain Trail (the hike turnaround spot), it descends slightly to meet the Hughes River. At the intersection, the Nicholson Hollow Trail continues right to follow the river, and the Corbin Mountain Trail crosses the river straight ahead. Head back to the car and enjoy the scenery along the trail from the opposite direction, noticing something different on the way back than you did on your trek out.

WHITEOAK CANYON AND CEDAR RUN LOOP

BEFORE YOU GO
Map: Available at the NPS shed on weekends (spring through fall) or on the park's website
Contact: Shenandoah National Park (charges a fee)
Nearest city: Syria, VA

ABOUT THE HIKE
Moderate, spring to fall
Length: 2.2 miles, loop (plus optional 1.6 mile extension)
Hiking time: 1½–2 hours
High point/elevation gain: 1300 feet/150 feet
Access: Compact soil and rock, not passable for jogging strollers

GETTING THERE

From I-495 (Capital Beltway), take the exit for I-66. Drive 22 miles, and take exit 43A for US 29 toward Gainsville. Drive 11 miles to Warrenton, and stay right to take US 211 west toward Luray. Drive 29 miles to Sperryville, and turn left onto US 522 (Sperryville Pike). After 0.8 mile, turn right onto VA 231 (Fort Valley Road). Drive 10 miles, and turn right onto Etlan Road (VA 643). Drive 4 miles, and turn right onto VA 600 (Weakley Hollow Road). Drive almost 4 miles to the trailhead parking lot on the left.

ON THE TRAIL

Whiteoak Canyon is one of the most popular places in Shenandoah National Park to hike besides Old Rag, a strenuous 9-mile loop with a challenging rock scramble at the top—not a great choice if you have kids younger than ten. However, Shenandoah offers a number of family-friendly hikes, such as the 2.2-mile Whiteoak Canyon and Cedar Run loop with a 1.6-mile out-and-back extension to the lower falls on the

The lower falls along Whiteoak Canyon trail

Whiteoak Canyon Trail. On most weekends, this trailhead parking lot is crowded. The area's cascading streams, large rocks, and waterfalls attract the young and old alike.

On spring, summer, and fall weekends, a ranger stationed in a National Park Service (NPS) shed adjacent to the trailhead kiosk provides maps, collects fees, and answers questions. The parking lot, which holds about thirty cars, is on private property; the NPS has permission to use the land through an easement. Cars are prohibited from parking on VA 600. Hikers enter park property a short distance from the trailhead. Shenandoah's park boundary is marked by large orange dots painted on tree trunks.

After your hike, you and your kids might enjoy picking apples at the Graves Mountain Orchard, nearby on VA 670. Or you might go wine tasting at the family-friendly DuCard Vineyards on Etlan Road (VA 643).

The hike starts on the blue-blazed Whiteoak Canyon Trail at the trailhead kiosk. The first 0.4 mile is relatively level. The trail tread, which is made up of soil, tree roots, and rocks, is characteristic of this hike's surface. Toward the end of the first 0.2 mile, turn right and walk over a long metal bridge that spans Cedar Run. After the bridge, the Whiteoak Canyon Trail intersects the Cedar Run Trail.

In Shenandoah National Park, which has more than 500 miles of trails, each trail intersection is marked with a large, square cement pillar with an embossed metal band at the top. Each metal band lists the trail names, their direction, and the mileage to the next intersection. A trail post at the junction of Cedar Run and Whiteoak Canyon indicates that the Cedar Run Trail is to the left, which is the direction you are going, and that the intersection with the Cedar Run Link Trail is 0.4 mile away.

The Cedar Run Trail starts out mostly level with a few areas where it rises and curves. The trail follows Cedar Run, and kids have many opportunities to climb the glacial-strewn boulders along its banks. The peaceful trail features the sound of cascading water with less foot traffic than the Whitoak Canyon Trail. Most people cut to the chase and hike the Whiteoak Canyon Trail to and from the falls, but Cedar Run and this connector trail offer more tranquility.

A few hundred feet before the Cedar Run Trail's junction with the Cedar Run Link Trail, the trail gains elevation and raises your heart rate. At the intersection with the Cedar Run Link Trail, make a hard right and go up three steps. This trail runs perpendicular to the slope of the mountain for 0.8 mile, undulating gently along the 1300-foot elevation line before it intersects with the Whiteoak Canyon Trail. As you hike the Link Trail, the sound of cascading Cedar Run fades into the sounds of the forest—creaking trees, chirping birds, and the rustle of leaves. Soon though, the sound of rushing water returns as you approach Whiteoak Canyon.

The Link Trail meets the streambank in Whiteoak Canyon about 25 feet above the water. Pause and savor the sight of the small cascade. The trail makes a left and follows the bank for 100 yards as it descends to the stream. Cross the stream atop evenly spaced large boulders; use caution because they are slippery when wet. Before turning on the Whiteoak Canyon Trail, stop for some fun, a snack, or picnic lunch here. (Don't forget that Shenandoah National Park is a pack-in, pack-out your garbage park.)

If you want to stick to the 2.2-mile loop, turn right on the Whiteoak Canyon Trail, and hike 0.8 mile back to the parking lot. The trail gradually descends 100 feet over a half mile at which point it rises gently over a hill and back down to a bridge over the stream. Cross the bridge, and hike the level land between the two streams. During wet periods, this area can be muddy.

The Whiteoak Canyon Trail connects with the Cedar Run Trail. Continue straight and over the second bridge to Cedar Run. The parking lot is less than 0.2 mile away.

Extension to the Lower Falls

To visit the lower falls (and upper falls, which is not covered in this book), turn left on the Whiteoak Canyon Trail at its junction with the Link Trail. This extension adds 1.6 miles to your total hiking distance, between an hour and an hour and a half to your hiking time, and 300 feet of elevation gain to reach a high point of 1600 feet. Most of the elevation gain is gradual with a few switchbacks up small hills and a final ascent of less than 100 feet in 100 yards, mostly up rock steps.

The trail rises over inclines along the right side of the stream four times, most of which are short switchbacks that are double blazed to indicate a change in direction. The first switchback is marked with a double blaze; however, if you do not pay attention, you may walk straight up a rock slab instead of turning right and ascending eight rock steps. But this rock slab is a great place to stop and observe the view of the small cascade flowing into a big pool of water. On hot summer days, it makes a great swimming hole.

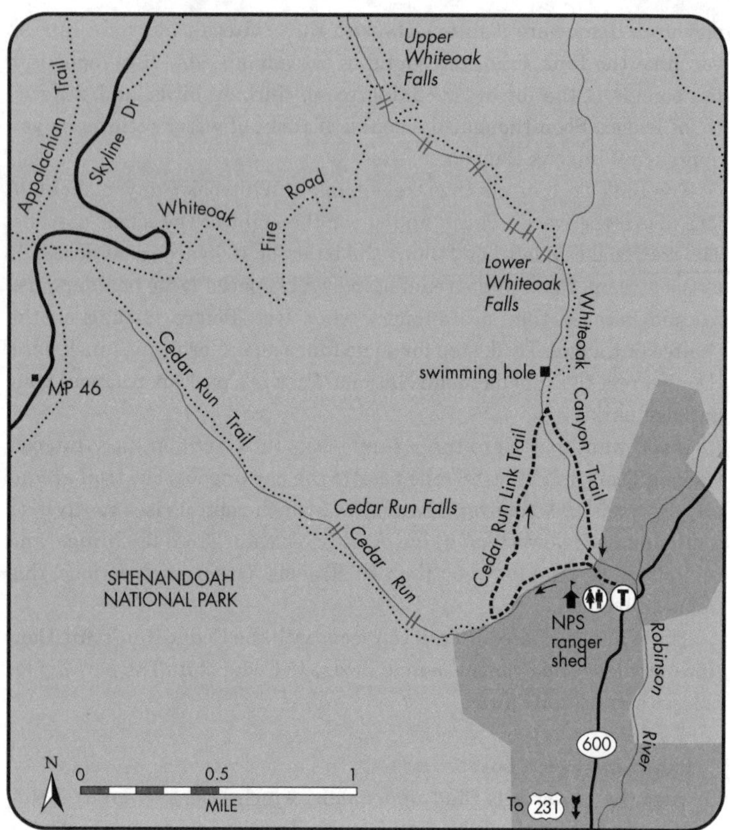

At the top of the fourth incline, you get your first sneak peak at the lower falls. Hike a short distance to cross the mouth of a feeder stream on four large rocks. Walk 100 feet to the blue double blaze, and make a sharp right to climb about a dozen rock steps and a large rock slab. Use caution here; a small spring leaches through the rocks on the steps, which can make them slippery. The lower cascade of the lower falls is at the base of the rock steps, while the taller cascade falls from above. There are large boulders in both areas where you can observe the falls' beauty and listen to their peaceful sound.

When you have had your fill of the falls, head back to the intersection of the Whiteoak Canyon Trail and the Cedar Run Link Trail. Continue straight on the Whiteoak Canyon Trail 0.8 mile back to the parking lot.

GRAVES MILL TRAIL

BEFORE YOU GO
Map: Park map #10 is available for purchase on the Potomac Appalachian Trail Club website
Contact: Shenandoah National Park (charges a fee)
Nearest city: Madison, VA

ABOUT THE HIKE
Moderate/difficult, spring to fall
Length: 4.2 miles, out and back
Hiking time: 3–3½ hours
High point/elevation gain: 1300 feet/400 feet
Access: Compact soil and rock, not passable for jogging strollers

GETTING THERE

From I-495 (Capital Beltway), take the exit for I-66. Take exit 43A for US 29 (Lee Highway) south toward Warrenton. Drive 11.5 miles to Warrenton; stay left at the split with US 211. Drive 45 miles south on US 29, and turn right onto VA 230 (Wolftown-Hood Road). After almost 4 miles, turn right onto Graves Mill Road (VA 662). Drive 5 miles, and turn right to stay on VA 662, which becomes dirt Graves Road. Drive 1 mile until it dead-ends at the trailhead parking lot. Note: Parking is allowed in this lot only.

ON THE TRAIL

The Graves Mill Trail is a beautiful hike along the Rapidan River. The trail was once a fire road in Shenandoah National Park. However, severe storms dumped 24 inches of rain in the area in June 1995, and the Rapidan and Staunton watersheds flooded, causing enormous damage to the forests, roads, and trails surrounding its streams and rivers. Park management decided not to rebuild the road and instead designated it a horse trail blazed in yellow. The trail width on this 4.2-mile, out-and-back hike fluctuates, demonstrating natural succession of almost two decades.

The trailhead is at the north end of a small parking lot adjacent to the Rapidan River. The Rapidan glides over glacial boulders, many of which are accessible via the trail. Shortly after the trailhead, a car-sized boulder along the river's edge is a great spot for kids to climb and feel

Hikers follow the rocks across the Staunton River.

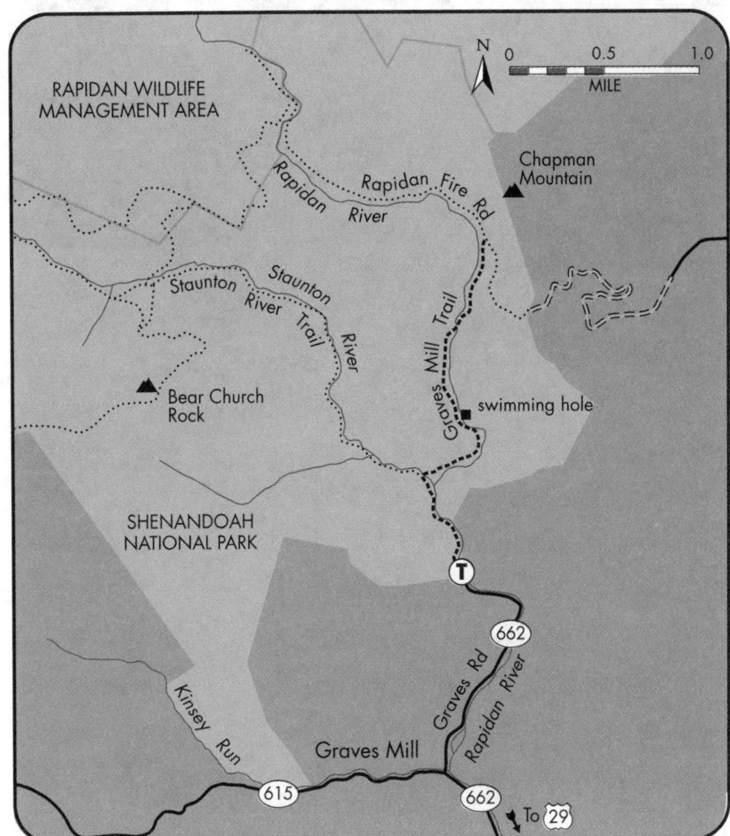

like kings and queens of the hill. You encounter more boulders, most of which are a little smaller, as the trail climbs next to the river. Here, kids can rock hop along the river if the water is low.

Within 0.2 mile, the trail bends away from the river and then shortly thereafter returns to the riverbank at 0.5 mile. Here the Graves Mill Trail intersects the Staunton River Trail on the left. Stay straight on the Graves Mill Trail. Within 0.1 mile between the Staunton River Trail and the Staunton River, you and your kids can spot "pencil points," evidence that beavers have used their sharp teeth to cut down trees to build a dam in the river and a lodge. Beavers build dams in narrow and shallow areas of streams to create deep pools for protection from predators like coyotes. With their webbed feet and flat tails, beavers are more

Crushing ice with rocks and sticks on the Rapidan River

adapted to live in the water than on land. There are additional dams within 0.1 mile upstream.

To continue heading north on Graves Mill, cross the Staunton River on rocks. Most kids will be fine, but little ones may need a hand to hold. Before you cross, take a look at the trees within 20 feet of the river. The forest is densely packed with young trees competing for sunlight. During the 1995 flood, a majority of the trees were uprooted and swept away by raging water. One large old beech tree that withstood the flood sits majestically on the bank of the Rapidan River at its intersection with the Staunton.

After you cross the Staunton River, the trail starts to climb gently, but most of the elevation gain, 300 feet, occurs later (between miles 2 and 3).

About 0.9 mile into the hike, a large rocky beach appears on the right of the trail along the Rapidan. It is next to a pool in the river—perfect for taking a summer dip, skipping rocks, crushing ice in winter, and stopping for a snack or picnic.

The trail gains more elevation and reaches a rock crossing of the Rapidan River at about 1.2 miles. The large boulders are mostly easy for kids to stride across; however, two wide gaps present a challenge, particularly when the water is high, like it is in the spring. Some large, accessible tree trunks and large boulders upstream from the crossing provide a great natural playground for kids, particularly when the water is low.

The remainder of the 0.8 mile of the Graves Mill Trail is wide and rises 200 feet to meet the Rapidan Fire Road. On this stretch, there is a backcountry campsite, established by previous backpackers. Backcountry campsites are first-come, first-served and not designated, but you must get a free permit to stay in one. The Graves Mill Trail rises above the river, which is inaccessible until the trail intersects the Rapidan Fire Road. Turn around at the fire road, and head back to the trailhead.

BEARFENCE TRAIL LOOP

BEFORE YOU GO
Map: Available at the park entrance station
Contact: Shenandoah National Park (charges a fee)
Nearest city: Stanardsville, VA

ABOUT THE HIKE
Difficult, spring to fall
Length: 1.2 miles, loop
Hiking time: 1½–2 hours
High point/elevation gain: 3560 feet/265 feet
Access: Compact soil and rock, not passable for jogging strollers

GETTING THERE

From I-495 (Capital Beltway), take the exit for I-66. Take exit 43A for US 29 (Lee Highway) south toward Warrenton for 11.5 miles. In Warrenton, stay left at the split with US 211. Drive 28 miles, and turn right onto VA 33 (Spotswood Trail). After 14 miles, take the exit for Shenandoah National Park. Turn left onto Skyline Drive, and drive 9 miles. The parking lot is on the left between mile markers 56 and 57.

ON THE TRAIL

The Bearfence Trail loop offers a challenging and engaging hike with a rock scramble to 360-degree views on its ridge. On a clear day, you can see the Shenandoah peaks from north to south and east to west, in addition to the Shenandoah Valley to the west and the Piedmont Plateau to the east. You may also observe hawks, vultures, and eagles riding the thermals above the peaks. On a cloudy day, you may be immersed in clouds blowing up and down the east and west ridges of the Shenandoah.

Bearfence Trail is not for the faint of heart and mind, but for the adventurer. If your kids have the physical ability and little or no fear of heights (although some fear keeps their abilities in check), plan to set aside a half day for this trail, which offers you and your kids a

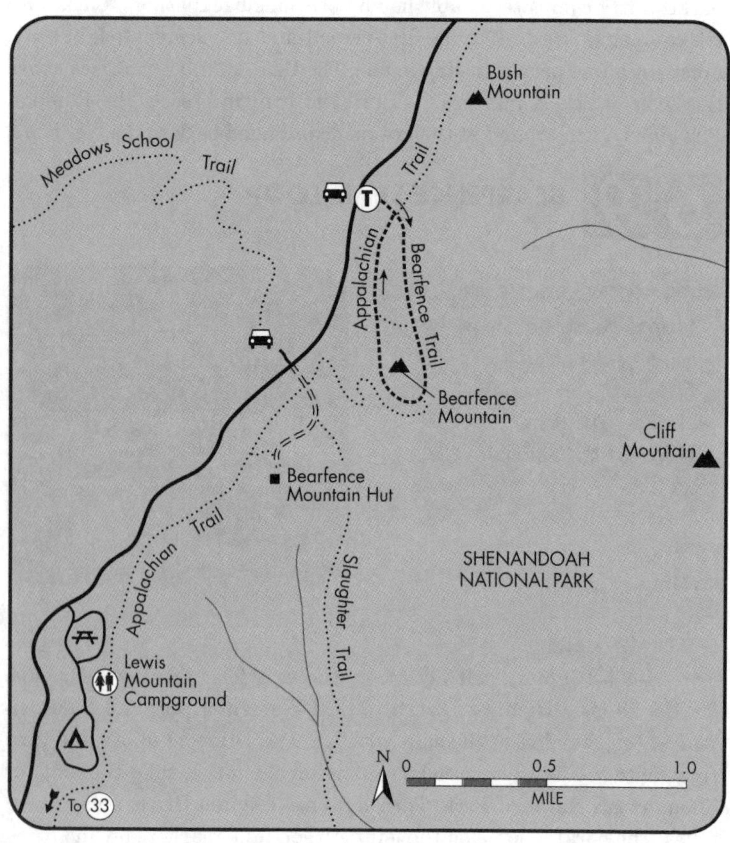

Climbing the spine of rocks on the Bearfence Trail takes courage but is rewarding for all hikers.

natural playground of rocks and crevices to explore and share quality time. Even though your canine friends might like the agility challenge this trail presents, Shenandoah National Park prohibits dogs on the Bearfence Trail.

At the parking lot on Skyline Drive, carefully cross the road and walk up the beautifully built steps that provide safe tread for hikers and decrease erosion on Bearfence Mountain. On this slope, you climb 100 feet in 0.1 mile. At the intersection with the Appalachian Trail (AT), continue straight on the Bearfence Trail. The blue-blazed Bearfence Trail makes up the first half of this hike, while the white-blazed AT makes up the second half. Follow the dirt trail another 0.1 mile to begin the rock scramble along the spine of the ridge.

At first, the scramble seems innocent, but with each step, it draws you into its more complicated hand- and footholds. Physically, it demands the use of two hands, two feet, and an occasional knee and butt. Mentally, it demands focus and a positive mind, especially if anyone in your party has a fear of heights. While you are scrambling, make sure to follow the single and double blazes painted on the rocks. Some are less obvious than others, and it is easy to stray off course.

After you reach what seems to be (but isn't) the top of Bearfence Mountain, a large cluster of boulders offers an amazing 360-degree view. Be prepared to linger. On a beautiful day, many hikers may share a spot; on a chilly, overcast day, you may find more solitude.

As you step over the crest of this 360-degree viewpoint, the dragon's spine of this trail comes into full view. From below on the AT, you might visually describe this part of the ridge as the points on a queen's crown. This view of the ridge from its highest point can be mentally challenging, particularly for people who suffer even slightly from acrophobia. Fear not—this is most kids' favorite spot on this trail. Beyond this spine sits Bearfence Mountain, your next destination.

Coming off the rock, you reach the sure footing of compact soil again. Within 0.1 mile, a trail marker appears. For a shortcut back to the AT, you can turn right, but you will miss Bearfence Mountain. Instead continue hiking straight along Bearfence Trail for another 0.2 mile until it dead-ends into the AT. Along the way, you reach another viewpoint with 180 degrees of scenery to the east. At the intersection with the AT, turn right and hike 0.7 mile on the AT back to the parking lot.

CONTACT INFORMATION

Accotink Bay Wildlife Refuge

Virginia Department of Game and Inland Fisheries

www.dgif.virginia.gov/vbwt/site.asp?trail=1&loop=CMN&site=CMN05

703-805-3972

Appalachian Trail: Annapolis Rocks

National Park Service

www.nps.gov/appa

Maryland Department of Natural Resources

www.dnr.state.md.us/publiclands/at.asp

Balls Bluff Battlefield Regional Park

Northern Virginia Regional Park Authority

www.nvrpa.org/park/ball_s_bluff

Banshee Reeks Nature Preserve

www.bansheereeksnp.org

703-669-0316

Preserve is open Saturday and Sunday only, 8:00 AM to 4:00 PM. Visitor center is open the third Saturday and Sunday of each month, 8:00 AM to 4:00 PM.

Battle Creek Cypress Swamp Sanctuary

www.calvertparks.org/bccss.html

410-535-5327

Park is open daily from 9:00 AM to 4:30 PM.

Bears Den Trail Center

www.bearsdencenter.org

540-554-8708

Day use parking is $3 per car.

Black Hill Regional Park

Montgomery Parks

www.montgomeryparks.org/PPSD/ParkTrails/trails_MAPS/black_hill.shtm

301-972-3476

Blockhouse Point Conservation Park

Montgomery Parks

www.montgomeryparks.org/PPSD/ParkTrails/trails_MAPS/blockhouse_point.shtm

301-670-8080

Blue Mash Trails

Montgomery Parks

www.montgomeryparks.org/PPSD/ParkTrails/trails_MAPS/blue_mash.shtm

Blue Ridge Center for Environmental Stewardship

www.blueridgecenter.org

540-668-7640

Bucklodge Forest Conservation Park

Montgomery Parks

www.montgomeryparks.org/PPSD/ParkTrails/trails_MAPS/Bucklodge_Trails.shtm

Bull Run Regional Park

Northern Virginia Regional Park Authority

www.nvrpa.org/park/bull_run

703-631-0550

Park charges an entrance fee.

Cabin John Regional Park

Montgomery Parks

www.montgomeryparks.org/PPSD/ParkTrails/trails_MAPS/cabin_john.shtm

301-299-0024

Cabin John Stream Valley Park

Montgomery Parks

www.montgomeryparks.org/PPSD/ParkTrails/trails_MAPS/cabin_john_svu.shtm

301-299-0024

Calvert Cliffs State Park

Maryland Department of Natural Resources

www.dnr.state.md.us/publiclands/southern/calvertcliffs.asp

301-743-7613

Park charges an entrance fee and a map fee.

Chesapeake and Ohio Canal National Historical Park

National Park Service
www.nps.gov/choh
301-767-3714
Park charges an entrance fee.

Claude Moore Park

www.loudoun.gov/index.aspx?nid=1285
571-258-3700
Visitor center open 9:00 AM to 5:00 PM daily; park open 7:00 AM to dusk

Cunningham Falls State Park

Maryland Department of Natural Resources
www.dnr.state.md.us/publiclands/western/cunningham.asp
301-271-7574
Park charges an entrance fee and a map fee.

Dyke Marsh Wildlife Preserve

National Park Service
www.nps.gov/gwmp/planyourvisit/dykemarsh.htm
703-289-2500
Preserve is open 6:00 AM to 10:00 PM.

Elizabeth Hartwell Mason Neck National Wildlife Refuge

National Fish and Wildlife Service
www.fws.gov/refuge/mason_neck
703-490-4979

Fairland Recreational Park

Montgomery Parks
www.montgomeryparks.org/PPSD/ParkTrails/trails_MAPS/Fairland.shtm
301-670-8080

Fort Dupont National Park

National Park Service
www.nps.gov/fodu
(202) 426-7723

Fort Washington Park

National Park Service
www.nps.gov/fowa
301-763-4600
Park charges an entrance fee.

Great Falls Park

National Park Service

www.nps.gov/grfa

703-285-2965

Park is open from 7:00 AM to dark; visitor center is open from 10:00 AM to 4:00 PM. Park charges a fee.

Greenbelt Park

National Park Service

www.nps.gov/gree

301-344-3948

Hemlock Overlook Regional Park

Northern Virginia Regional Park Authority

www.nvrpa.org/park/hemlock_overlook

Adventure Links operates an outdoor education center in the park; learn about it at www.adventurelinks.net.

Huntley Meadows Park

Fairfax County Park Authority

www.fairfaxcounty.gov/parks/huntley-meadows-park/

703-768-2525

Visitor center is closed on Tuesdays; park is open from dawn to dusk.

Kenilworth Aquatic Gardens

National Park Service

www.nps.gov/keaq

202-426-6905

From spring through fall, park is open 7:00 AM to 5:00 PM; in winter, it is open 7:00 AM to 4:00 PM.

Manassas National Battlefield Park

National Park Service

www.nps.gov/mana

703-754-1861

Visitor center is open daily from 8:30 AM to 5:00 PM.

Mason Neck State Park

Virginia Department of Conservation and Recreation

www.dcr.virginia.gov/state_parks/mas.shtml

703-339-2385

Park charges an entrance fee.

Muddy Branch Stream Valley Park

Montgomery Parks

www.montgomeryparks.org/PPSD/ParkTrails/trails_MAPS/muddy-branch-greenway-trail.shtm

301-972-6581

Northwest Branch Stream Valley Park

Montgomery Parks

Rachel Carson Greenway Trail

www.montgomeryparks.org/PPSD/ParkTrails/trails_MAPS/Rachel_Carson_Greenway_trails.shtm

301-627-7207

Underground Railroad Trail

www.montgomeryparks.org/PPSD/ParkTrails/trails_MAPS/Rural_legacy.shtm

301-774-6255

Patapsco Valley State Park

Maryland Department of Natural Resources

www.dnr.state.md.us/publiclands/central/patapsco.asp

800-830-3974

Park charges an entrance fee.

Patuxent Research Refuge and National Wildlife Center

US Fish and Wildlife Service

www.fws.gov/northeast/patuxent

301-497-5580

Trail is open daily (except federal holidays) from sunrise to 4:30 PM. National Wildlife Museum is open 9:00 AM to 4:30 PM.

Patuxent River Park

Prince Georges County Department of Parks and Recreation

www.pgparks.com/Things_To_Do/Nature/Jug_Bay_Natural_Area.htm

301-627-6074

Park is open daily from 8:00 AM to dusk. Pets prohibited on Brown Trail.

Piscataway Park

National Park Service

www.nps.gov/pisc

301-763-4600

Potomac Overlook Regional Park

Northern Virginia Regional Park Authority

www.nvrpa.org/park/potomac_overlook

703-528-5406

Prince Georges County Department of Parks and Recreation /Lake Artemesia

www.pgparks.com/page328.aspx

301-627-7755

Rachel Carson Conservation Park

Montgomery Parks

www.montgomeryparks.org/PPSD/ParkTrails/trails_MAPS/Rachel_Carson.shtm

301-670-8080

Red Rock Wilderness Overlook Regional Park

Northern Virginia Regional Park Authority

www.nvrpa.org/park/red_rock_widerness_overlook

Riverbend Park

Fairfax County Park Authority

www.fairfaxcounty.gov/parks/riverbend-park/

703-759-9018

Visitor center is closed on Tuesdays. In spring, summer, and fall, weekdays hours are 9:00 AM to 5:00 PM; weekends 12:00 PM to 5:00 PM. In winter, weekday and weekend hours are 11:00 AM to 4:00 PM

Rock Creek National Park

National Park Service

www.nps.gov/rocr

202-895-6070

Nature center is open Wednesday through Sunday, 9:00 AM to 5:00 PM.

Rock Creek Regional Park

Montgomery Parks

www.montgomeryparks.org/PPSD/ParkTrails/trails_MAPS/rock_creek.shtm

Lake Needwood

301-948-5305

Boat center is open May through September.

Lake Frank

301-258-4030

Nature center is open Tuesday to Saturday, 9:00 AM to 5:00 PM.

Rust Nature Sanctuary

Audubon Naturalist Society

www.anshome.org/index.php/about-ans/sanctuaries/rust-leesburg-va

703-669-0000

Scotts Run Nature Preserve

Fairfax County Park Authority

www.fairfaxcounty.gov/parks/scottsrun

Shenandoah National Park

National Park Service

www.nps.gov/shen

540-999-3500

Park charges an entrance fee.

Sugarloaf Mountain Park

Stronghold Incorporated

www.sugarloafmd.com

301-869-7846

Park is open 8:00 AM to sunset.

Theodore Roosevelt Island Park

National Park Service

www.nps.gov/this

703-289-2553

Turkey Run Park

National Park Service

www.nps.gov/gwmp/planyourvisit/turkeyrun.htm

703-289-2500

US National Arboretum

www.usna.usda.gov

202-245-2726

Upton Hill Regional Park

Northern Virginia Regional Park Authority

www.nvrpa.org/park/upton_hill

703-534-3437

Wheaton Regional Park

Montgomery Parks

www.montgomeryparks.org/PPSD/ParkTrails/trails_MAPS/wheaton.shtm

301-962-1480

Nature center is open Tuesday to Saturday 9:00 AM to 5:00 PM and Sundays 1:00 PM to 5:00 PM.

Wolf Trap National Park for the Performing Arts

National Park Service

www.nps.gov/wotr

703-255-1800

Woodend Sanctuary

Audubon Naturalist Society

www.anshome.org/index.php/about-ans/sanctuaries/woodend-chevy-chase-md

301-652-9188

Pets are prohibited.

RESOURCES

The Washington, DC, region is rich with parkland managed by local, state, and national governments that provide thousands of miles of trails where you can hike, mountain bike, and ride horses. These parks provide families in the region with accessible and unique opportunities to play among a large variety of natural resources. All three government entities have a big job to manage and maintain the vast acreage of parkland, oftentimes relying on volunteers to clear trees and brush from a trail, maintain its surface to improve safety and reduce the trail's impact on the ecosystem, and build stream crossings (such as rock steps or bridges) for easier access. Many land managers and organizations provide excellent opportunities and programs—such as the National Park Service Junior Ranger program and Kids in Parks, which offers self-guided brochures and activities—to help families engage with the outdoors. The government and nonprofit organizations listed below provide valuable resources for families who want to take a hike.

US GOVERNMENT AGENCIES

National Park Service, www.nps.gov
US Fish and Wildlife, www.fws.gov
US Forest Service, www.fs.fed.us

STATE AND DC AGENCIES

District of Columbia Parks, www.dpr.dc.gov
Maryland State Parks, www.dnr.state.md.us/publiclands
Virginia State Parks, www.dcr.virginia.gov/state_parks

COUNTY AGENCIES

Arlington County Parks, www.arlingtonva.us
Fairfax Country Parks, www.fairfaxcounty.gov/parks
Loudoun County Parks, www.loudoun.gov-index.aspx?NID=122
Montgomery County Parks, www.montgomeryparks.org
Prince Georges County Parks, www.pgparks.com

ORGANIZATIONS FOR TRAILS AND HIKING

American Hiking Society, www.americanhiking.org
Appalachian Mountain Club, www.amc-dc.org

Appalachian Trail Conservancy, www.appalachiantrail.org
Capital Hiking Club, www.capitalhikingclub.org
C&O Canal Trust, www.canaltrust.org
Hiking Upward, www.hikingupward.com
Leave No Trace, www.lnt.org
Potomac Appalachian Trail Club, www.patc.net
Potomac Heritage Trail Association, www.potomactrail.org
Rock Creek Conservancy, www.rockcreekconservancy.org
Seneca Greenway Trail, www.senecatrail.info
Sierra Club, www.dc.sierraclub.org
Wanderbirds Hiking Club, www.wanderbirds.org

ORGANIZATIONS FOR KIDS AND OUTDOORS

Audubon Naturalist Society, www.anshome.org
Children & Nature Network: Natural Families, www.childrenandnature.org
Discover the Forest, www.discovertheforest.org
Hiking Along, www.hikingalong.com
Kids in Parks, www.kidsinparks.com
National Wildlife Federation: Hike and Seek, www.nwf.org/Hike-And-Seek.aspx
Nature Rocks, www.naturerocks.org

INDEX

R

S

T

U

V

W